NO GREATER LOVE

NO GREATER LOVE

The Story of Michael Crescenz, Philadelphia's Only
Medal of Honor Recipient of the Vietnam War

JOHN A. SIEGFRIED AND KEVIN FERRIS

CASEMATE

Philadelphia & Oxford

AN AUSA BOOK
Association of the United States Army
2425 Wilson Boulevard, Arlington, Virginia, 22201, USA

Published in the United States of America and Great Britain in 2022 by
CASEMATE PUBLISHERS
1950 Lawrence Road, Havertown, PA 19083, USA
and
The Old Music Hall, 106–108 Cowley Road, Oxford OX4 1JE, UK

Copyright 2022 © John A. Siegfried, Kevin Ferris, Joe and Valerie Crescenz

Hardback Edition: ISBN 978-1-63624-222-4
Digital Edition: ISBN 978-1-63624-223-1

A CIP record for this book is available from the British Library

Printed and bound in the United States by Integrated Books International

Typeset in India by Lapiz Digital Services, Chennai.

For a complete list of Casemate titles, please contact:

CASEMATE PUBLISHERS (US)
Telephone (610) 853-9131
Fax (610) 853-9146
Email: casemate@casematepublishers.com
www.casematepublishers.com

CASEMATE PUBLISHERS (UK)
Telephone (01865) 241249
Email: casemate-uk@casematepublishers.co.uk
www.casematepublishers.co.uk

Back cover photo provided by Patrick Hughes

My continued journey to write the stories of the Vietnam generation would not be possible without my friend. Thank you, Kevin Ferris, for your part in this wonderful testament to a Philly kid.
—John A. Siegfried

To Michael Crescenz and his brothers.
—Kevin Ferris

Contents

Foreword

Dear Mike,

It has been almost 54 years since I answered the knock on the door of our family's home in Northwest Philadelphia and all our lives were changed forever. I was 12, watching a soldier tell Mom and Dad that you had been killed in Vietnam. In country barely two months. Nineteen years old.

We didn't get details until much later. That your unit was pinned down. That you grabbed a machine gun and charged the enemy. That you saved the lives of your fellow soldiers. That you were a hero.

Even as a kid you were always looking out for others, as our parents and our faith instructed us.

A lot has happened since then. Your five brothers grew up, got married, had families, and got to live full lives. Mom, Dad, Charlie, and Pete are gone, but you already knew that. Philly, our West Oak Lane neighborhood, our St. Athanasius parish are all so different.

Two things that have not changed are how much I miss you and how proud I am to have you for my brother.

As painful as it was to lose you, the brother I idolized, a lot of good has come of it. I may have lost one brother, but I have gained a whole bunch of new ones. The men that you saved on that final day of your life have gone on to have children and grandchildren of their own. These men are my brothers now—especially Bill "Doc" Stafford. You have inspired more people in more ways than you could have ever imagined.

No one would ever think you were too lucky when you were sent to Vietnam, but one thing was very lucky—having Lt. Col. Sam Wetzel for your commanding officer. He was so inspired by what you did on November 20, 1968, that he nominated you for the Medal of Honor.

He wound up becoming the commander of Fort Benning, Georgia, and had the weapons pool there named for you. He also became a three-star general. He, too, is gone now, but I am proud to have called him my friend.

Your buddies from the old neighborhood will never forget you. I am in touch with some of the "old heads" from the Samuel Pennypacker Elementary School yard and Simons Community Recreation Center: Jack Norton, Jim Engler, Ron Burke, Tom Robinson, Tom Stanton, and others. A bunch of us from St. A's just met up for lunch not long ago, and the stories come out about you and Charlie and the rest of the gang. It is almost like you are there, but not quite.

Of course, no one who ever met you could ever forget you. But there are many others, fellow Vietnam guys, who never met you but were so inspired by what you did that they wanted to make sure you would always be remembered. Veterans of Foreign Wars Post 2819, Rising Sun, was renamed to honor you. Frank Tacey, another Philly Vietnam vet, made it his personal mission to get the Philadelphia Veterans Medical Center renamed for you. It took him five years, but he got it done! He is my brother now.

You will be pretty amused by this—the Philadelphia City Council recognized you with a proclamation designating a "Cpl. Michael J. Crescenz Day." It was at that council session that I met Tom Roberts, a Vietnam vet who insisted that there should be a statue of you at the Philadelphia Vietnam Veterans Memorial. He spearheaded a fundraising campaign that did not include any politicians. The Philadelphia Vietnam Veterans Memorial Society got it done. It also put a bronze memorial plaque on its "hooch" in the city's Bridesburg section. They wanted to make sure you would not be forgotten. Your statue stands guard over your 648 brothers whose names are on the memorial wall.

Across the river, there is a mural honoring you and your awards in American Legion Post 129, Toms River, New Jersey. This was the project of Ray Miller, who was the commander of the post and Charlie's very close friend. They served together in the New Jersey State Police.

You would also be delighted to see the street sign with your name at 46th Street and Landis Avenue in Sea Isle City, designating the block where Pop-Pop's house was. Joe Griffies, a fellow Cardinal Dougherty High School grad and Vietnam vet, made it his mission for the community to remember you, a special son of Sea Isle who spent all of your summers there. He got it done. Joe also got Sea Isle to do a special beach admission tag in 2020 for only veterans to wear, featuring your likeness with the Medal of Honor around your neck, courtesy of your old pal Jeff Jacobs and his computer skills.

I never got the chance to tell you how proud I always was to be your brother, and how proud I continue to be. You have left quite a legacy, not in children and grandchildren, but in brothers.

Love,
Joe

PROLOGUE

Fortress in the Clouds

It was known as the fortress in the clouds, a jagged set of peaks called Nui Chom Mountain, so tall that on a clear night it was possible to see the South China Sea, 35 miles to the east. The mountain was tucked away in the northwestern corner of South Vietnam, not far from the borders with North Vietnam and Laos to the west—making it an all-important crossroads for communists looking to resupply their forces below the demilitarized zone separating the two warring nations.

Steep-sided, and coated with thick elephant grass and vines that gave way to triple-canopy jungle at the higher altitudes, the mountain posed many hidden dangers to mere mortals year round, but monsoon season made it almost impenetrable.

"One way or another, an infantryman gets wet and stays wet during the monsoons," Sgt. George Hawkins wrote in *American* magazine in May 1969.[1] "If it's not the rain, it's the rain-soaked jungle he cuts his way through; if it's not a river-crossing, it's an assault across a rice paddy; or it's simply his own sweat soaking into his jungle fatigues as he climbs a rugged mountain trail."

"It was heavily overgrown," recalled William "Doc" Stafford, a medic in Alpha Company.[2] "It was jungle, it was mountainous, it was rocky. There were a lot of tree roots. I remember because I fell down a few times." In fact parts of the mountain were so steep and rocky that the men "had to crawl hand over hand, sometimes taking more than an hour to move 100 meters"—a little more than the length of a football field.[3]

In November 1968, the mission of 4th Battalion, 31st Infantry, was to take Nui Chom from well-supplied and deeply entrenched North Vietnamese forces. At sunrise on November 20, Alpha Company prepared to pit itself once more against the mountain. It was its turn to walk point, but it had progressed only 100 meters up the steep slopes when all hell broke loose.

Walking right into a fortified bunker complex, four soldiers were hit almost immediately and the company was pinned down. Doc Stafford was called forward to help a wounded soldier lying in the open under heavy fire. While he managed to reach the man, he couldn't get him back to safety. Doc realized he could not even stand up under such heavy fire and, in desperation, dragged the man to a nearby bunker. While this offered some temporary protection, it would soon prove a trap, but every attempt to move attracted more fire, and the injured man was hit again.

The two men were alone in a sea of smoke and noise. Time seemed meaningless in such intense chaos—it could have been seconds, minutes, or even hours before Doc tried once more to pull the man to safety. But it was useless: the ground was too rough, and the bullets were unrelenting. There was nothing more he could do other than pray for deliverance.

Suddenly, Pfc. Michael Joseph Crescenz, a big, broad-shouldered 19-year-old out of Philadelphia, loomed over the medic and his charge brandishing an M60 machine gun, as enemy fire filled the air around them.

"I got this, Doc, no problem," he said.[4]

CHAPTER I

Family

Charles Crescenz Jr. and Mary Ann McLaughlin met down the Shore. For any true Philadelphian, it's always just "down the Shore." Never "the beach." And not "the *Jersey* Shore." No adjective or geographic reference is needed. Charles was born in the City of Brotherly Love on August 6, 1921, to Charles and Cecilia Crescenzo, not long after his father had finished his service with the U.S. Army during World War I. The older Charles, also known as Carmine, was born in Philadelphia too, on South Eighth Street, to Angelo and Antonia Crescenzo, in 1889.

Young Charles Crescenz—family members are not clear on when or why the name was shortened and Americanized—grew up in Roxborough, a neighborhood just northwest of Center City. Then it was still considered almost a suburb, though it had been officially part of Philly since the 1850s. Carmine did well in the beer business and, along with many other Italian Americans in Philly before and since, sent his son to local Catholic schools. First, he attended St. John the Baptist Elementary, and then off to the Jesuits at the all-boys' St. Joseph's Preparatory School, which boasts both famous and infamous politicians among the alumni who have walked its halls since the school was founded in 1851. Charles decided to stick with the Jesuits after graduation, attending St. Joseph's College—later St. Joseph's University.

While at St. Joe's, he worked summers as a lifeguard in Sea Isle City, New Jersey, where his parents owned a Shore home on 46th Street. There he met the tall, slender, and beautiful Mary Ann McLaughlin. Her father, Martin McLaughlin, was a Marine veteran of the First World War who also owned a home in Sea Isle. But home base for the McLaughlins was Cecil Street in West Philadelphia. Martin was a fixture in the Streets Department—Mary Ann would say a "big shot"—back in the days when Republicans ruled the city and patronage jobs were doled out to loyalists who helped them keep control of the town.

The McLaughlins were members of Transfiguration of Our Lord Roman Catholic Church on Cedar Avenue, which wasn't even two decades old when Mary Ann was born on October 11, 1923. She graduated from West Catholic High School for Girls, the archdiocese's second girls' high school, founded in 1927 to accommodate Philadelphia's rapidly growing Catholic population. After graduation she headed west—just about 20 miles—to Immaculata, built among the hills of bucolic Chester County right after World War I as the first college for Catholic women in the Philadelphia area.[1]

Like her three brothers, Mary Ann was tall—she was 5 foot 9—and her sons remembered her as old-fashioned, almost Victorian, in her ways, but kind and always doing for others, treating them as she wished to be treated. Two of her many nieces, Kathleen Zippilli and Mary Lou Allen, fondly recall how good she was to all the children when the clans assembled for picnics at Cooper River Park or other family gatherings. And while she always seemed to have more than enough to do, she took time to listen to the kids—and, maybe more importantly, feed them. "She was the sweetest, kindest woman, very much loved," Mary Lou said. "And what a wonderful cook. There was always plenty of food, huge bowls of food."[2]

Kindness. Family first. Caring for others. Making time for all. They were all traits she learned as the third of six children and ones that she, in turn, drilled into her six boys.

But before there were her boys, there was the courtship, with the handsome, athletic Charles Jr. He loved playing tennis and would later try to teach his sons, finally giving up when they insisted on whacking the balls with all their might high over the fence behind their opponents. At least he always had Wimbledon to watch. He admired golf, but never swung a club. However, the young man could swim. He was powerful and fearless, especially as a youngster, often pushing himself so far out that he worried his fellow lifeguards, who called out from the shore, urging him back.

As with so many other couples, their courtship, and any future plans together, were put on hold by World War II. Charles served in Europe and forever kept his experiences to himself, at least as far as his sons were concerned. Not long after he returned home, Charles and Mary Ann finally married, on September 23, 1946—a Wednesday, so as not to interfere with Carmine's busy weekend days in the beer business. Eleven months later, their first son, Charles, was born. Five more boys would follow: Michael (1949), Peter (1951), Joseph (1956), Steve (1960), and Chris (1961).

Postwar life was good to the Crescenzes. Charles joined his dad in the beer business, promising Mary Ann she wouldn't have to work outside the home. He was active in the local bowling league and it provided a welcome night out for the couple as their family grew. Friday nights they played pinochle with neighbors, the various families taking turns hosting. They bought a three-bedroom, one-bath brick twin in the city's West Oak Lane neighborhood, at 7443 Thouron Avenue. Mom and Dad had the back bedroom, and divided the boys—and the bunk beds—evenly in the other two, Charlie, Mike, and Peter in the front room and Joe, Steve, and Chris in the middle one.

Mary Ann bore the day-to-day brunt of running a busy household with six rowdy boys while Dad was at work. "The moms were kind of like the field generals in the house," her son Joe said,[3] noting how both parents were tough on the kids. Everybody was expected to pitch in, and that meant the older boys sometimes kept the younger ones in line. It might, at first, have been at their parents' urging, but over time it was just instinct. Looking out for others was a way of life in Philly's West Oak Lane in the '50s. Yes, each batch of kids had their own parents to answer to, but every other mom and dad in the neighborhood was also keeping watch, and they weren't shy about letting you know when you crossed a line. Even neighbors who weren't parents felt free to set wayward kids straight, as would older brothers and sisters, and your friends' older brothers and sisters. It was a community that looked after its own.

"The older they got, Charlie and Mike, they took on more and more responsibility," Joe told Bob Moran of the *Philadelphia Inquirer* as part of a series of interviews on Michael Crescenz in 2013—pronouncing his oldest brother's name as "Chollie." "And they didn't put up with too much crap from the younger brothers. I used to get some of those old knuckle sandwiches, or they'd dig their knuckles with their high school rings into my head, if I got smart with Mom. They protected her that way."[4]

She needed protection. To an extent. Mary Ann was a formidable Irish woman in her own right, and more than familiar with the chaos that comes with growing up in a big family. But most of the time it was her versus six growing, increasingly rowdy boys. Kathleen Zippilli described the Crescenz household as "bedlam."

"They were boys.... They would throw the football around inside the house, occasionally, from one room to the next," Kathleen told television anchor and reporter Samantha Crawford for the 2015 documentary, *Michael Crescenz: Never Forgotten*.[5] "I remember my sister saying they used to ride their tricycles all over the house, inside the house. It was bedlam, but it was fun."

There were limits to the fun. The boys knew they could only push Mom so far. The last thing they wanted to do was force her into deploying the ultimate punishment—"Wait 'til your father gets home."

"You didn't pull that nonsense when he came home, from the oldest all the way down," Joe said, and that was true even when the sons started to tower over their father. "When we pissed Dad off, all hell broke loose. We got the hell out of there, because Pop would lay you low, buddy. He was a tough little half-Irish, half-Italian kind of guy, with these big-barrel Popeye arms from lifting kegs and cases of beer all day."

Joe chuckles at the memory.

"That anger," he said with a smile and a shake of his head. "Unfortunately, us Crescenz boys, we all inherited that pretty crazy side of us from our father."[6]

They inherited other things as well, including a strong work ethic and a clear understanding of their responsibilities within the family and their community.

"My father was a hard worker and he loved the beer business," Joe says. "Him and his father, my Italian grandfather, had such a rapport with the neighbors and with their customers. I remember they had these two big, distinct key rings, and they were so they could get into people's homes and businesses and deliver beer. He was a businessman, no nonsense, but he enjoyed being out there with the people. It was a customer-service business and he loved it. And my older brothers would help on occasion during the holidays or when my dad needed extra help."[7]

One of Mike's closest friends, Ron Burke, has fond memories of greeting Mr. Crescenz each week when he was making deliveries for Dallas Beverage.

"It was no secret that my father Tom loved his 16-ounce Esslinger beer," Ron said. "My job every Saturday morning was to go to the basement, unlock the back door, and take money down to give to Mr. Crescenz when he delivered the case of beer. I would always thank him for delivering, gave him the money and he would put the case in the exact spot my father designated. Little did he know my father would have it finished by Monday morning. I would always make sure I said, 'Thanks, Mr. Crescenz, my father will be *real* happy you delivered so early.' He would laugh. And he would ask every week, 'What are you and Michael up to today? Do you have any games this week?' He was always interested in what Michael and I had planned."[8]

Mr. Crescenz also went out of his way to show his appreciation when he saw others working hard. "My older brother Roger delivered the *Evening Bulletin* newspaper to the Crescenz family household every day," Ron said. "He would come home and tell me he saw Charlie or Mike all the time. He always said they were great people and that either Mr. Crescenz or Mrs. Crescenz would always find a way to give him a tip on weekly collection day. He knew Mr. Crescenz worked multiple jobs but he was thrilled to get the tip every week."[9]

Charles and Mary Ann's efforts made an impression on their sons. "So, you start to get the work ethic, because Dad, like most men of the day—they grew up in the Depression—had nothing, and they gave us kids everything," Joe said. "Mom and Dad scrimped and saved to put a roof over our head, to clothe us, to feed us—and don't forget my mom was cooking for seven men. They were some feasts. We never knew what hunger was. We were very fortunate."[10]

Here's one other thing Charles and Mary Ann Crescenz gave their sons, the chance to grow up in a postwar neighborhood full of hardworking families that provided a seemingly endless supply of children that kept one another out of their mothers' hair, out of trouble (mostly), and out on the playing fields. It was a time before cellphones and computers, even calculators and color TVs.

"With six boys, we were thrown out of the house in the morning—'Come back at dinner time,'" their first born, Charlie, told Crawford in *Michael Crescenz: Never Forgotten*.[11]

"It was a great neighborhood, great to grow up in, very pretty," Joe says. "Everybody played the street games back then, the old stickball, Wiffle ball, half ball, wall ball, step ball, you name it. We invented some games and others we learned from our older brothers and sisters in the local school yard where we played ball. And we played from sunup to sundown. Moms didn't have to worry because everybody looked out for each other."

As the fourth of six sons, Joe followed his older brothers onto the streets and ball fields and to this day, more than 60 years later, is in awe of all he saw and experienced.

"I was just amazed at how great the athleticism was in our neighborhood. Everybody could play ball, and my brothers were no exception," Joe says proudly of Charlie and Mike.

Charlie is remembered as solid, quiet, respected—at home, in school, and on the playing fields.

"He let his playing do his talking for him," Joe says, "He wasn't loud, he wasn't emotional, just very businesslike."

Joe still marvels at how fast, strong, and athletic his oldest brother was. "He was quick as all get out, and so talented. I remember as a kid he could walk on his hands. Yeah, he'd get up, invert himself, and he'd be walking on his hands. The guy had incredible balance."[12]

Jim Engler was another close friend of Mike's. They were classmates at the local parish grade school, St. Athanasius—a mouthful of a name for kids or adults so it is always shortened to St. A's in conversation—and later Cardinal Dougherty High School. Jim vividly remembers how multitalented Charlie was on the football field:

"One particular memory I have of Charlie was in a St. A's football game. He was in eighth grade, Mike and I were in seventh. By the way, Mike was the only seventh grader to start on that team. He was a pretty good football player in those days. Charlie was playing as one of the defensive backs. The opposing runner was running full speed up the sideline. Charlie threw the most beautiful body block to take down the runner and anyone else in the way. It was a great tackle. He was originally a running back (halfback in those days), but when our two quarterbacks were injured and out for the season, he became our quarterback and played well."[13]

If he seemed more grown up then his peers, it might have come from his parents' expectations. "I think he had a lot put on him, like the eldest in any family does," Joe says. "The father and mother expect a lot more out of their oldest child."

Born just 17 months after Charlie, Michael, too, was expected to do his share of helping around the house, including looking after his younger siblings and keeping them in line. "It was the pecking order," Joe says. "They didn't want me to be a smart ass as a kid, especially around our mom, so you learn from your older brothers. I think every family ran that system."

Where Charlie had a quiet authority, Mike could be a little more vocal. If Charlie was speed and grace, Mike was more of a "slam-bang power" kind of guy, as Joe puts it. "He had a different type of athleticism, and his personality fit that." But what they shared, Joe said, was they were both excellent athletes, very strong and powerful.

"As a kid I watched them play with their peers in the school yards and the sand lots in Philadelphia, playing their baseball, football and basketball, and I could see how fantastic they were," Joe says.

Their differences complemented each other.

"Michael had this strength," Joe says. "Not that Charlie didn't but I'd say he was more like a gazelle, swift and agile. Mike was more, not a gorilla, but he had that upper-body strength and he knew how to use it if he had to defend himself."[14] That was just as true when he was a skinny young kid, often the tallest in his class, as evidenced by old class photos, and even more so as a teen, when he worked out and started to develop.

Though Charlie and Mike had to be stand-in disciplinarians at times for their younger brothers, they didn't let others mess with them. They were extremely loyal and protective.

"His family was his backbone," Jim Engler said of Mike.[15]

"He was my best friend," Pete Crescenz said of his brother Mike. "He used to take care of me all the time, any kind of trouble I got in."[16]

"They were there for you," Joe says. "If something happened in the neighborhood, the older brothers were there. They had your back. Charlie and Mike, they protected the younger and the weaker. I guess it was just built into them, or maybe Mom and Dad instilled that in them. I don't know. But they didn't put up with too much crap out on the streets."[17]

Or from each other. Charlie, in the documentary, *Never Forgotten,* looked back at his rivalry with Michael: "We had some battles royal between the two of us while we were growing up. He was the strong one. I was the fast one. And typical brother stuff, like we'd be out and we'd be playing something and I'll say something to him and he'll get mad. He hit me over the head—we had incredible fights—he hit me over the head with a milk bottle, broke it over my head. I threw a pair of baseball spikes and stuck them in his back. Stuff like that. We took doors down in the house when we were fighting."[18]

"They were both sports guys, both very, very active," Mike's friend Ron Burke said in an interview with the *Inquirer.* "They were very competitive in just about everything they did."[19]

Jack Norton, a West Oak Lane neighbor and friend, saw the Crescenz brothers' rivalry in action, and it had its entertaining side.

"We used to climb the trees on Pennypacker school lawn," he said, "and when we got to the highest point that would hold our bulking 75-pound bodies, Charlie would start egging on Michael to climb higher. And Mike, being Mike, would rise to the challenge and climb out on a limb that would only support a squirrel. I watched Mike fall through so many trees and was on hand for the subsequent battling. Those were the days, my friend."[20]

That energy and passion found other outlets as well.

Joe particularly remembers how Michael would step in if he saw someone being bullied. "I heard stories in the neighborhood, how he'd approach one or two different guys and say, 'Hey, knock it off, leave that kid alone.' And I do believe he got in quite a few scraps that way, fending for the weaker kids who were being bullied. So yeah, he was a scrapper. Mike was a strong guy and if he didn't like what he saw or heard, he did scrap. He was a fighter and he had somewhat of a reputation within his circle. Don't mess with him, don't get him pissed off."

"Justice was swift," Joe recalls with a chuckle. "The kids handled their justice out on the street and you kept it out on the street. You didn't dare bring it home."

But once justice had been administered, the issue was forgotten. "You had to get over it," Joe said. "We didn't hold any grudges. That was the thing. We liked the camaraderie of our friends. It was important to have that growing up on the streets."[21]

It was that camaraderie, the sense of community defined by families and neighbors, parish and schools, rec centers and sports leagues, that in many ways shaped their character and destiny—including, in Michael's case, an act of valor above and beyond the call of duty that would be recognized with the Medal of Honor.

CHAPTER II

Community

The life Michael J. Crescenz lived, and the impact he had on others, is echoed in a passage written by another hero of the Vietnam War, Senator John McCain of Arizona, in his book *Character is Destiny: Inspiring Stories Every Young Person Should Know and Every Adult Should Remember*. One chapter honors the patriotism and courage of Pat Tillman, the legendary NFL player who gave up his football career to serve his country after the terrorist attacks on September 11, 2001. Tillman was killed by friendly fire in April 2004 while serving as an Army Ranger in Afghanistan. McCain wrote:

> He was quite a man, tough, honest, overachieving, intense, colorful, daring.... He came from a good family, who were as close as a family could be. His parents were strict, but fun and encouraging. He was raised to be brave, work hard, not to brag but to believe in himself.... He is remembered as the first one to help a friend in trouble, to stand up to a bully, to try to do the right thing. He thought for himself, and had, without doubt, the courage of his convictions.[1]

It's no surprise that such sentiments apply to more than one warrior who gave his life in the service of his country.

Michael Crescenz had a heartbreakingly short life. He was only 19 when he died more than half a century ago, on November 20, 1968. And yet the memories of him, and the impact he had on family and friends who watched him grow up, have not faded with the passing of the decades.

"The first thing you would normally probably see is his big grin," his cousin Kathleen Zippilli told television anchor and reporter Samantha

Crawford about the fun that she and her family would have when visiting her cousins on Thouron Avenue. "His smile was infectious. That's the first. As soon as he would see anybody come in, he would have this big smile on his face.... He was funny. They were..." and she stops herself, smiling at the memory of Michael and his five brothers. "They were boys," she says with a laugh. "Let me tell you it was a whole group of them. They were funny."[2]

Jim Engler met Mike in first grade at their parish school at St. Athanasius. The school was just a half mile from the Crescenz home and when Michael started attending in the 1950s, it was bursting at the seams. It hosted grades one through eight, often with three sections per grade, and 60 or more kids per section. The daily parade of uniformed Catholic school kids trudging to school or home happened four times a day—before school, after school, and back and forth for lunch. Jim lived on the edge of the parish, three blocks over from Thouron on Woolston Road. From age 6 through 14, Mike and Jim hiked back and forth together, sometimes having to hustle to be back before the lunchtime bell rang.

"It was pretty common for kids in the neighborhood to walk to and from school four times a day," Jim told Bob Moran of the *Philadelphia Inquirer*. "I think that's why our legs were so strong. Because it was so crowded in the Catholic schools there was no staying for lunch. Most of the parents—the mothers—were stay-at-home moms, so we were able to go home and eat our lunch, although we had to rush back a lot of times. Mike lived near the end of the parish and I was in the very end, next block up. So, it was probably a nine-block walk, eight to nine city blocks to get to school."

Depending on the route, that walk could take them past the row homes common to the West Oak Lane neighborhood, or twins like the one the Crescenz family lived in. Around those homes were temples and churches, corner groceries, dry cleaner shops, pizza parlors and kosher meat markets, and a local Irish bar open on Sundays—thanks to its hotel license—making it very popular with even the non-Irish in a state (Pennsylvania) whose blue laws kept bars closed on the Sabbath.

"I remember, not vividly, but I remember certainly being in class with Mike," Jim says, "but more often it was our walks home from school and back to school that were most memorable, because we were just always walking together."[3]

But one incident from those first years at St. A's school is quite vivid, what Jim calls one of the earliest encounters between him and Mike. The class was lined up at the water fountain, each student waiting a turn, some patiently, and some not so patiently. "You know when you're six or seven your teeth are falling out," Jim recalls with a smile. "And you know we were, like they say, horsing around and somehow I got pushed and my loose tooth came out. I don't know whether it was because of Mike pushing me, but the nun thought the 'horsing around' caused it to be knocked out and thought Mike was the culprit. He got in some trouble for it."[4]

When they weren't in school hanging out, they were free to explore the neighborhood, often playing army, basing their adventures on what they learned about the military from the big screen, almost never from their tight-lipped fathers who served in World War II. "We played army all the time," Jim says, "I'd say from second, third, fourth, fifth grades. Up on the same block Mike lived on there was an empty lot. It was always overgrown and probably pretty narrow though we thought it was wide, and it ran all the way back to the next block over, Forrest Avenue. We dug foxholes in there, and there were foxholes from older kids who had played there before us. It was really our playground for activities when we were that young, which included army, but also king of the hill, buck-buck,"[5] the latter a popular Philly street game where friends piled atop one another until they collapsed in a giggling, writhing heap.

Ron Burke also met Mike during their early years at St. A's, which he calls a "great little parish school." "We all did pretty good there," he said, "and then worked our way to high school."[6] Ron credits those early lessons learned at St. Athanasius with setting their direction in life. "It helped us be more disciplined in life and made us better people," he said.

He laughs now, thinking about him and Mike hanging out together, the skinny Mike, who was always among the tallest kids in the class, towering over his much shorter friend. "Mutt and Jeff," Ron says, likening the oddly matched grade school friends to the two characters of the old comic strip. "I was the smallest. He was the tallest." But they hit it off right away and stayed close all through their years in Catholic school.

"I met Michael in first grade and we lived a couple of blocks away from him, so I didn't see him every day after school, but the end result was I knew him in first grade, second grade, all the way up—and that included when we got active on the sports side, which was especially in seventh and eighth grade, where we were all active in football, baseball, and basketball—and then obviously going to Cardinal Dougherty High School," Ron told Bob Moran.

"Michael, he was a guy who always liked to have fun. He always liked to laugh," Ron said.

"He always had a tremendous smile and he had a terrific personality. And he and I, there were a couple of years there, I believe it was seventh and eighth grade, where we sat very close to each other all day, so we would—I would never get good marks on self-control—we would always be goofing off. We would talk, laugh, pass notes, joke around, and do anything and everything we could get away with.

"The girls liked him a lot. He was a handsome guy and you can clearly see that from his pictures. The girls enjoyed him. We would have some parties where, again, it wasn't the whole class, it was maybe eight or nine of us, and we all had girlfriends and, you know, Mike would be the favorite of lots of girls in the school. He was very—I'm not finding the right words here, but the girls all liked him. That's for sure."[7]

And Michael liked them.

Ron says, "In eighth grade, he was seat one, I was seat two. Seat three was one of the prettiest girls in our class, Eileen Coor. Even to this day she is beautiful, as is Alexis Tarsi, who sat in the last seat. I can only tell you that every boy in the class had the hots for Alexis. To top it off, in front of Alexis was Connie Arcaro, who was also very pretty. Thus, Mike and I felt that every day we were in the 'good guy' aisle and he couldn't wait until he had to hand out tests and other paperwork, especially to the girls. There were times he would bypass me just to get to the back of the aisle faster. We would joke about this all the time."[8]

Unlike some friends who drift apart as they grow older and their interests change, the bond between Ron and Mike stayed solid.

"I never saw him change. He was the Michael I knew from first grade to senior year. His demeanor was always the same, he was always friendly, he was always smiling, he was always there to help you if you needed it. And that's why we got along so well. There was a group of us—Jimmy Engler, Mark Brady, Dick Osborne—we were all a bunch of guys that were together all the time, and it was just a fun time in our lives to have friends like this and to grow up with them.

"But he always had this presence about him too. I don't know if it was because of his height or just his overall demeanor, but everybody looked up to Mike as a leader, and he demonstrated that to me all the way through grade school and high school."[9]

Grownups also noticed that presence. Another neighborhood friend, Tom Stanton, lived across the street from St. A's, and his mom made a point of keeping an eye on the children as they trooped back and forth to school every day, ensuring an adult presence would keep any mischief to a minimum. Of course, in the West Oak Lane neighborhood of the time, she wasn't alone.

In an email to Joe Crescenz, Tom wrote, "Mom called me to the window one day and said to me, 'Look at those boys,' referring to your brothers Mike and Charlie. She was so impressed with the way they walked in time and always had perfect crewcut haircuts. 'Look at those boys.' She knew there was something special about both of them. Mom seemed to have a sense to recognize good people.... I will never forget my mom's words, 'Look at those fine boys.'"[10]

That presence was a combination of their own natural gifts and abilities, but also clearly reflected their upbringing.

Joe Lynch remembers not just the influence Mike and Charlie had on him growing up, but also how Mr. Crescenz looked after his sons' friends.

"In the neighborhood, your dad was well known to enjoy playing baseball and softball with his sons, Chollie and Mike, as well as with anyone else they could entice to join them to widen the experience," Joe wrote to Joe Crescenz. "I was a chubby, slow, uncoordinated neighborhood kid without a glove who watched from the sidelines. Your dad noticed this and made it a point to get me on the field.... He encouraged me to practice the fundamentals and made sure that Chollie and Mike assisted me and kept encouraging me. Never got to the level of Mike or Chollie, but did slim down, speed up a bit and get coordinated enough to progress to basketball and rise to the level of the last person to be picked in pickup games at the Rec Center."[11]

Once they hit a certain age, sports dominated the social life of the boys and young men of the West Oak Lane neighborhood in the 1950s and '60s. Some of it took the form of official leagues, at St. A's, local Boys Clubs, and later the teams at Cardinal Dougherty High School. More often it was self-organized, stickball and Wiffle ball on the streets where they lived. They played after school games at the yard at Samuel Pennypacker Elementary on Washington Lane. They enjoyed organizing marathon dawn-to-dusk pickup games of baseball, basketball, football, and more—and it didn't matter what the official season was—at the sprawling Simons Community Recreation Center, known affectionately as the Rec. Tom Corcoran, a contemporary of Mike's described the Rec as "our magical place…. There, we were free of all worries!!!"[12] A home away from home for generations of Philadelphia youth, it is still one of the city's largest recreation centers, boasting basketball courts, and four baseball fields in the corners of the massive complex, with room enough for a football field in the middle.

Ron Burke called the Rec "the center of the universe, where just about everybody from all over the West Oak Lane area met…almost daily, to play any type of sports with any type of weather."[13]

Jim Engler regularly met up with Mike early on Saturday mornings and headed over to the Rec. "It was usually locked when we got there, that's how early we got out," he says. "So, we would climb the fence to get into the recreation center and then just hang out there."[14]

Mike was a gifted athlete, one whose height and great strength gave him an advantage in almost any sport he played.

"Mike was a terrific baseball player," Ron said. "I played with him on the seventh and eighth grade team for St. Athanasius, but he progressed. He was more talented at baseball than most of us and actually ended up, I believe, on the Cardinal Dougherty High School team, becoming one of their star players…. I can remember him playing several different positions. I know he pitched for a while, he played first base, and he was one of our power hitters. At least on the eighth-grade team, he certainly won us a couple of games with his bat."[15]

Jim Engler is painfully aware of Mike's hitting skills.

"A vivid recollection I have was playing baseball on the midget field at Finley Playground on Upsal Street. I was a member of the West Oak Lane Boys Club at that time—I played there for about four years before switching over to the Ogontz Boys Club. Finley was our home field. I was pitching against Ogontz that day and was ahead 5 to 4 late in the game. Mike came up to bat with two runners on base and hit a triple to the right field fence to put Ogontz ahead 6 to 5. That's how the game ended. Funny thing, my father always remembered that and would bring it up once in a while—much to my chagrin."[16]

Ron has a distinct memory of Mike's strength, demonstrated during a game at the Rec, with its four baseball diamonds in the four corners of the massive field.

"I saw the two longest homers ever hit from the diamond," he says. "One was hit by a player named Jackie Dougherty. The other was hit by Michael. He hit the ball so far over the center fielder's head that it actually rolled close to the baseball diamond by the basketball courts. In all honesty, Mike could have walked the bases and would not even have a throw to the plate. Mike was either 13 or 14 at the time but his power and strength were unbelievable. He was an outstanding player in high school."[17]

Others experienced his strength on the football field. William Peglow, who was a year behind Mike and Ron at both St. A's and Cardinal Dougherty, was one of those players.

"I still remember those 'head-ons' during practice sessions with the running backs like Mike running straight into one on one with people like me," William said. "Trying to tackle Mike was like trying to tackle a tank. Needless to say, Mike ran over me like a tank. But occasionally I tackled him—occasionally."[18]

Another friend, Rick Gallagher, called Mike "the big kid on the Ogontz Boys Club team." "When he got up to bat the coaches yelled, 'Back up, back up.' And guess what? He still hit it over our heads." But pitchers occasionally had some success against Mike's bat. "One game I pitched in relief and we were getting beat again," Rick recalls. "Mike came up and I struck him out. When we met again in high school, he came up to me and remembered I struck him out. I guess he was mad."[19]

Whatever his feelings about being struck out, they didn't keep him from coming to the aid of a teammate.

"When we played for Cardinal Dougherty High School, I wasn't a favorite of the coach," Rick said. "And against West Catholic, I broke my glasses and of course the coach sends me out to right field. As I ran out, I stopped at first base where Mike played. I told him I couldn't see shit with this gray, overcast sky. Mike said no problem, he would let me know if it was coming my way. So, first pitch, here it comes, high pop up. Mike ran into right pointing up and, thank God, I caught it. Two pitches later, there's a ground ball past Mike between first and second and he helped me again."[20]

Mike had a very clear sense of right and wrong, and he was always willing to back up his convictions.

Jeff Jacobs describes a softball game at the Pennypacker schoolyard when he and Mike were about 10 years old. As co-captains of one of the teams, they were taking turns choosing up sides, naturally starting with those they considered the best players and working their way through the rest. As they got toward the end, Jeff made a call without consulting Mike.

"My neighbor, a few years younger than Mike and I, was in the remaining player pool," Jeff wrote to Joe Crescenz. "We both knew he had virtually no baseball skills, but he lived just a few doors down from me on Nolan Street, and his dad used to drive us to school in the morning so I wanted to include him. The only thing worse than being picked last is not being picked at all."

"We choose Harry," Jeff announced.

Mike instantly retorted, "Oh, no, we don't."

Jeff shot back, "Yes, we do."

"Back and forth it went until Mike asked the question you never want to hear but to which you can never answer 'No,'" Jeff wrote. "And that was, 'You wanna fight about it?' I reluctantly gave the obligatory answer: yes."

It turned out to be a carefully considered battle. Their first decision was to move the fight off the concrete playground and onto grass—"There was less chance of getting any scrapes or tears in our clothes we'd have to explain to our parents later and for which we'd most certainly suffer," Jeff wrote. Then the ground rules: no face punching, no groin hits—evidence on the face would show and the other would just hurt too much.

The others, picked or not for the game, formed a circle, and the two captains went at it.

"'Fought' is actually taking more than a few liberties as not a single punch was thrown," Jeff wrote. "We grappled and fell to the ground, each with a head lock on the other; each straining to gain advantage. Neither one of us really wanted to hurt the other, but we'd gotten ourselves into that mess, so there we were. After what seemed like a half hour, but in reality was more likely a few minutes of maximum exertion in trying for submission, we were both exhausted. Then…one of us (and I cannot remember which) asked, 'Have you had enough of this?' to which the reply was, 'Yes.' That ended the 'big fight.'… We stood up, went back to the playground and played the game."[21]

"That is typical of how we dealt with stuff like that, instead of running home crying to your mom," Joe Crescenz says. "Our moms and dads would tell you to go back and settle the issue among ourselves."[22]

And after the issue had been settled, and the game commenced, did Harry get to play? Jeff didn't remember.

It wasn't Mike's first fight, or his last.

Jim Engler describes his friend as one of the tougher kids in the neighborhood.

"I'd say he had a pretty serious nature," Jim says. "He was competitive. He didn't tease and he wasn't a bully, but he was tough. Invariably there were fights in grade school. One in particular happened when we were in eighth grade and up at the Recreation Center. I was there with Mike. There were these two brothers. I wasn't involved and don't remember what triggered it. But, somehow, we got into it. I knew Mike was tougher than the one brother, but I didn't think he could beat both of them. But he did. He took care of business."[23]

His strength was put to use in other ways too. Sometimes a game at Pennypacker might have to be called because someone sent a ball—often the only ball available—soaring over the boys' heads and onto the roof of the school. Game over. Unless the Crescenz boys were on hand.

"We would often play baseball or softball in the summertime with a bunch of older guys in the neighborhood down at the Pennypacker school yard," Jim Engler said, "and invariably we hit the ball up on the roofs of the school. Now a lot of the public schools in Philadelphia had a common footprint, with a wing sticking out that was usually for the auditorium. And if you hit a ball high and far enough, it went up on that roof."[24]

"One feat that few in the neighborhood could do was to climb up onto that auditorium roof. It took lots of confidence, strength and, more importantly, GUTS. Both Charlie and Mike could do it."[25]

Ron Burke echoes Engler's description of Mike. "I'll use the words 'lean and mean,'" he says. "Michael was aggressive, strong, very strong."[26]

It took all the height, strength, and agility the Crescenz boys had to clamber onto the auditorium roof. Charlie or Mike would first have to stand on the railing of the steps and then reach up to the cyclone fence. They scaled that fence to the very top, balanced themselves and reached up to grab the lip of the roof. From that tentative handhold, they pulled themselves up and over onto the roof. "All that risk to throw off the collection of softballs and any other stuff that was up there," Jim Engler says.[27]

"But like I say, there were very few kids that would even chance it, or were strong enough to do it, because it was pretty high up, especially going from the cyclone fence up to the roof ledge. I'm sure Charlie did it first but Mike probably matched him because he did it. There was always a sibling competition. But it wasn't something I would ever do. They were two athletic kids, Mike and Charlie, and pretty strong for their size."[28]

That strength and size came in handy for another big neighborhood sport, basketball. Whether in an organized league or in a pickup game among friends and friendly rivals, sportsmanship, camaraderie, and teamwork were the orders of the day.

"Mike was good in all sports but especially basketball and baseball," Ron Burke says. "At the end of grade school, we put a team together to play in the Rec League that had just started up. We called our team the Magnificent 7—though we actually had eight players, John Bangert,

Mark Brady, Ron Burke, Mike Crescenz, Jimmy Engler, Dick Osborne, Joe Lepko and Joe Leonardo. We had a great time playing together and were always competitive. The year following, we added really good players, Jack McPhilemy and Tommy McDermott. Our team was now called Dallas Beverage—sponsored by Mark Brady's father, who was the owner, and Mr. Crescenz, who delivered for them. This added some good height and we were really competitive. That was probably one of our best memories because we turned out to be a pretty good team—though there was always that one team that we couldn't beat."[29]

Around the same time, in 1961, they were eligible to try out for the team at St. A's, a squad that usually consisted mostly of eighth graders. Rarely did a seventh grader make the grade. But Mike and his friends were determined and ready to do what was necessary.

"The biggest problem we had that year was that Mike's older brother Charlie was in eighth grade and one of the better players on the team, along with some really good players like Jack McPhilemy, Bill Ziegler and some others," Ron says. "All of us knew the open slots would be limited. I won't say we made a pact but I honestly believe all five of us were determined to make the team no matter what. With Michael being the tallest, we assumed he would be a lock.

"The coach was Mike Cosgrove and without a doubt he was one of the best players ever at Simons Rec. Practices were tough and grueling but I think Mike played a huge part in all of us pushing hard to make the team. I know all of us were getting better."

As the deadline for final picks neared, the coach pulled Ron aside, to work on dribbling skills, he said. Ron was sure he was about to be cut. But the conversation didn't go as expected.

"He told me that more than likely Jimmy Engler, Dick Osborne and I were probably going to make the team," Ron says. "He was a guard when playing and based on our size and quickness he needed guards for next year also. I remember asking him about Mike and Mark, saying I hoped they were going to make it also. He didn't answer me at the time and we ended up talking about my oldest brother Roger. He was a good player, and had been on the 1958 team, but always had the tendency to have his outside shot hit the abutment of the low ceiling at our gym. So, coach said make sure Jimmy and Dick knew not to shoot the basketball too high, and also to keep practicing our lay-ups."

Finally, the tight-knit group learned that the hours and hours of practice and drills had paid off.

"When he picked the team, the great news was that all five of us had made it as seventh graders," Ron said. "I had always hoped that my conversation that day with Coach Cosgrove helped—it wasn't until years later that I realized I might have been a tag-along because my brother Roger and Coach Cosgrove's sister Marie were dating. Anyway, I never looked back and I know I improved as a player each year. I think all of us would agree that Mike Cosgrove was real instrumental in getting us started. He helped build in us the determination to play hard and play as a team.

"From that cut day forward, Michael, Jimmy, Dick, Mark and myself were linked as a team in almost every sport we played. For almost eight years we all played on the same basketball teams and developed as players. Most importantly, we developed as very good friends."[30]

And it was as friends and teammates that they faced their most challenging times together. In the Rec League, for example, there was always that one team they just couldn't beat—until inspiration struck.

"We were in a pretty intense game against this team we really struggled against and at one point in the game one of their point guards fouled me and knocked me down pretty hard," Ron says. "I was pretty feisty back then and I got right back up and was ready to retaliate. That's my first reaction: 'I'm gonna jump up and knock his block off.' Even though he was obviously a little bit bigger than I was."

Not just bigger. Soon that point guard had his whole team behind him, ready to do battle. And then, just as suddenly, Ron wasn't alone either.

"The first person there was Mike Crescenz," Ron says. "He stepped in and made sure that that other fella knew that nobody was going to be able to touch me or hit me. If there was going to be a fight, he would be the one to deal with it."[31]

"Mike, he was the anti-bully guy," Charlie told the *Philadelphia Inquirer*. "Our father ingrained that in us—that you never pick on people." If someone went too far, they got a warning from Michael, Charlie said, adding, "If you didn't listen to the warning, then you had a problem."[32]

"I'll never forget that. It was one of those things—he wasn't my brother but that day he was my big brother and probably saved me from getting my head beat in," Ron says with a chuckle. "That type of presence and demeanor was the foundation of his courage. No wonder he was a Medal of Honor recipient. Always the guardian then and still watching over me today."[33]

For Ron, the incident on the court made a solid lifelong friendship even stronger, but it wasn't the only significant memory of the day.

"The end result is we finally beat that team and it was one of the pleasures of our basketball careers because we just could not beat this team on a regular basis and that day, we found a way," Ron says. "Maybe the fight instilled that in us both, but who knows? It was a game that we both played really well in and it was a good win for us."[34]

Mike's loyalty knew no limits, as reflected in another time he was out with his friend Jimmy Engler.

"In grade school we hiked up to Scout Woods behind Gimbels [department store]," Jim says. "We were headed down the steep incline alongside the concrete spillway and I tripped and went tumbling down the hill. I got cut and all scratched up. Mike helped me back up the hill and we proceeded to return home so I could get tended to. Needless to say, his day of fun ended prematurely, but he didn't complain. He showed the kind of concern that he would demonstrate for the rest of his shortened life."[35]

Pinochle was the sport of choice during rainy days at the Rec, where teams would play cards under the canopy at the concession stand.

"Michael was my partner on many occasions," Ron says. "We were both at Cardinal Dougherty High School at the time and we used CDHS as our signal to each other for strength of hand—clubs, diamond, hearts, spades. That made it real easy to remember how we would bid. It was great when Mike and I were partners but when Rick and Ron Burke played against Mike and Charlie Crescenz, it sure changed the process. Still, Mike and I would roll our eyes and smile at each other even though we were playing against each other."[36]

The weather inspired another adventure for the group of friends. One winter day, though they might've preferred a pickup game indoors, they were hard at a game of tackle football, which was a good way to keep warm.

"In the cold winter months, it was hard to play basketball at the Rec," Ron says. "It was too cold or too windy or even too icy. We always wished we could go to an inside gym but there was none available to us."

During a break in the football game at St. A's, they found themselves on the massive grates—5 by 10 feet covering holes 8 to 10 feet deep—in front of the building. They were peering down and wondering. Was there a way into the closed school? There didn't appear to be through the heavy grates and the block glass below it. But...

"When we got up to play again, I think it was Tommy Stanton who pointed to the manhole. It was about 24 inches in diameter and raised up on concrete about a foot high," Ron says. "I remember that cement part real well because when playing there a year later I was tackled right onto that manhole. Got banged up real bad and missed a week of school. Anyway, going down into the manhole actually led to the boiler room of the school and, low and behold, a few steps through that room, into the gym. Awesome. We now had a place to play basketball and be warm. We played that day, got away with it, and decided to do it again the following week."

But for the next go-round they wanted a full-court game with two full teams of five. So they invited others along. The expanded group entered the same way the boys had the week before and the game commenced.

"As we were playing, we suddenly realized that there were kids watching us, kids running around on the stage, running up and down the stairwell. Where did everyone come from?" Ron says. "Turns out that one kid told another kid and then another kid and so on and so on. Obviously, word really got out. Eventually, there were over forty kids running all over. They were opening the doors, running in and out and our entire secrecy was blown. I didn't curse much back then but I remember saying to Mike and Billy that we would be in deep shit if we got caught.

"Thank goodness we were smart enough to stop. We got everyone out and then got out ourselves. We agreed to keep this between ourselves. If Mr. Burke, Mr. Crescenz or Mrs. Stanton had found out about what we did there would have been hell to pay. Luckily, we weren't caught by the nuns either or we would still be sitting in the cloak room with our hands sore from being whacked by a yard stick."[37]

One highlight in the countdown to graduation at Cardinal Dougherty, as with almost any high school, is senior prom. And it was no different for the Class of 1966. As with everything at Dougherty then, prom was a massive undertaking. The school, then just 10 years old, was in its heyday, with a peak enrollment of almost 6,000 students, requiring staggered schedules to accommodate them all. School and Archdiocese of Philadelphia officials claimed it was the biggest high school in the world. It certainly was world-renowned. Its marching band, color guard, and drill team—200 strong—performed for Pope Paul VI at the Vatican, for President Lyndon Johnson's inauguration in January 1965, for the 1962 NFL championship game (not then the Super Bowl), and for Princess Grace of Monaco, the Philadelphia-born actress Grace Kelly, who first became Hollywood royalty and then went on to marry a real-life prince. Two years before Mike and his friends graduated, the band won a world music championship in the Netherlands.

Though he was older than his best friend by almost four weeks, Ron didn't have his driver's license. But Mike did. Also, while the Burke family didn't own a car, the Crescenzes had a '65 Plymouth. Mike had permission to use it for the prom and he asked Ron if he wanted to double. Ron eagerly agreed, and they got to work.

"The two of us planned every step of the way together," Ron says. "In fact, we spent two full days washing, shining and polishing his dad's black and white Plymouth. The night of the prom it was whistle-clean. It looked like a brand-new car."

That Plymouth saw them through the seemingly endless rounds of photos, good wishes, and warnings to be careful, starting at the Crescenz home on Thouron Avenue, then with Ron's family, and finally at each girl's house. Through it all, there was one twist to the evening the boys' dates might not have been expecting.

"I think the girls were shocked when we put them in the back and I rode shotgun with Mike up front," Ron says with a smile. "I think they got the message that Mike and I were best of friends."

After they had posed for their last family photo, it was off to the big time, Philadelphia's Municipal Auditorium, the Art Deco landmark on Civic Center Boulevard at what was then the edge of the campus of the University of Pennsylvania. Over the years it had become known as the Philadelphia Convention Hall, having hosted four national political conventions in the 1930s and '40s. It was home to professional and college basketball and, in just the two years before the Class of '66 descended for prom night, the hall had hosted a sold-out show for the Beatles, to be followed by the Rolling Stones the next year. President Johnson made a campaign appearance there during his reelection effort in '64.

"Getting there was a unique experience because I had never driven directly down there, so Mike did his best to navigate and get us down the Schuylkill Expressway and out to the Penn campus area where the building was," Ron says. "We had no idea where to park so we drove around the block a couple of times and that was kind of comical. But eventually we parked, got into the prom and had a great night there."

After a night of dancing and fun with their classmates, they were off to the Venus Lounge on Broad and Reed Streets in South Philly, original home of famous disc jockey Jerry "The Geator with the Heater" Blavat. "That's where we hooked up with our favorite circle of friends and had a great party. Roast beef and sodas and everything else—we certainly couldn't have alcohol in those days. But we stayed there for another couple of hours and it was a good night had by all. I know it was the wee hours of the morning when Michael dropped me off at 2103 Walnut Lane and he headed to Thouron Avenue. Great time."[38]

In another month they were posing again, for and with their proud parents, this time in bright garnet high school graduation gowns. Times were changing rapidly, as the Crescenz family was all too aware. The year Mike graduated, brother Charlie enlisted in the Marines Corps, and soon he was off for a 13-month deployment to Vietnam.

CHAPTER III

Call to Service

In 1966, when Michael Crescenz and the West Oak Lane gang graduated from Cardinal Dougherty High School, the stirring words of America's first Catholic president, the late John F. Kennedy, still resonated with a generation looking to find their way in the world: "Ask not what your country can do for you—ask what you can do for your country."

This message—doing for others, taking care of your own, living up to your responsibilities—had been drilled into Michael and his circle of friends at home from birth and was at the heart of their 12 years of Catholic school education. They watched their parents, teachers, and coaches, as well as countless priests and nuns, live up to the credo, even if it wasn't always preached aloud. Actions often spoke louder than words. And those actions made an impression as the recent graduates considered their options: more school, work, or the military.

"We didn't talk about joining the military, although many of us, many of the kids in our class, had firsthand knowledge of what it was like for veterans of World War II," Jim Engler said. "My father served in World War II in the Army and Mike's father was a veteran of the Army too. You knew that they had served—though of course you didn't have any details—and it was a source of pride that you served in the military. I know in my mom's family, she talked about her five brothers, and the next thing she knew, in a couple of years four of them were in the service.

"So, it was pretty commonplace to expect to be in the military at some point, especially with the draft not being [ended] yet, and they were drafting people."[1]

That fall after graduation, Ron Burke began work on his associate's degree at nearby Temple University in North Philly, the city's option for working-class Philadelphians seeking to further their education. Michael went to work. He landed a job right over the city line in neighboring Montgomery County with L. B. Smith Inc. in Plymouth Meeting and began training as a welder.

His brother Charlie, who had graduated the year before, gave college a shot, signing up for a semester to study marketing at the Community College of Philadelphia. But he quickly decided it wasn't for him. He and a close friend opted for what was a common route for high school graduates at the time, the military, enlisting in the Marine Corps on the buddy system. They shipped off to the famous Marine Corps Recruit Depot, Parris Island, in South Carolina for boot camp on September 15, 1966, eight days before Charlie's parents would celebrate their 20th wedding anniversary. He was 19. In a very short time, he would begin a 13-month tour of duty in Vietnam.

Charlie's experience in the Marines had an impact on Jim when it came time to decide how best to serve his country.

"I wasn't as close to Charlie as I was to Mike since he was a year older than us," Jim Engler said. "But I do remember when he returned from boot camp at Parris Island, and him telling me how demanding and tough it was. Right then I thought if it was tough on Charlie then I wondered how I would handle it. It probably played a role in my decision to forego joining the Marines and join the Navy instead."[2]

But he had nothing but respect for Charlie's service. "I often think that because of Mike's heroic actions and recognition for such, that what Charlie went through in Vietnam as a member of a rifle company for thirteen months may have been overlooked somewhat. Having read many books and accounts of life as a 'grunt' in Vietnam, it was truly remarkable and worthy of much adulation to have survived such an ordeal. Many veterans served in Vietnam but few experienced the constant drudgery and danger that the grunt experienced each and every day while on the line. I remember seeing Charlie at the Crescenz house when he first got back in April 1968 and thinking it really was tough to get back to a normal state of mind after serving in combat for an entire tour in Vietnam."[3]

Jimmy Engler enlisted in the Navy in January 1967. Many others from the neighborhood would also enlist, or be drafted.

"The fun years for many of us occurred from the early 1950s to the mid-'60s. Then the reality of post high school years and the U.S. at war started to change the face of the neighborhood," Ron Burke says. "Charlie Crescenz, Michael Crescenz, Rick Burke, Ron Burke, Mickey McKenzie, Tommy Robinson, Billy Ziegler, Bud Laurich, Joe Cosgrove, Mike McBride, Jimmy Engler, Jack Norton, Joe Lynch, Charlie McGlinchy and many more were some of the people from the Rec who were off to various military services and shipped out to war or other hostile places.

"Of all the names I mentioned, there was not one of us who balked, challenged or objected to being drafted. There was not one of us who did not answer the call with remarkable pride and courage. Each one of us has fond memories and each one of us has our horror stories of being impacted by the Vietnam War, the Vietnam era, and the challenges of the time. Some had been wounded, some have had issues for many years, but all served with dignity and honor."[4]

In a documentary about his brother Michael, Charlie said, "I was in the Marine Corps, so I volunteered. The majority of guys who went to Vietnam were drafted so you kind of differentiated between them. Some people say you're an idiot for volunteering but I felt that's what I should do. Guys who were drafted I feel kind of sorry for, because that's not what they wanted to do. But the guys did serve so we're all the same."[5]

"When we started seeing our older brothers go off to war, we were thinking, 'I guess it's sort of like *Combat!* the TV series about the old World War II guys fighting the Germans," says Joe Crescenz, who had just turned 10 when Charlie enlisted. "That was my image of what war was and I really didn't have a sense of what Charlie went through, especially going through Marine Corps boot camp. It's still probably the toughest boot camp and back then probably even more so because they knew, soon as most of them were done, boom, right over to Nam."[6]

Joe knew about Vietnam from watching the six o'clock evening news each day, or reading about it in the paper. He even wrote to Charlie, but can't imagine now what he had to say to a brother in a war zone. The reality of his older brother's situation didn't register for him at that age.

"You just felt, 'Eh, they'll be home within a year,' and you went about your business. You still went and played your street games, you went to school. Mom and Dad, they went about their business the best they could, so you didn't have that sense they were probably praying to the good Lord every gosh damn night to bring their son on home uninjured and alive. We didn't know Mom and Dad were going through that."[7]

Still, there were certainly reminders close to home of what was happening on the other side of the world. Joe vividly recalls attending a funeral Mass for one recent Cardinal Dougherty grad, LCpl. John J. Murphy, who was killed in Vietnam on January 7, 1967. All the classes from St. Athanasius were packed into the church as a show of support for the Murphy family. The young Marine, just 21 when he was shipped overseas, had been in Vietnam a little over a week.

As terrible as the news was, Joe says with regret, "It didn't really hit home for me. I just thought, 'Oh man, a guy got killed.' It was terrible but it didn't sink in. And it sounds horrible, horrible, horrible of me to say this but my heart didn't go out to that family like it should have. The older I've gotten, it's like, 'Oh man.' But as a kid, I don't think it clicks unless it happens to somebody that's close to you. And it eventually did. It affected me for the rest of my life in a way that I didn't even realize."[8]

While Charlie was still in the thick of his tour of Vietnam, Michael was thinking about his next steps. Work was going well. By all accounts, he was enjoying welding and his work at Smith. He and his girlfriend Christine Carol were getting serious.

Joe had a chance to join Mike and Chrissy on a date one night. "They took me bowling," he says. "That was pretty cool that they allowed some little brother to tag along because I did love bowling. Got that from my father, who was a pretty good bowler. They didn't have to do that but it was neat, having an older brother and his girlfriend take me out on their date. Made me feel like I was her little brother, too. Very lovely girl."[9]

But as good as things were, Mike clearly believed he had more to do.

"He wanted to get on with his life, but he felt this call to duty," Joe says. "Like his older brother and all the other older guys in the neighborhood, who all felt it was their duty to serve our country—whether it was a just war or a right war, it was their duty to serve this country and they dealt with it as it came to them."[10]

"I talked to Mike right as he was going in," Ron Burke said, "and he seemed anxious to do it. He seemed ready to do whatever the country asked him to do at the time, and was proud to serve."[11]

The decision to go Army instead of the Marine Corps, Joe believes, might have been a continuation of the years of one-upmanship between his two oldest brothers.

"I think because of that sibling rivalry, Mike just had to go opposite," Joe says with a chuckle. "Mike and Charlie used to go back and forth with each other in a funny, jokingly, and brotherly love sort of way. And Mike probably figured, 'I'm gonna prove to Charlie that the Marines ain't the best. I'm going Army.' And he didn't want to wait for the draft. Nam wasn't getting any easier. The troop buildup was happening when he joined, Charlie was still overseas, so I guess he felt, 'Hey, now it's my turn.'"[12]

At the time, the Armed Forces Examination and Entrance Station was in Center City Philadelphia, at 401 North Broad Street, just four blocks from City Hall, which would be the backdrop of its share of protests during the Vietnam War. Michael reported for his preinduction physical on January 17, 1968, three days after his 19th birthday. He was just over 6 feet tall—later records would say 6 foot 2—and 187 pounds, and while the doctors noted that he'd broken his right hand at some point and had some fluid on his left knee, probably left over from his time on the gridiron, he was overall in good health. Less than a month later, on Valentine's Day, Michael took the oath of enlistment.

He joined just two weeks after what came to be known as the Tet Offensive, one of the largest military campaigns of the war, had erupted across South Vietnam. North Vietnamese and Viet Cong forces launched attacks in dozens of cities across the war-torn country, even blasting a hole in the wall of the U.S. Embassy in Saigon. U.S. and South Vietnamese forces would eventually prevail, but at great cost. It took 24 days just to recapture the city of Hue, in one of the bloodiest battles of the war. All told, Allied troops suffered almost 3,500 dead and more than 12,000 wounded during Tet—and the offensive would do its share of damage on the home front as well. After it, there was a loss of support for the war effort among many dispirited Americans that would never be regained.

This was the maelstrom Michael was volunteering to be part of when he raised his right hand and swore to "support and defend the Constitution of the United States against all enemies." He was shipped south, one of more than 200,000 young soldiers who underwent basic training in the late '60s at Fort Bragg, North Carolina—home of the famed 82nd Airborne Division and headquarters for U.S. Special Forces—and among more than 2.7 million American men and women who served in Vietnam.

The next few weeks were a whirlwind of training in the basics of soldiering. For Michael, some of this would be new, such as learning how to use and care for a variety of weapons. He would qualify as an "expert" on the M14, the semi-automatic rifle that was initially used in Vietnam, and receive the same rating later on the M16. It was 2 pounds lighter than the M14, with a smaller round that allowed soldiers to carry more ammunition in the field. He also learned how to use a bayonet and a grenade, and got the feel and taste of tear gas. In the classroom, they were drilled in the code of military conduct, chemical and biological weapons, the Geneva Convention, military justice.

But so much of what was demanded of him in North Carolina he'd spent a lifetime preparing for, both as a student at St. A's and Cardinal Dougherty and as an athlete on the ball fields of the Rec and schoolyards around the city. Basic turns civilians into soldiers with an onslaught of physical readiness training, endless road marches and formation drills, and confidence building. If Michael had anything, it was confidence, the quiet kind, as so many of his friends had observed over the years. He'd been doing isometrics through high school to make himself even more physically imposing for sports. Caring for and wearing a uniform? He'd had 12 years of that in Catholic school and on the numerous baseball, football, and basketball teams he'd joined. Discipline, teamwork, and values? That training began at home with his parents on Thouron Avenue and continued with nuns, priests, and coaches he'd met along the way, reinforced with every game shared with his core group of friends and teammates.

All those experiences had helped shape him into a good brother, son, and man, a responsible citizen ready to take on his duties at home, church, school and for his country. In fact, all that came before he enlisted contributed to his desire and willingness to serve. The Army would reinforce the values of good citizenship he'd learned, but its training has a much more immediate and important aim: preparing young soldiers like Michael Crescenz not only to complete their missions but also to survive them.

By the time Michael was ready to graduate from basic, in May, Charlie was home from Vietnam, and eager to check in on his younger brother—now also a brother in arms. "The last time I saw Michael was when I went to his graduation at Fort Bragg," Charlie told Samantha Crawford. "And then I guess he had additional training and after that he was sent to Vietnam."[13]

He was temporarily assigned to Company A, 1st Battalion, 2nd Brigade, U.S. Army Training Center at Fort Ord, California, and promoted to private first class while there on June 25. The next month he returned to the East Coast, this time to Fort Benning, Georgia, for advanced infantry training. There, the young soldiers reviewed and rehearsed all they learned in basic, in addition to receiving specialized training in small unit tactics and how to engage the enemy and advance on it as a team. Of course, there was more physical training—never again in their lives would they be in such shape. And there was more on weapons, drills repeated over and over again until their use and care became almost instinctual. It was here that Michael and his fellow infantrymen in training became intimately familiar with the M60, a gas-operated, air-cooled, belt-fed machine gun. It was known as "the Pig" or "the Hog" because of its grunting sound when firing; its size—at 23 pounds, it weighed three times more than an M16; and the way it chewed up and spit out ammo—up to 650 rounds per minute. It usually required a crew of two or three soldiers, who divided the ammunition among themselves while in the field and carried extra barrels, to replace—never as easily as advertised—overheated ones in the middle of a firefight.

Overarching the daily stresses and demands of training was the reason behind it all. It was no secret where many of these young soldiers would be assigned next. And one had only to watch the evening news to be reminded of the risks. Once in country, these newly minted infantrymen would have missions to perform. The training, the discipline, the attention to detail, pushing them mentally and physically beyond what they ever imagined they could do, was all designed to ensure they completed those wartime missions successfully and—most important of all—returned home safe and sound to family and friends.

On August 2, Michael received his final vaccination, this one for cholera, before being shipped overseas. He'd already been inoculated for tetanus, yellow fever, smallpox, typhoid and typhus.

Now, Vietnam awaited, but it would have to wait just a little longer. After six long months away, Pfc. Michael J. Crescenz was going home on leave to Philadelphia.

Joe doesn't recall a going-away party when Michael enlisted in early 1968. "There was no big deal made of it," he says. "Everything was low-key. Maybe it was a sign of the times."[14]

But it was different when Michael came home that summer. For one thing, Charlie had been back from Vietnam since April. And now a second Crescenz son was going off to war. There was reason to gather, count the family's blessings, and pray for another safe return.

"Before Michael shipped off, Mom and Dad had a big family gathering with friends, neighbors, and guys that Mike and Charlie grew up with," Joe says. "I'll never forget this: We found out that Michael had proposed to his high school sweetheart and she accepted. At first, Michael wanted to get married before he went overseas. When we had the party, Mom begged him not to, and she finally approached her father-in-law. My Italian grandfather spoke to him and made a little more sense to him. He told Michael, 'Look, you're giving your mother a hard time here. Don't. If that girl loves you, she can wait another year till you get home. You do your time. Come home. We'll throw you a big wedding. Don't you worry about it. If that girl loves you, she'll be here for you when you get home.' And that was that. Michael said, 'Okay, Pop-Pop, I guess I'll have to wait.'

"Mike, of course, being fond of Pop-Pop, he listened to him. It's funny he listened to Pop-Pop more than he listened to Mom at that time.

Cause Mike was pretty headstrong. He wanted to get married before he shipped out, but my grandfather spoke some sense into him—knocked some sense into him, I should say."[15]

Some of his closest friends from the neighborhood didn't make it to the party. They, too, were in the military at that point. Among them was Ron Burke. He was drafted into the Army after completing his associate's degree and was already at Fort Bragg for his own turn at basic training when Michael was home on leave. Jim Engler had joined the Navy six months after they had graduated from Dougherty, so he wasn't around when Michael first came home.

"I missed that party," Jim says, "but was on leave from the Navy before Mike left for the West Coast in September and we hooked up."[16]

Jim would never forget that night, the last time they would see each other. They met not just as old high school friends, but as soldier and sailor. Their first stop was the neighborhood pizza hangout and eventually they ended up in front of the Crescenz home on Thouron Avenue.

"We sat out in my car in front of a pizza parlor where I used to work, Jimmy's, talking and drinking beer—Mike always got served because he was so tall and looked older than most of us. It's funny, we both had owned Mercury Comets before entering the service. I think we talked about that. He bought a nicer one than I had. Mine went to my brother when I went in the service. I don't know what happened to Mike's car.

"He also told me he had gotten engaged to Chris. My wife Anna was my girlfriend by then. We were both looking ahead, maturing at a very fast pace. I guess it was the times we lived in and the way we were brought up.

"I don't remember how long we sat there, parked in front of his house. Just shot the breeze and he didn't show any trepidation or concerns, you know, about going to Vietnam. I guess Mike wasn't really one to share his feelings and maybe he never had any doubts. I don't know. Mike always had confidence, he really did. Maybe he was born with it, maybe it was the fact that he had to compete with Charlie and that drove him a little further. But he didn't doubt himself. Maybe that was part of the heroic deeds, that he chose to not fall prey to his own fears. I don't know. But he was a tough kid. He was strong and he was tough.

"But certainly, many of us had doubts about what would happen if you went to Vietnam. It prevented me. At one time, after Charlie went through Marine basic training I thought, 'Boy, that sharp uniform. I'd like to join him.' But reality sunk in and going to Vietnam as a combat troop didn't sound like the best choice. The Navy seemed a better fit for me anyway."[17]

After 10 days among those he loved, Michael flew out of Philadelphia International Airport on September 18, 1968, landing in Oakland, California, a few hours later. Along the way, he met and took an instant liking to a fellow private first class, Bob Gleason, from Buffalo, New York.

"Mike and I met and we hit it off immediately, since I had nine brothers and he had five," Bob recalled decades later. "I was the third oldest. We were both heavily involved with baseball, grew up in a large Irish family. To this day I still remember that Mike went to Cardinal Dougherty High School."[18]

Bob went to a two-year college after high school, played baseball there, and then matriculated to the University of Buffalo. He had a full-time day job, so he took classes at night. "Big family, no money," he says frankly. "I dropped one course—one—and a month later I was drafted."[19]

Like Mike, he was shipped to Fort Bragg for basic, but received his advance infantry training at Fort Polk, Louisiana. From there, again like Mike, and countless others, he stopped in Oakland en route to Vietnam.

"We arrived and were sent to an airplane hangar," Bob recalls of the 12 hours he and Mike spent in Oakland. "It was a cluster fuck. Guys all over the place. We wanted to get a beer but that didn't happen. We were among hundreds of servicemen bunked down on cots and finally boarded a bus to Travis Air Force Base—57 miles away—early the next day."[20]

Many of the men in the hangar endured a wait of a week or more before hearing their names called. Mike and Bob were relatively lucky, forced to hang around for just 12 hours. But the time was well spent—they used it as an opportunity to talk almost nonstop.

At Travis they boarded a commercial flight run by the Flying Tiger Line, an airline the government used to transport personnel and cargo back and forth from Vietnam. It was named for the legendary fliers who defended China against the Japanese during World War II. The attendants for the flights to Vietnam were often the last civilians the troops saw, and years later the women remembered how difficult those trips could be. One former attendant, during a reunion in 2014, told NBC Bay Area, "If they tried to engage us in any kind of emotional conversation, we just changed the subject. And said, 'Oh, there's more of you guys coming home than you can imagine.'" Another remembered the men filling out postcards to loved ones during the flight. "It was really tear-jerking stuff," she said. "I'd sit there in the back jump seat reading these things, crying my eyes out."[21]

"On the plane, the seats were three across," Bob said, "with Mike, me, and this guy who was a mortician. Mike and I looked at each other and decided we didn't want to talk to him."[22]

As Mike had done his whole life with people back home in Philadelphia, he made a strong impression on Bob.

"Mike was kind of gung-ho," Bob said. "I noticed that Mike had fatigues on. He told me about his brother Charlie who already was 'over there' and then I see he has these fatigues on. He had two of everything and was reading a field manual on military tactics."[23]

After a stop-off in Anchorage, Alaska, they landed in Long Bien, South Vietnam, officially "in country" as of September 22, 1968, assigned to the 23rd Administration Company, Replacement Detachment, U.S. Army Pacific.

"You'd see them walk off," a Flying Tigers attendant told the NBC affiliate, "and you'd kind of go, 'Oh, will we take them home?'"[24]

Mike and Bob were sent to Chu Lai, a sprawling Marine Corps base in central Vietnam just south of Da Nang that was home to the Army's 23rd (American) Division. "When we arrived at Chu Lai, we both went through additional training at the combat center—booby traps, pop-up targets, that kind of stuff," Bob said. "So, we trained together for a week or two when we first hit Vietnam. And then we were trying to go to the same company or unit, and Mike created quite a stir about it when we were split up."[25]

The American Division was comprised of three light infantry brigades—the 11th, the 196th, and the 198th—and the 16th Aviation Regiment, as well as other units. Each of the brigades had three or four infantry battalions, with each battalion having 500 to 800 soldiers. The 196th, which was known as the fire brigade because it was sent to so many of the division's hot spots, had three battalions—3rd Battalion, 21st Infantry; 4th Battalion, 31st Infantry; and 2nd Battalion, 1st Infantry.

Mike and Bob were both assigned to the "fire brigade," but different battalions, despite their request to be stationed together, and Mike created a stir when informed their request was denied. Bob went to Charlie Company, 2nd Battalion, 1st Infantry, while Mike drew Alpha Company, 4th Battalion, 31st Infantry. Bob would never forget his new-found friend, but he never saw Mike again after they shipped out to their respective units.

Sergeant First Class Jim Willard had been in Vietnam eight months when Mike was assigned to his 3rd Platoon, a weapons squad. Jim had worked his way up from ammo bearer, assistant gunner, gunner, and then finally squad leader.

"I remember my first impression upon meeting Mike," he said. "We were both strong believers that our faith would get us through the war. Mike was Catholic; I am a Baptist. I fully appreciated his dedication to what he was doing. I really believed he was doing what he thought was best, for us and the Lord. It was our purpose for being there.

"He was gung-ho. He never shared why he joined, but Mike believed in what we were doing, and why we—the United States—were there. With his attitude, Mike could have won the war single-handedly if anyone could. There were times when he was out on point or patrol, and he did some heroic things, which I would say, 'Why would you do that?' To which he would reply, 'For God and country. And to protect my guys.' And *we were his guys*. Mike had a total neglect for himself—it was solely to protect us."[26]

William "Doc" Stafford arrived at the 196th the same month as Michael. He had enlisted right after high school, was trained as a medic at Fort Sam Houston in Texas, and volunteered for Vietnam. Like Michael, he was assigned to Alpha Company's 3rd Platoon.

He remembers the young man from Philadelphia well. "First impression? Handlebar mustache, big, thick handle. And he was growing a beard. You could get away without shaving for a week, two weeks. But

I remember that mustache, thick and bushy, thicker than mine. There is one picture of him, I guess it was taken in boot camp or something, that shows him as this baby-faced kid, which he was. But that's why people thought it was great to have hair on your face at that age. You were a man or whatever. It was a sign of maturity.

"And he was a pretty good-sized guy, big guy, 200 pounds plus, I think. I remember that he was engaged. He was so excited about that, and that he had a big family. He loved his family. He was very family-oriented. He was proud to be from Philadelphia. He was proud to be there. He was a good guy."[27]

Doc, too, recalls a gung-ho side of Michael, but Mike wasn't alone. "A lot of people were kind of gung-ho," Doc says. "I was gung-ho until I got there and somebody started shooting at me and I said, 'Ah, so this is what it's like.' This book I had read about Custer and Patton and Eisenhower, and all the books I'd read, it's not exactly the same. What they portray in words about war and real life were a little different.

"And Mike was enthusiastic he could do it all, but that also comes with the age, being that young and being kind of naive, really, and being a male, thinking you could do it. Everybody could be Audie Murphy [the heavily decorated World War II hero], which wasn't the case. Mike sure tried, though. I don't think he thought—he just thought he was doing the right thing and that's what he was there for, and in reality, he was."[28]

Doc felt the same way. He had already registered for college and was headed in that direction, but he reconsidered, in part because of friends who had served in Vietnam.

"It was the right thing to do," he says. "At that point in time, the Vietnam War was popular, or it was accepted. My father had been in World War II, his father in World War I, and before that, family members had served in prior wars. I didn't see anything wrong with it. I had no clue what it was like. That was for sure.

"War is not a pretty thing. War is not a very good thing. If one can avoid it, it's a good idea because it can not only hurt you or kill you or maim you. It can also psychologically hurt you, and you have to live with it for the rest of your life. But my initial thing there: I was excited and I'm ready to go. The Army had done a pretty good job, psychologically, of getting me to want to do my job. The people I met and formed a relationship with, such as Michael and others, it was a good thing. The camaraderie was great. Everybody was together. There was no race, color, religion. It was just people, comrades. That was a good thing."[29]

Mike and Doc had landed in central Vietnam just in time for the monsoon season, when the countryside could get slammed almost daily and see up to 24 inches of rain. Temperatures in this tropical climate run into the 80s, with humidity often hovering around 85 percent. The soldiers of the 196th were out in the pouring rain and unrelenting heat regularly, frequently making contact with the enemy.

"It took some time to get acclimated to the weather in Vietnam," says Doc, who was assigned as one of two or three platoon medics in his company. "It was hot, muggy. They kept you up in Long Binh, a holding facility, for the first week or so to get acclimated."[30]

But it wasn't just the weather that took getting used to.

"I can remember being apprehensive but also being excited about being in a new place," Doc says. "I was, at that point, 19 years old and I hadn't been anywhere. It was just totally different. Different smell, area. People were different."[31]

Once assigned to the 196th, he and his fellow soldiers were regularly sent out on long, rigorous patrols.

"There was a lot of physical exertion, a lot of walking," he recalls. "We walked everywhere. And I carried a lot of weight—food, ammunition, and for me, I had a medical bag that weighed thirty pounds or so—and I had to get used to walking and get used to the people I was around. It was all new to me. It was all fresh. In the beginning, it was exciting, I thought, but now thinking about it 40 years later, it wasn't that exciting. I could have done without it."[32]

His fellow soldiers may not have had medical bags, but still had plenty of gear to haul around.

Infantrymen like Michael had their M16, but also three hand grenades, 20-plus magazines, with 20 rounds in each, cans of C rations for several days, water, a claymore mine, a foldable shovel for digging foxholes (known as an entrenching tool), meal prep utensils, and C4, which could be used to heat up meals.

"Our mission in the area of operation (AO) was trying more to harass the North Vietnamese Army (NVA), not search and destroy," Willard said. "Our battalion units were deployed for harassment missions—to both make, then break, contact as frequently as possible—to prevent them from fortifying potential supply lines, such as the Ho Chi Minh Trail along the Laotian border."[33]

Lieutenant Colonel Sam Wetzel, a Korean War veteran and former Reserve Officer Training Corps (ROTC) instructor, had assumed command of 4th Battalion, 31st Infantry, that July. In his six months as battalion commander—the standard rotation for command officers, while the troops usually served a year in country—he was hands-on, out with his troops each day, constantly emphasizing training, believing that it, above all, would see his men through their mission and safely home.

If there were losses among his command, he took them deeply personally. Decades after he retired from 34 years in the military as a lieutenant general, Wetzel told an interviewer he took a list of the men who died while he commanded the 31st to Mass with him each week. His list included their names, ranks, hometowns, dates of death, and, in some cases, coordinates for the exact location where they fell. "I pray for these guys every Saturday night," he said.[34]

Given what his soldiers faced, it's almost miraculous the list is not considerably longer.

"We had contact practically every day with North Vietnamese regulars—some sort of firefight at low level, like a squad or platoon level," he told the *Inquirer*'s Bob Moran. "We were way out, 35 miles northwest of Chu Lai in southwestern Da Nang, up in the mountains of the northern part of South Vietnam. We had no way of getting vehicles out to us, everything had to come by helicopter: resupply, ammunition, replacements, evacuation of killed and wounded, and so forth. Everything was done by helicopter, even bringing in big water buffaloes, as we called them [water tanks on wheels], with water out to the bases."[35]

Wetzel was in his command-and-control helicopter every morning, visiting troops in the field, scouting for NVA and Viet Cong, leading supply and evacuation missions, and alerting his rifle companies to nearby enemy forces and their movements.

Missions through the dense jungle, regular contact with the enemy, the heat and rain, all could get to even the most gung-ho of soldiers.

Joe Crescenz remembers an exhausted Mike writing home to the family in Philadelphia.

"In one of the few letters we got from Vietnam—don't forget he was only there a little under two months—he talked about how tired they were," Joe said. "Him and his platoon were on the move, day and night, constantly, for weeks at a time. Part of it was because he thought the commander in chief, who was Lyndon Baines Johnson at the time, had pulled a bone-headed move by halting the bombing of Hanoi. The NVA were busy building up their troops, their weaponry and all that, I presume on the Ho Chi Minh Trail near where Mike's guys were operating, and they felt, these guys out in the boonies, humping it as foot soldiers, as grunts, they weren't getting the proper support from back home.

"I remember because my father was commenting on it to my mother at the dinner table. I was surprised because Dad and Mom kept everything pretty tight. They didn't say too much in front of us younger kids about anything, especially the war and what our older brother was writing home about."[36]

So tight-lipped were Charles and Mary Ann about what they were hearing from Michael that Joe was quite eager to sneak a peek at a letter he spied one day on his father's bedside table, especially when he saw who it was from. But his hopes of finding out more were dashed. Someone started coming up the stairs, and Joe quickly put the letter back exactly as he'd found it. "I threw it back where it was supposed to have gone," Joe says. "So I really didn't get a good grasp of what it was, but it was definitely a letter that Michael sent from Vietnam."[37]

Looking back, Joe is sure his parents kept things from the younger children because they had their own worries about what Michael was going through.

"Charlie came home in April and four months later Michael was getting his orders to go over," Joe said. "So, I think it was taking a toll on our mother. Imagine having a second son go back over to that craziness. I'm sure that brought a lot of angst, a lot of anxiety, just like any mother of a soldier or Marine, airman, or sailor that gets the call to go overseas and do what their country has asked them to do.

"I don't know how she did it. I don't know how I would have reacted if any of my kids went off to a foreign land to do their thing. You'd worry every gosh damn day, day and night. I'm sure my parents didn't sleep well, especially my mom. How could you get a restful sleep knowing that you had sons back-to-back going over to Nam like that? And I'm sure my parents weren't the only ones who went through that."[38]

Joe, as a kid, didn't really connect the war he watched on the nightly news with the experiences of his brothers.

"Watching it on TV with my dad, it was like watching a movie," Joe said. "My head wasn't into the actual horrors of the war. It was just like I was viewing a TV show or movie. Unfortunately, that's the way my mind worked at that young age. I heard guys were getting killed but it wasn't affecting me because it didn't affect anybody in our household at that time. At least from what I could see. It wasn't registering like it would for our parents, especially my dad being a combat veteran of World War II. Don't know what he thought—he never spoke about it, of course—but I know that it had to affect him, seeing these young men over there fighting."[39]

Two letters Michael sent home from Vietnam survive. One, dated October 31, is mostly responding to news he received of his brothers in letters sent to him from Philadelphia.

> Dear Mom and Dad,
> I received a letter from you yesterday, it was a welcome sight, they didn't bring mail out to us for four days and everyone was glad to see some. I'm glad to hear that everybody is doing well and that there is no bad news.
> I see in your letter that Peter is trying to be a hippie, well tell him that I said he is a strap. And if he doesn't like that tell him that's too bad because the truth hurts. Let me know what he says.
> So Chollie wants to get an Olds 442, does he? Well, tell him it's going to cost because they are pretty nice cars. Tell him to put a big deposit on it or they will rob him on interest. I guess dad has explained that already to him. Did he get his license yet? You better also tell him that he should get to be an experienced driver before he gets a nice car like that. Because if he cracks that up, he will be in a jam.

I think you're doing right by letting him do what he wants to do. Then he can determine how much things cost these days. Tell dad for me, not to worry about it because if he goes into debt, it's his own prerogative. Then maybe he'll admit you were right. Then again, I think he'll be able to swing it pretty good. Ask him if he has been working overtime. That's where he can get extra money. Ask him also if Wayne or anybody else is giving him trouble. Because Wayne is a bum and if he lets him, he'll let Chollie do all the work while he sits back and watches. Tell him to write me and let me know about his car, job, and the school he is going to. I'd like to know what he is going to do. And how he's doing.

Well, I guess that's about all for the time being, be sure to take care of yourselves and may God bless all of you. Tell the little ones I said hi.

With love,
Your son
P.S. Don't gain too much weight mom. You looked good when you were thin. Keep off the beer a bit.[40]

In the second, dated November 19, he asks about family but there is more about the war, and what he and his fellow soldiers are experiencing. The battle of Nui Chom Mountain had been raging for two days at this point.

Dear Mom and Dad,

How's everything going with you lately? I've been quite busy lately. We have been in two firefights in two days. We practically wiped out about a half of a regiment of NVA yesterday and we only had a few wounded men. We lucked out but they didn't. Thank God.

Well enough of that. We have a system for mail and re-supply during the monsoon, we don't get anything but once every three days. So please be patient with my mail, it's not my fault. It's this lousy system they have.

How has everything been going with all of you back home? I hope the weather isn't too bad. Here it's surprising, they say this monsoon has been the most irregular one they have ever had. It has rained a lot but it hasn't been anything compared to last year's. That's why no one can understand why we can't get re-supplied more often. Well, the monsoon is about half over and this system ends at the end of monsoon. I hope to get your package today when we get our re-supply shipment, our mail comes in when we get re-supplied. So, now you know why I don't get mail that often. I hope you sent me some goodies because I'm half-starved anymore. I hope you got that letter from me asking for the soup and ravioli because it sure will be appreciated when I do get it.

The NVA kept us up all last night so right now I'm pretty tired. I've been pretty busy for the last couple of days. I've shot about 8,000 rounds in two days, that's a pretty lot wouldn't you say? I think I nailed a few on the run yesterday but I didn't put my head up to look.

Well, let me know if you've had any exciting news, until next time be sure to take care and may God bless all of you.

Love, Mike[41]

Two years before, another soldier, 1st Lt. John F. Cochrane, a 25-year-old platoon leader, wrote to his parents on the eve of battle:

Tonight...I am awaiting an attack. Yes, that's right.... Your only son, who you didn't raise to be stupid, is 11,000 miles away from home, sitting here beneath a shadowed Coleman lantern on top of a hill awaiting a visit from friend "Charlie." ...Here I sit, so afraid that my stomach is a solid knot, yet laughing, joking, kidding around with the 18 troops with me—and even writing a letter to the folks back home as if I haven't a care in the world. What I really want to do is to load up these men...and get out of here.... I have offered every excuse in the world, but I know why I am here and why I couldn't be any other place. The reason is because I do believe we should be here and I do believe that...basic principles are enough for a man to die for.... We are here because we actually believe that our country is good enough to fight, and even to die, for. All we ask is that some good come out of it....

Charlie is a formidable enemy.... It really seems that God has turned his back on mankind when one is in a situation like this. With all the intellect and intelligence and scientific discovery he has endowed man with, it boils down to two soldiers on opposite sides, sworn to kill each other....

I am going to take one last look around and then I am going to try to get some sleep. If all goes well, I will finish this tomorrow. Thank goodness I can call on God at a moment like this.[42]

The next morning, he added to the letter: "I wonder if we will ever know what makes man work. What causes him to do things he does."

Nine days later, on October 24, 1966, Cochrane was killed by a sniper. His letter home was read aloud that year at the White House tree-lighting ceremony by President Johnson. The commander in chief added, "I have known many brave men and wise men, but I wish I had known Lieutenant John Cochrane. Then I would have known the best of men."[43]

One of the men in Cochrane's unit, Charlie Becker, had graduated from Cardinal Dougherty High School a few years ahead of the oldest Crescenz brothers. He would be one of many Vietnam vets from the

Philadelphia area who would help the Crescenz family honor Michael in later years.

What Michael did not mention in his last letter home was that he and the other tired soldiers of 3rd Platoon, A Company, 4th Battalion, 31st Infantry, would be going deeper into Nui Chom Mountain the next day. The NVA were waiting for them.

CHAPTER IV

The Battle of Nui Chom Mountain

When he wrote home for the last time, on November 19, 1968, Michael Crescenz was sending a first-person account of a small part of what became known as the battle of Nui Chom Mountain.

Elements of the North Vietnamese Army first made contact with the 4th Battalion, 31st Infantry, commanded by Lt. Col. Sam Wetzel, two days before. A history of the 31st Infantry, compiled by men who had served in the unit, described the opening hours of the battle: "On November 17 at 1000 hours, Company D, commanded by Captain Sidney Ordway… made contact with the enemy at the base of Nui Chom. Moving up the mountain they found ever increasing enemy emplacements. At 1345 hours, the company encountered a large base camp with a stream flowing through the middle, sleeping positions, and spider holes everywhere…."[1]

The account began:

> The 1st Platoon was walking point along the base of Nui Chom. The experienced men in the platoon felt in their guts that they were in a bad place. Lieutenant Dolan stopped the company and sent out two teams to do a flank recon. When they returned, he took a fire team…on a deep flank recon up toward the Nui Chom ridgeline. They discovered a well-worn trail cut into the ground, wide enough for wheeled carts. They smelled smoke and came to another trail leading directly up the mountain. Soon they saw several armed, well-equipped men in NVA uniforms. The fire team was then engaged by the NVA.[2]

John Dolan talked to the *Ledger-Enquirer* of Columbus, Georgia, for a series on the 50th anniversary of the battle: "We hadn't gone very far up that trail when I could see in the distance several well equipped men in uniforms sitting around a small cooking fire, talking softly. We moved closer and got behind a large rock. Then all hell broke loose."³

The history of the 31st Infantry continued:

> Lieutenant Dolan and his group returned fire, hitting some of the enemy. The enemy scattered and left behind two AKs [AK47 assault rifles] and a radio. The retreating enemy left a blood trail up the mountain. Lieutenant Dolan radioed his platoon and the company commander. It was obvious that the fire team had found an outpost of a large NVA force. The company command group linked up with the 1st Platoon fire team at the site of the NVA outpost. Lieutenant Dolan left his RTO [regimental transport officer] at the trail junction below the site of the initial contact with orders to guide his platoon and the rest of the company to his location farther up the mountain.⁴

The recon team, reinforced by the command group, which included Captain Ordway and 1st Sgt. John Neely, set off in pursuit of the NVA.

"I mean, we were running hard," radio operator Butch Harris would tell the *Ledger-Enquirer*. "We had dropped our packs and left two platoons to secure the packs and guard the trail. As we took off running, the blood kept getting better and better."⁵

"The fire team lost the blood trail but continued up the trail," the 31st history continues. "One of the fire team noticed a dozen or more strands of communication wire, a likely sign of a large enemy headquarters, alongside the trail going up the mountain. Further up the mountain the trail and the communications wire divided. The two groups split up, and soon both groups were engaged with the enemy."⁶

"Captain Ordway went down almost immediately," Harris told the *Ledger-Enquirer*. "The first sergeant yelled he was hit and folded over. The rest of us started to return fire in the direction to the front of us."⁷

Ordway was wounded across the forehead and blinded. He never regained his sight. Neely's hand was torn up badly.

Wetzel was nearby, in his command-and-control helicopter, when Harris radioed the dire situation. "We're in heavy contact, need help," Harris told him. "My commander has been hit, my first sergeant has been hit, and they're down and we're in heavy contact here. We need air strikes." Wetzel obliged, with both air and artillery support.

Years later, Wetzel was still impressed with how the young radio operator took command. "He, in fact, was running the company," the retired general said. "He was a specialist four, the equivalent of a corporal, but he was passing my instructions down."[8]

Harris had Ordway and Neely evacuated to a secure rear position and they immediately prepared the area for a medevac helicopter. The specialist was also coordinating with platoons to pull back from the camp and set up a defensive perimeter.

An *Americal* article published about six months after the battle reported:

> Assuming command with cool efficiency, Harris radioed the platoons and relayed LTC Wetzel's orders. Instructing the forward platoons to mark their positions with smoke grenades, he then coordinated with 'Blue Ghost' gunships of F Troop, 8th Cav, for air support.
>
> The helicopters came in with mini-guns and machine guns blazing, and after they hosed down the area expending their ammo, artillery fire was called in.[9]

"The pilot said that he could see the NVA soldiers running and to keep our heads down," Harris told the *Ledger-Enquirer*. "The choppers started to work with the M79, M60s, rockets and mini-gun on the side. Man, what a beautiful sight."[10]

The retreating enemy also came in contact with Alpha Company—Michael Crescenz's unit—and the running firefight continued.

Lieutenant Dolan reflected on how the men of Delta Company kept their heads amid the chaos.

"The leaders and men of my platoon and Delta had to act on their own initiative that day," Dolan said. "The CO [commanding officer] was seriously wounded and I did not have a radio when the heaviest contact was taking place. Men and leaders literally moved toward the sound of the gunfire and then took the action that they saw needed to be taken. In so doing, they insured that the lead elements were supported, enemy fire was suppressed, casualties were moved to safety and evacuated, and the NVA force that was fighting from fixed positions and greatly outnumbered our company chose to break contact and withdraw rather than continue the fight."[11]

Harris mentioned the bravery of one soldier in particular that day. "It seemed like everything happened just after Captain Ordway was wounded," he told Hawkins for the *Americal* article.

"He got hit in the open. I ran to him and started dragging him to cover when a friend of mine from First Platoon (Spc. Jim 'Homeboy' Williams) started running through the exposed area to our front.

"I kept yelling, 'Get back, Homeboy, get back. I got him,' but Homeboy kept firing at the fighting position where machine-gun fire was coming. He kept their heads down long enough for me to drag the captain to safety. Homeboy was one of the last to pull back.

"He had only eight days to go in the field, and I kept thinking, 'Don't get hit now, Homeboy, not now.' When he finally pulled back to the rear security platoons he had two AK47 bullets lodged in an M16 magazine in the bandolier slung over his shoulder. I remember we both smoked about three packs of cigarettes that afternoon."[12]

As Wetzel ordered Harris and his men back to regroup, he was already formulating his plan to move all four of his companies back up to take Nui Chom and inflict as much damage on the enemy as possible.

"I wanted to keep contact with the enemy so we could move other companies up the fingers of the mountain," he told the *Ledger-Enquirer*. "The mission was to take that hill and kill as many North Vietnamese as we could."[13]

But at that point, he wasn't aware of just how deeply entrenched the NVA were—"I had no idea they had more than 250 bunkers in the area," he said later.[14]

His plan to take Nui Chom was inspired by the World War II battle of San Pietro in Italy. Wetzel knew the battle well. He had taught it as an ROTC instructor a dozen years earlier at Idaho State University. The confrontation during the Second World War featured a mountain similar to Nui Chom, defended by heavily fortified German forces. In that battle, it took American GIs nine days to prevail, but at the cost of brutally high numbers of wounded and killed in action.

While Wetzel saw the similarities in terrain and a potential line of attack between San Pietro and Nui Chom, he wasn't about to expose his guys to the same high casualty rate the GIs of the World War II battle endured.

"I wanted to have as few casualties as possible with lots of air strikes, artillery and mortars," Wetzel told the *Ledger-Enquirer*.[15]

He envisioned three routes of attack. Alpha and Delta Companies would work their way up the mountain from the eastern left flank, Bravo from the west, and Charlie in the center.

"I looked at the map and saw that there were three fingers going up Nui Chom, and attacking with three companies would get as many infantry fighters going up together as possible, supported by the air strikes, artillery and mortars," Wetzel told the *Ledger-Enquirer*. "It worked. I also knew we needed another company from the right flank on up the hill and I asked Col. (Frederick) Kroesen for a company from 2/1 Infantry [2nd Battalion, 1st Infantry] to assist us. He agreed."[16]

Even with the air strikes and artillery bombardment pounding enemy positions before the Americans' ascent of Nui Chom, they would find the going every bit as difficult as their counterparts had in their assault on San Pietro almost 25 years before.

"Nui Chom was a very steep mountain, a very high mountain, with some very difficult terrain," Wetzel told the *Inquirer*'s Bob Moran.

"And what people don't realize is, we're out in the jungle, we're 35 miles from the South China Sea, northwest of Chu Lai in southwest Da Nang, up in the northern part of South Vietnam. No roads out there. It's all helicopter-supplied, for people or ammunition or whatever. It rains a lot, and we're just in November, so it's right after the monsoon season, and everything is slippery as the devil. And the mountain, it's literally this steep, and fighting up that mountain, we had to go on our hands and knees, crawling practically, inch by inch. These are infantrymen, on foot, and they are sliding like crazy all the time and practically crawling up this mountain.

"And it's the jungle, so it's hot, and these guys, of course, are sweating all the time in the process of climbing up rocks and slippery slopes in a triple-canopy jungle so you can't see. There's not too much daylight either coming through these big, tall trees, jungle trees. So, you're in the jungle but you're on a mountain also. There's not wide-open spaces at all, so you can't see very far in front of you, and night is just pitch black....

"So that's why it took so long, it took six days. And I just said, 'We're gonna do this inch by inch with lots of artillery, lots of mortars, lots of air strikes, and even the USS *New Jersey*, the battleship, firing for us from out in the South China Sea. So, we had lots and lots of help.'"[17]

But even that formidable firepower wasn't enough to eradicate the machine gunners hidden in well-fortified bunkers throughout the mountain. Hawkins wrote, "The enemy was well entrenched in camouflaged fighting positions and sunken bunkers 10 to 15 meters off the main trail. The bullet-spitting fortifications had bamboo covers camouflaged with dirt and foliage." One well-placed bunker, with a .30-caliber machine gun, could stall a unit's progress for hours.[18]

"We more or less leap-frogged up the trail knocking out the enemy bunkers as we went," Staff Sergeant Phillip Madlin of 1st Platoon told Hawkins.

"One of our biggest problems," he continued, "and one that really slowed us up, was that the enemy bunkers were always above us. They were about three-fourths below ground, and when you first looked at them, they looked like an ordinary rise in the ground. Our point men usually couldn't spot them until they were fired upon."[19]

Once a position was identified, the Americans moved in a machine gun team of their own to level suppressive fire against the enemy. As they blasted away with hundred-round belts of ammo, other squad members maneuvered closer to the bunker, attempting to silence it with grenades and their M16s.

Alpha Company medic Doc Stafford remembers his unit moving into position before the assault on Nui Chom.

"We came in off helicopters, off into a jungle, but it was flat, and had trails. We walked for hours until we got to the mountain. I remember camping at the base of it. It got cold for Vietnam, because it would be 100/110 degrees and then it would go to 70, and that was cold. I think it was raining. Many times, it would rain every day, it would rain for 10 minutes, it would rain for an hour."

In the quiet of the evening before their ascent, Doc made his rounds.

"I remember checking on the guys," he said. "One of my responsibilities was checking people's feet and things like that, you know, making sure they took their malaria pills and making sure they felt okay, and just giving them—not consoling them—but just paying attention to them, making sure they were feeling good. That was part of my job.

"And I remember some apprehension because we knew something was going to happen for sure, because we'd heard the intelligence reports and we knew that other companies had already been in contact with the enemy. The unit knew that we were going into battle. How big a battle? No one knew."[20]

"We all knew we were in a very bad place," said Jack Bisbee, another member of Alpha Company. "Late that afternoon, they choppered in a chaplain, a Catholic priest. He set up his portable stand and said a 5-minute Mass on the trail. I will never forget it. It was like yesterday. He said, 'Tomorrow you men are going into battle, and many of you are going to die, please receive Jesus.' Everyone had Communion. I showed some non-Catholic kids how to hold out their hands or they could receive the Host on their tongue. In Vietnam we weren't hung up on denominations. The next morning, the 20th, we got up at sunrise. It was our squad's turn to walk point. We walked about 100 meters up the mountain and all hell broke loose."[21]

Alpha Company had followed a trail right into a fortified bunker complex, with half of 1st Platoon walking into the trap before the NVA opened fire. Four soldiers were hit almost immediately. Sergeant Danny Hudson, who had been walking point, was killed and Sergeant James Larrick, a squad leader, was wounded. Two other men were also hit. The lead squad was pinned down, and the fire was so intense it seemed impossible for others to move forward to support or rescue them.

First Lieutenant Kevin Burke asked for volunteers to help him retrieve the dead and wounded. More than a dozen hands went up. "When he explained the situation to us, every man said, 'Let's go,'" Rodney McFee would later tell the *Ledger-Enquirer*.

After crawling just 15 meters, they spotted one of the wounded. Burke ordered cover fire from his men, got into a crouched position, and headed for his fallen comrade. He didn't make it. "I can still see him going for that man, the helmet jolt back and the lieutenant dropping," McFee said.[22]

As a medic, Doc Stafford was usually somewhere in the middle of a line of march, making him accessible to wounded or injured in either direction. This day on Nui Chom Mountain, he was called forward to help a soldier he only recalls as "Smiley," who had been shot above his wrist.

"Fire broke out, heavy fire, and they yelled for a medic to come up," Stafford said. "I came up. There was a gap of maybe 15 or 20 feet or 30 feet. There was somebody down. They said, 'You gotta go get him,' so that's what I did. They gave me some covering fire. I got down there, I treated the guy, and I was trying to bring him back. I couldn't get back. The fire intensified so much that there was no way I was gonna get back, not if I stood. If I stood up, I wasn't gonna be around. So, I stayed down. I noticed close by there were bunkers—enemy bunkers. I dragged the guy into the bunker so we were out of the line of fire pretty much."[23]

The *Ledger-Enquirer* wrote: "He found himself in a sea of noise and smoke and alone with an injured soldier. Stafford…was doing what he normally did when taking enemy fire, 'I was praying they didn't hit me.'" But, he realized that he and the wounded soldier "were pinned down in a way that was probably not going to end well."[24]

He remembers the intensity of the chaos around him. "You have hundreds of people shooting at each other, and just this tremendous volume of noise," he said of the rattling of the M16s and AK47s, "and if there was artillery there it was deafening. Plus, this acrid smoke from the weapons. It's hard to think sometimes with all that noise. It can really heighten your fear and the adrenaline because there's all this stuff going on and you realize you have no control over anything. It's a scary thing."[25]

Somewhere behind him, Alpha Company was pinned down. One member of the 3rd Platoon, Pfc. Michael Crescenz, apparently decided that something had to be done. The young soldier from Philly seized an M60 machine gun, a weapon usually manned by two soldiers, that had been dropped or discarded in the fray. And then he charged the enemy positions about a hundred yards away. Firing a continuous spray of 7.62mm shells into the front gun port, he took on one bunker until it went silent, with two NVA soldiers dead. Michael then attacked a second bunker, entering from the rear and killing two more NVA.

The remaining NVA positions were now focused on Michael, yet on he charged, crashing through the brush up the hill to a third bunker. A bullet ripped into his thigh, barely slowing him. He knocked out the third position, with two more kills.

In the meantime, Stafford was becoming more and more desperate to get Smiley and himself out of the line of fire to safety. But each time he attempted to move the wounded soldier, more shots from the NVA bunkers crashed around them. Smiley was hit again, this time in the leg.

"It continued, for me, it seemed like hours," Stafford told the *Inquirer's* Bob Moran. "It could've been minutes or seconds. I pulled Smiley out again and tried to bring him back up.

"But I couldn't pick him up anymore. I thought I could but I had no strength. I couldn't even stand up. I could pull him a little bit but the terrain was so rough and the bullets were flying around so there was no way I could do it.

"And that's when Michael showed up.

"I had heard him behind me. He had an M60. He was shooting a machine gun. Then he stepped forward in front of me."[26]

Doc said there seemed just a split second of calm. As if Michael's assault on the three enemy positions had stunned the enemy into silence or submission. But automatic weapons fire suddenly resumed.

Michael turned to Doc, looming over him as the medic willed himself and Smiley deeper into the protective cover of the ground.

"I got this, Doc, no problem," Michael said, and then stepped in front of the medic as he turned to a fourth bunker.[27]

"Crescenz quickly realized the danger to his buddies and, with his machine gun under his arm, attacked a fourth enemy position," Hawkins wrote. "Before he could silence the NVA, the courageous GI was hit again by machine gun fire five meters from the bunker and mortally wounded."[28]

"Shots rang out and he was done," Doc said. "He was in front of me and he fell. I could see he was gone. It was on the spot. There was nothing I could do about it. He took a head shot. This was just instant, went right through. He hit the ground and he was dead."[29]

Instinctively, Doc reached out and checked for a pulse, but he was still taken aback by the experience.

"I had never been that close to anyone being killed on the spot like that," he said. "He was just a couple of feet in front of me. I was close enough where the brains and the blood were all over me. That freaked me out. It was a source of nightmares for years."[30] And along with the nightmares, came survivor's guilt.

"He took a bullet that might have been mine," Doc said. "He definitely saved my life. There's no doubt about that. So, I would assume God had something for him to do that day. And I was not called."[31]

Wetzel, who would nominate Michael for the Medal of Honor for his actions that day, said, "What he did to save his buddies by going up to four bunkers to take them out so they could move up the hill, was the most heroic thing I have ever seen in combat."

But 50 years later, Wetzel still had one burning question: "Why did he all of a sudden pick up that machine gun?"[32]

"What was his thought process?" Wetzel asked Bob Moran. "I don't know, but he did it and he did it on his own. It wasn't the squad leader telling him to do anything. It wasn't the platoon leader telling him to do it. It was Michael Crescenz alone who took that action to help A Company then move on up the hill."[33]

Thanks to Michael's act of valor, Alpha Company was able to press forward into the bunker complex, taking out the remaining enemy positions.

But it didn't happen immediately. Though Doc's life had been saved by Michael, he and Smiley were not yet safe. And the battle for the mountain itself would rage for three more days.

Smiley had gone into shock and Doc was frantically trying to keep the soldier stable. Though they had managed to find some cover in an NVA bunker, Stafford at some point decided that it was too dangerous to stay put. He gathered the strength to lift his charge and began to move, but tripped over a root and fell. He felt a thud against his helmet. A bullet had grazed it. Dizzy, his strength gone, Doc called for help but couldn't be heard over the din. He fired his M16, and then his .45 sidearm, until he ran out of ammo.[34]

"I could see some shadows moving around, and I shot what I had," Doc said. "I didn't carry that much ammunition, that wasn't my primary job. I had four, five clips, maybe 100 rounds and I used them up right away. Those M16s, as fast as you pull the trigger the bullet was there—maybe 20 rounds gone in two, three seconds. It went pretty quick."[35]

As darkness fell, he was still separated from the main force, out of ammunition, and he could hear the enemy soldiers talking. He wasn't sure that he and Smiley would make it through the night.

Yet they did—"but for the grace of God," Doc says. The next morning, they were recovered by their fellow soldiers. Smiley was put on a medical helicopter and Doc could have joined him because of his own wounds but decided to stay with his platoon. Alpha Company was also able to recover the bodies of Crescenz, Hudson, and Burke.[36] To their great relief, Larrick, though shot five times, was still alive and hiding in a knocked out NVA bunker—"a wonderful gift to us all," Dolan would tell the *Ledger-Enquirer*. During the night, two enemy soldiers had actually entered the bunker and rifled through his pockets, thinking the GI dead.[37]

As the fighting continued, the enemy remained formidable. Two more Americans were killed in the days to come—Spc. Thomas Dickerson and Cpl. Harold Glover. The terrain was relentlessly difficult. At one point, Wetzel was lowering chainsaws down to his troops from his chopper so they could clear landing areas for supply and medevac helicopters. Farther up the mountain, fog and clouds prevented chopper crews from dropping packs and supplies to the men on the ground.[38]

Undeterred, the Americans had control of Nui Chom by the morning of November 23. Along the way, it became even clearer how deeply entrenched and well fortified the enemy had been and why they had fought so hard. Alpha Company discovered an underground command post and headquarters measuring 50 feet square. "We found numerous papers and documents in their high command post," Captain Braswell, Alpha CO, told Hawkins for this 1969 *American* magazine article, "plus a telephone switchboard and a small motor, which was probably used as a generator. There was commo [communications] wire running all over the mountain, and each of the more than 200 bunkers were connected."[39]

A few hundred meters east of the command post, Charlie Company captured an extensive field hospital, as well as an NVA doctor and two nurses. Spc. 5 Tony LaPalio described it for Hawkins:

"It was about 20 by 50 feet, with a storage tunnel connected to it. It was made mostly of bamboo, but had a green canvas over the roof. Inside there was an operating room and table, a well-stocked pharmacy, and an area for sterilizing surgical equipment.

"We found more than 30 different kinds of medicines ranging from morphine to penicillin, four complete sets of surgical equipment, and dozens of medical texts and journals, some written in Chinese and others in Vietnamese.... They had more than fifty bamboo hootches nearby, each with two beds, and there were about 120 fighting bunkers encircling the hospital."[40]

The bloody clothing and bandages scattered about the hospital indicated the extent of NVA casualties during the assault on Nui Chom. The captured doctor reported treating at least five dozen wounded, with slightly more than that number killed. The Americans suffered 5 killed and 38 wounded during the battle.

A few days after the 4th Battalion, 31st Infantry, secured Nui Chom, choppers were dropping food crates on the mountaintop for the troops' Thanksgiving celebration. One soldier, Stan Satcher, told the *Ledger-Enquirer* 50 years later exactly what he was thankful for that day:

"Being able to wake up that morning."[41]

Lieutenant Dolan, who went from a platoon leader in Delta Company to commander of Alpha Company during the battle, would say long after that Thanksgiving, "I feel eternal gratitude for the gift of having been able to serve my country in ground combat with such extraordinary men. I believe all of us who served in 4-31 Infantry [4th Battalion, 31st Infantry] at Nui Chom, and at any time in the second half of 1968, were specially blessed to have had Lieutenant Colonel Sam Wetzel leading our battalion in battle."[42]

Wetzel, for his part, is equally effusive in praise of the men he led. When Jack Bisbee visited then lieutenant general Wetzel many years later at Fort Benning, Georgia, he confessed to his old commander that he wasn't sure he'd been a good soldier.

"I'll never forget what he told me in his house," Bisbee told the *Ledger-Enquirer*. "'Every guy in my battalion is a hero. Every one of them.' That stuck with me and made me feel a lot better."[43]

When asked by the newspaper if he had a message for all those men from his past, Wetzel, by then a long-retired three-star general, said, "You were the most gallant fighting soldiers I saw in my entire thirty-four years in the Army. I am proud of every one of you. What you did on Nui Chom Mountain and elsewhere was really unbelievable and hard for people to understand."[44]

Doc Stafford did two tours in Vietnam, and he was wounded twice, receiving the Purple Heart in each case. He thought often of Michael and once back in the States thought about reaching out to the Crescenz family in Philadelphia. He never did.

"Twice I was going to go to Philly to meet his parents but I couldn't do it," he said. "For over twenty-five years I thought about calling or writing Michael's family, but I could not face the fact that I was living because of him."[45]

But what the young soldier from West Oak Lane did that day will never be forgotten by Stafford.

"Many times, I think, war comes down to your comrades," Stafford said. "You fight to survive. You're fighting for a principle, yeah, but that's an abstract thing. Fighting for comrades is real, and that day it was really real, for me anyway.

"Michael was proud to be there. He was a good guy. We all were. We were all good guys, and we all had a story to tell. Some didn't have a long time to be able to tell a longer story, and I've been lucky. I got to tell a long story."[46]

That was thanks to Michael Crescenz, whose story would continue long after his life ended on a mountainside in Vietnam on November 20, 1968.

CHAPTER V

Medal of Honor

Joe Crescenz will never forget that Saturday morning in November. The family was inside their brick twin on Thouron Avenue, easing into the late autumn weekend, a hint of the holidays rapidly approaching in the air. Outside, a soldier in his dress green uniform had driven through the quiet, dark Philadelphia streets and found number 7443. He parked nearby and slowly made his way toward the house. There were seven steps from the sidewalk to the small front yard, and then four more to the stone porch.

It was early, just after sunrise. Mom was in the kitchen, but Dad hadn't come down yet. Steve and Chris, the youngest brothers, were still in bed. Joe, then 12, was downstairs.

"It was a little after 7 o'clock," Joe said. "My dad was upstairs shaving in the bathroom, getting ready for work. He was going to take me to the bowling alley, for my bowling league with Ogontz Boys Club. We had a 9 o'clock meet. And mom was in the kitchen getting breakfast ready for me and Dad."

Then the knock.

"I opened the door and then the screen door and there was this guy in uniform," Joe said, "and I asked, 'Sir, can I help you?'"

"Is this the Crescenz residence?" he asked.

"Yes, sir, it is."

"I need to speak to your mother and father. Are Mr. and Mrs. Crescenz here?

"Yes, sir, they are."

As Joe was opening the door for the man to enter, he heard his dad bellowing from upstairs, "Who the hell's at the door at this time in the morning? Who the hell is bothering us this time of day?"

Joe yelled back, "Dad, it's somebody from the Army."

A frying pan crashed to the floor in the kitchen.

"Mom had to know right away when I said it was a man from the Army," Joe recalls.[1]

Charlie, upstairs in his room, was wide awake. "I immediately knew what it was," he said. "I could hear what was going on downstairs, and I knew immediately what it was."[2]

"Son, can I come in?"

"Yes, sir."

As Joe was letting the soldier and his news into the house, Dad was rushing down the stairs, Mom from the kitchen. Then the horrible, life-numbing official notification. Their son, Pfc. Michael Crescenz, had been killed in action on November 20…

"I don't know what else was said because your mind just goes elsewhere," Joe said. "It becomes numb. And Mom was just…. It wasn't good that was for sure."[3]

"You can imagine, my mother went crazy," Charlie said. "My father, now he's gotta calm—he's upset too but he's gotta calm my mother down."[4]

"And things changed from that day on," Joe said. "You take life for granted. I was a 12-year-old kid. I'd seen my grandparents die, my uncle and aunts, and people like that. You have a connection but you weren't as close. It sounds horrible to say but things are different when it's your mom or dad or one of your brothers. It's a different kind of hurt. And it really hit me. It was like, damn, Mike's not gonna be here anymore. I'm not gonna be able to say hi to Mike or ask him how to hit a baseball or just say, 'Hey, you wanna go to the bowling lane?'

"I'll never forget opening up that door. I can see that young guy, in his dress uniform, the look on that guy's face. What a crappy job he had bringing that sort of news to parents of a soldier. And to this day you wonder how that guy made it, if he's still alive and how he has dealt with that. Here he was alive and well, but delivering that news to parents of a fellow soldier, that their soldier wasn't coming home, except for being in a coffin provided by the U.S. government."[5]

It didn't take long for the devastating news to spread through the West Oak Lane neighborhood, the St. Athanasius parish community, and beyond.

Ron Burke had been drafted not long after completing his associate's degree at Temple. At the same time Michael was heading to Vietnam, Ron was en route to Fort Bragg, North Carolina, for basic training.

"I was in my third month of training when I got the horrible news that Mike was killed in Vietnam," Ron said. "It was the most devastating day of my life.

"My mother sent me a letter and she included an article about Michael—we had a local newspaper called the *Leader*, which was published once a week—and I opened it up, and I gotta tell you—I'm stumbling even now—I opened it up and I absolutely broke down in tears. I didn't know what to think. I felt utterly helpless and began to cry uncontrollably. I had some fellow soldiers come over and ask me what was the matter."[6]

His grief was soon worsened by the realization that he wouldn't be able to go home and join Michael's family and friends in paying their final respects.

"I was so bad and so depressed that my platoon leader sent me to the commanding officer to explain the news I'd gotten. I actually took the article with me to see him. I asked if I could have emergency leave so that I could go home but he said that, because Michael was not a family member, they would not permit that at all. At that point I broke down and cried for over 20 minutes right there in his office. I just found out my best friend was dead and I could do nothing about it.

"Knowing him as a friend and a buddy, I wanted to be able to at least get home, but I had to stay with my platoon in training. I quickly wrote back to my parents to see if they could help me out with anything on that end but there wasn't a thing anyone could do. I was at the tail end of my training at Fort Bragg and they just wouldn't let me go.

"That was probably the most troubling letter I ever received, and I saved a copy of it because I always wanted it as a memory of Mike, and I know he knows how I feel. I just never was able to recover from that for a while."[7]

Jim Engler was aboard the newly commissioned USS *John F. Kennedy*, a crew member in the aviation fuel division. He, too, received a letter from home and more than anything wanted to be there for his friend.

"It was one of the saddest days of my life when I received the news," he said. "We were in the Caribbean—it was actually our first cruise with the *Kennedy*—and I got a letter from my parents in November 1968 that Mike had died, had been killed. I couldn't believe it. It brought immediate tears to my eyes.

"It was upsetting because Mike and I were good friends and it was just a shame. He was 19 years old. We were pretty young, just staring out. So, I was hoping I could get home, for at least maybe the funeral. I went to the chaplain and he explained that's just not what they would give you emergency leave for. If it was your parents, that was something different, but he convinced me that there would be no way I could get leave to come home."[8]

Jack Norton was also in the service, stationed in Vietnam, and heard the news from someone who recognized him from the old Philly neighborhood.

"Sometime in late 1968, I was on convoy duty," he said. They were in the Marble Mountains area, just south of Da Nang. "As we waited for Seabees to clear Route 1, a security force jeep stopped by our deuce-and-a-half [2.5-ton] truck. The guy recognized me—more accurately he thought I was my brother. His comment was, 'Did you know Crescenz was killed?'

"This was very disturbing to me and I took it out on my family that was trying to spare me by not letting me know."[9]

Another friend, Rick Gallagher, was in Da Nang. He didn't hear the news from family, but read about Michael's death in *Stars and Stripes*, the military newspaper.[10]

Tom Corcoran was still in Pennsylvania, although his family had moved out of the city and into Horsham, in nearby Montgomery County.

"My mother received a phone call from someone, I don't remember who," he said. "This was the third time a family we knew had lost a son or a brother. My mother was upset, my father did not say too much. Later in life my mother and I had a long talk about those days. In 1966–67, her brother was in Vietnam and at one point he came home on emergency leave because my grandmother was on her death bed. In that conversation with my mom, she brought up Michael. She didn't exactly remember all the names but she did remember how the neighborhood was giving up too many young men. She told me her and my dad spent many a night talking about the war and myself. They knew I would be turning 19 right before I graduated. When her brother had to go back, he said to her, 'I don't know if I will make it back.' It was a time of bad things in our country, but it really hit our neighborhood."[11]

It wasn't just West Oak Lane. All of Philadelphia was hit hard during Vietnam. During the war the city suffered 648 service members either killed in action or reported missing. Philadelphia public and Catholic high schools bear the sad distinction of the highest number of Vietnam War casualties in the nation. Edison lost 64 alumni, while Father Judge and Michael's alma mater, Cardinal Dougherty, each lost 27.[12]

For Joe Crescenz, the days following the news of Michael's death are largely a blur, though some stories stand out.

He remembers Michael's body coming home through Dover Air Force Base in Delaware, and being brought to the Fitzpatrick Funeral Home on South Broad Street in Philadelphia. Charlie accompanied their dad to claim the body. And it was the son who counseled his dad not to look inside the coffin.

"Our father was pretty bullheaded," Joe said, "but Charlie told him, 'You don't want to look in there. Just remember Mike the way he was.' Because Charlie probably saw a lot of crap over there, a lot of death and destruction, and I'm sure my father did in the European campaign in World War II. And that had to be hard for my father, not to be able to see his son again, one last time, at least physically. Had to be real tough, on my brother Charlie too. And, of course, tough on Mom. But Charlie had to be the guy who breathed a little common sense to our father and just tell him, 'You don't want to see what's in that coffin.' Probably good advice. And at the wake the casket was closed, too."[13]

The funeral Mass was said at St. Athanasius, named for a defender of the faith of whom it was said, "His courage was of the sort that never falters"[14]—just like Michael Crescenz. The imposing stone edifice straddling a corner off Limekiln Pike was about a 10-minute walk from the Crescenz home. The church, established 40 years before by Cardinal Dennis Dougherty himself,[15] to this day hosts a school, the same one that Charlie, Michael, and their four younger brothers walked back and forth to daily from first through eighth grades.

"I'll never forget that day we buried him," Joe said.

It was a solemn service, Joe said, with the church "packed to the gills. It was standing room only." Family and friends were there, along with entire classes of St. A's school, allowing the classmates and buddies of the grieving brothers to attend.

"A lot of the neighborhood, a lot of the friends of the family came to not just honor Mike, but I think to give support to Mom and Dad since they lost their son," Joe said. "And then we went up to Holy Sepulchre Cemetery, to finally put Michael into the ground, and this is the part I'll never forget. It was cold, very bitterly cold and windy. It was a very surreal moment because here you were, you're finally gonna put your brother into the ground. And it was a final, final act to put his physical body into the ground.

"When the soldiers were firing the three-volley salute to honor their fallen brother it was starting to snow flurry. And it was windy in a wide-open part of the cemetery, with no wind break. While they were firing their rifles, the snow was flurrying around you, swirling around. The people were all huddled together because it was so cold."[16]

The graveside service was not as crowded as the Mass had been. The students, for example, had gone back to class. But still, many had come, with some notable exceptions.

"A lot of his neighborhood buddies, his boyhood chums, were still over in Vietnam fighting," Joe said. "They were there, not knowing that their buddy Mike, our brother, was being buried that day. A lot of them didn't know until they actually came home from their tour of duty. How awful is that, that they found out when they got the hell home that Mike didn't make it home, that he wasn't as fortunate as they were? And I think that still plays on some of those guys' heads, that here they're living their lives and their childhood buddy never made it home."[17]

For Joe and his family, life would never be the same.

"It was a shock to my system and I didn't know how to react," Joe said. "I know I cried like a gosh-damned baby at his wake the day before we had to bury him. And it affected me a lot. I didn't realize until recent years that I had a lot of freaking anger, a lot of rage. My world, as a 12-year-old kid, was never the same. The neighborhoods were changing. The country definitely changed. The '60s, or early '70s, were a crazy time in our nation. We, from our young eyes, started to see the world that we knew as younger kids, as 6-, 7-, and 8-year-olds, gone forever. That age of innocence? That every generation has? That was gone.

"There weren't any more innocent times for me and my boys back in the neighborhood, when we saw not just my brother's death, but I do believe there were at least two, maybe three, other men young men that also were killed in Vietnam. We saw our world being shattered bit by bit, piece by piece. It was a different world then. The coldness, the dark side of life started coming in because Mom and Dad couldn't protect you anymore. Because we came from a pretty protective shell, let's say. Most of the parents in our neighborhood raised their kids in somewhat of a protective atmosphere. But I think that because of what was going on in the world at that time it really changed all our views of the world and our lives back in the neighborhood. It just wasn't going to be the same."[18]

Not the same, but not stopping either. As devastated as they all were, life continued, in some ways very differently.

"Mom and Dad, to their credit, they kept the family moving forward as best they could," Joe said. "You lost one of your brothers in the war and somehow life goes on. I still played my sandlot baseball that spring. The following spring, I looked forward to the baseball season and watching the Phillies down in the old Connie Mack Stadium in North Philly. We didn't dwell on it. One thing, I look back, we didn't know how to grieve and it wasn't just our family. I think a lot of the families back then, they kept it in. There was no support system.... The moms and dads, they just went about their business, like, 'Okay, we had to bury our son. We gotta move on.' And that's kind of how they did the everyday, what you call humdrum life of growing up like we did in Philadelphia.

"And the neighborhood didn't make a big deal of it either. They kept it inside. It was internalized. But I was one angry SOB. I was always getting into fights. I was looking for fights. If anyone coming down the street, they looked at me the wrong way, I would say something real smart-assy and I would get in a brawl. Whether I'd get my butt kicked or not, that's the way it was. And I didn't know what was going on. I just thought, 'Hey, it was just me. My hormones are raging. I'm hitting those adolescent years.' You look back, your body is changing but I think it was a lot more. I look back and realize, yeah, Michael's death affected me a lot more than I thought. And you wonder how many other lives were affected—the other sons and daughters and moms and dads. How it affected those families from around the country. So, it wasn't just me. I'm not an isolated case. And you don't forget. You don't ever forget."[19]

At least from Joe's perspective, life changed for his parents as well.

"I look back, I don't think they socialized as much as they used to before any of their sons were in the military," Joe said. "I know they used to play the old pinochle [card game]. That was a big game with our parents in the day. They would host, maybe some of the other parents, or other couples that came to our house on Friday nights. They'd smoke and drink in the house. As younger kids we were sent up to bed early because it was adult time. And my mom and dad would go out too. It sounds corny, but bowling banquets were a big thing then. So just a lot more socialization with our mom and dad before.

"But after Michael, I don't think they went out of their way to socialize as much as they used to. I think that's how they changed. Sure, we went out. We'd still visit our relatives and aunts and uncles. But things were just different. It was tough for them—and they kept it all in. They didn't talk about things in front of us."[20]

"She didn't want to hear or talk about the war," Joe's cousin Kathleen Zippilli says of her Aunt Mary Ann. Another cousin, Mary Lou Allen, noticed a difference in her aunt as well after Michael's death. "Great sadness, devastation," she said.[21]

"Nobody really talked a whole lot about it to each other when you would see them," Zippilli said. "And I think it was due to the fact that Aunt Mary—the parents—they didn't really talk about it a whole lot either. I think it was just too hard for them."[22]

A close friend of Joe's later wrote of that time in the West Oak Lane community, "One of the childhood memories seared into my soul is the shock and sadness that swept over our neighborhood when Mike was killed in Vietnam.... Every time I walked by the Crescenz home, I could feel the immense sadness and the pain coming from their house."[23]

The family was inundated with sympathy cards and condolence letters. One, dated just six days after Michael was killed, came from John Cardinal Krol, leader of the Catholic Archdiocese of Philadelphia:

Dear Mr. and Mrs. Crescenz:
No words of mine can possibly assuage the grief or minimize the loss caused by the death of your dear son, Michael, in the Vietnam War.
However, may I assure you of my deepest sympathies and compassion in your bereavement, and my fervent prayers that God may grant you the courage to bear and the wisdom to understand this cross, and that He may grant eternal rest to your son and to all who made the supreme sacrifice for their country.

Devotedly yours in Christ,
John Cardinal Krol
Archbishop of Philadelphia[24]

Soon after, a letter dated November 29 arrived from the White House:

Dear Mr. and Mrs. Crescenz:
I have learned with deep regret of the death of your son, Private First Class Michael J. Crescenz.
Your son, like many of our fine Americans, has given his life toward the attainment of peace. He will be greatly missed not only by you, but by his friends as well. Our Nation, which shares your loss, is grateful for your son's contribution.
Mrs. Johnson joins me in extending to you our heartfelt sympathy in the loss of your son.

Sincerely,
Lyndon B. Johnson[25]

Early in the new year, this letter arrived:

Dear Mr. and Mrs. Crescenz:

I fully understand the depth of your grief and I share the burden of your family tragedy, as all Philadelphians must do.

The loss of your son, Michael, who gave up his life heroically in an ugly war many thousands of miles away, is a price we must pay for the preservation of those freedoms which all Americans cherish.

He gave his life in a just and honorable cause. That consolation can do very little to lessen the impact of his loss, to be sure, but as time tends to lessen the initial shock you can one day be proud of the valor of his service.

I pray that his sacrifice will not have been made in vain and I would like to extend my personal sympathy in this dark hour. If there is any way I can be of assistance at this time, I do hope you will grant me the opportunity.

Sincerely yours,
James J. Tate
Mayor[26]

That same month, a letter arrived at 7443 Thouron Avenue from 4th Battalion, 31st Infantry, headquarters:

Dear Mr. and Mrs. Crescenz:

It is with deepest sorrow that I extend to you the sympathy of the men of the 4th Battalion, 31st Infantry, for the loss of your son, Michael.

On the morning of November 20, 1968, Michael's unit was participating in a combat sweep operation near the village of Tan My, approximately 25 miles west of Tam Ky City, in Quang Tin Province, Republic of South Vietnam. At 7:55 a.m., Michael was mortally wounded when the unit came under intense automatic weapons fire from an enemy bunker line. I hope you gain some consolation in knowing that Michael was not subjected to any prolonged suffering.

I sincerely hope that the knowledge that Michael was an exemplary soldier who gave his life assisting his fellow man and in the service of his country will comfort you in this hour of great sorrow.

A memorial service was conducted for your son. Michael's comrades joined me in rendering military honors and final tribute to him....

The sincere sympathy of this unit is extended to you in your bereavement.

Sincerely yours,

Robert L. Wetzel
LTC, Infantry
Commanding[27]

There were no hints from these letters or other communications with the military at the time of the circumstances of Michael's death, or his extraordinary act of valor in taking on the enemy positions single-handedly, saving lives, and allowing the mission to go forward. It would be months before the family started to hear any of this. But Lieutenant Colonel Wetzel, while writing that letter of consolation to the Crescenzes, was well aware of Michael's gallantry. He was already determined to see that Michael's courage and sacrifice were honored, and had already set the process in motion.

As the commanding officer, Wetzel was kept apprised of all actions during the battle. And, as with every engagement with the enemy, there were any number of heroic acts to be recognized, in addition to the Purple Hearts that are awarded to all those wounded or killed while serving.

Acts of bravery are recognized in a number of ways by the U.S. Army. The Bronze Star can be given for valor as well as for merit and achievement during one's time in service, the Silver Star is presented for "gallantry in action," and the Distinguished Service Cross for "extraordinary heroism." The nation's highest military award, the Medal of Honor, is, according to the Defense Department, "presented by the President of the United States, in the name of Congress, and is conferred only upon members of the United States Armed Forces who distinguish themselves through conspicuous gallantry and intrepidity at the risk of life above and beyond the call of duty."[28]

The Medal of Honor is reserved for the most extraordinary acts of courage. Of millions who have served since this honor was created during the Civil War, only about 3,500 men and one woman (a Union surgeon and prisoner of war) have worn the medal. In almost all cases, the recipients had risked their own lives to save others. Many did not survive. The Congressional Medal of Honor Society estimates that the majority of the Medals of Honor presented since World War II have been awarded posthumously. Most recently, of eight Medals of Honor awarded for actions in Iraq during the War on Terror, six have been awarded posthumously.[29]

These numbers further illustrate how rare this honor is. During the Vietnam War, almost 720,000 Bronze Stars were awarded, about 170,000 for valor,[30] while about 21,600 Silver Stars were issued.[31] A little over 1,000 Distinguished Service Crosses were presented, with almost 400 of those posthumous.[32] Just 262 Medals of Honor were awarded during Vietnam, and well over half of the recipients—about 150—did not survive the action that led to their award.[33]

After a thorough review of the heroic actions by his men during the battle of Nui Chom, Wetzel gave serious consideration to recommending two for Medals of Honor. One for 1st Lt. Kevin Burke, who gave his life while trying to retrieve wounded soldiers, and another for Michael Crescenz. "But then I thought, 'No, Crescenz is unique, what he did is unique,'" Wetzel said. "First, he saved lives. That clearly happened. And secondly, he enabled the mission to be accomplished. What he did was above and beyond, the way I see awards."

He recommended Burke for the Distinguished Service Cross, which quickly made its way through the approval process. "They got that the following spring," Wetzel said. "I had a letter from his father telling me they'd received it. Somebody had come out to Iowa and presented it to them. So that was quick."[34]

For Michael's nomination for the Medal of Honor, the process started with Wetzel assigning a staff person to interview the men who had been on the ground on November 20 for eyewitness accounts. Those official statements came from four members of A Company: Capt. Billie J. Braswell, 1st Lt. Barry L. Brandon, 1st Sgt. Francis A. Duval, and Spc. 4 Donald L. Phelps. Though all tell the same story of heroism, with only a few lines that are different in the Brandon, Duval, and Phelps statements, Braswell's account is the most detailed. He wrote:

> PFC Michael J. Crescenz…at 0815 hours on 20 November 1968, came into contact with a late enemy force…. PFC Crescenz was a rifleman walking in the center of the third platoon of Company A when the NVA opened fire on the point element of his platoon. The two point men were immediately mortally wounded by automatic weapons fire. At this time, he was in a relatively safe position approximately 100 meters from the three fortified enemy positions to his front.
>
> As his comrades sought cover, PFC Crescenz, carrying his M60 machine gun (the other three accounts say, more accurately, 'Grabbing an M60 machine gun,' as Michael was a rifleman, not a machine gunner), rushed toward the still firing NVA. Machine gun fire and automatic weapons fire hit all around him.

PFC Crescenz, completely exposed to the enemy and supplying his own covering fire, advanced on the first enemy position. He killed the two NVA firing from inside the bunker and rushed toward the second bunker, his machine gun still firing. The second position met the fate of the first as PFC Crescenz daringly killed two more NVA soldiers.

Realizing the danger to his comrades, who at this time were unable to assist him, of the fire from the third bunker, he rushed toward it. With heavy enemy fire directed at him, PFC Crescenz still moved forward. The third NVA position was soon silenced and two more enemy lie dead.

At this time, he noticed a fourth previously unseen enemy position which had begun firing at him. Having advanced approximately 100 meters from his position when the initial contact began, PFC Crescenz bravely continued on with his machine gun still held under his arm, firing at the enemy.

Five meters from the enemy position, he was mortally wounded by NVA .30 caliber machine gun fire.

PFC Crescenz undoubtedly saved the lives of many of his comrades as he acted above and beyond the call of duty, sacrificing his own life by willingly exposing himself to heavy fire in order to silence the NVA fire.

With profound concern for his fellow soldiers, he demonstrated indomitable courage, conspicuous gallantry and extraordinary heroism and intrepidity at the cost of his own life.[35]

Specialist Phelps ended his statement with, "I certainly feel that this was above and beyond the call of duty, inspired all of his fellow soldiers, and saved most of our lives."[36]

The summary included in the recommendation noted the thick jungle growth and dense woods the soldiers fought in, as well as the weather—"Cloudy, visibility limited due to heavy ground fog and a low ceiling, 70 degrees F, light rain."

The enemy was described as "a large force of the 21st Regiment, 2nd North Vietnamese Army Division. Morale was high. Well-armed with AK47 rifles and .30-caliber machine guns."

"Company A," the summary continued, "was in pursuit of a large enemy force which had been located in the area of operations. The unit's morale was high."[37]

"Sometimes the Medal of Honor takes a long time," Wetzel observed, "starting with a recommendation from the commander and then going through the channels all the way back to Washington. This one took until 1970, from '68, so a couple of years."[38]

In some cases, the process can take much longer—years, even decades—after a battle. Teddy Roosevelt wasn't awarded his Medal of Honor until 2001, 103 years after leading his men up Kettle Hill, part of San Juan Heights, in Cuba, in 1898 during the Spanish-American War.[39] In contrast, the Medal of Honor awarded to the former president's son, Brigadier General Theodore Roosevelt Jr., was presented posthumously just three months after his heroic actions on D-Day, June 6, 1944.[40]

Sometimes the reason for the delay, though frustrating, is benign, a result of bureaucracy and red tape, or just the incredible amount of fact-checking that goes into ensuring the integrity of the medal. In other cases, medals have been delayed or initially denied because of the race, ethnicity, or religion of the intended recipient.

At other times there are gaps because a case has been reopened. A soldier may have received a Silver Star or Distinguished Service Cross for an action, but higher-ups or brothers in arms don't believe that's recognition enough, and they want the person's award upgraded to a Medal of Honor.

President Donald Trump presented two such Medals of Honor to heroes of the Vietnam War more than 40 years after U.S. involvement there ended. One went to James McCloughan on July 7, 2017, for his actions as an Army medic who, despite his own wounds, saved several lives at the risk of his own during a three-day battle near Tam Ky in May 1969.[41] The other went to retired Sergeant Major John Canley on October 17, 2018, for his courage, leadership, and efforts to save his fellow Marines in the battle of Hue from January 31 to February 6, 1968, during the Tet Offensive.[42] McCloughan had previously been awarded the Distinguished Service Cross and Canley the Navy Cross (the Navy's equivalent of the DSC).

It didn't take quite as long to upgrade the Silver Star awarded to the Army's SSgt. David Bellavia for his heroic actions in Iraq. Bellavia had been recognized for leading his men, and saving their lives, during the brutal house-to-house combat of the second battle of Fallujah in November 2004.[43] He was awarded the Medal of Honor 15 years later, on June 25, 2019.

The granting of such honors years after an individual's act of valor is not unique to modern times. According to the National Archives' *Prologue* magazine, the government was flooded with applications for Medals of Honor in the 1890s for acts of heroism during the Civil War—about 1,500 of the more than 3,500 total recipients are from the War Between the States. The application process in the late 19th century was much different from the rigorous, formal one of today, and not nearly as scrupulous in terms of witnesses and verification. The magazine writes:

> In 1890, 33 medals were awarded, which doubled the following year to 67, and mushroomed to 127 in 1894. More than five hundred medals were awarded between 1891 and 1897 for actions performed during the Civil War. Because the army had not established a system for applying for the medal (as the navy had done in 1862), some medals were awarded based on scant evidence. As word spread of the availability of the medal, veterans all over the country sought to secure a piece of glory for themselves. Because many of these honorees were not required to provide hard evidence of their heroics, some critics...felt the integrity of the medal was in jeopardy.[44]

Reforms began in 1897, with Secretary of War Russell A. Alger announcing that awards going forward would have to be based on "incontestable proof of the most distinguished gallantry in action"—and henceforth, recommendations for the medal would have to be submitted within a year of the action being honored.[45]

A more thorough review of Medals of Honor awarded came in the early 20th century, with the government evaluating the circumstances of each recipient's wartime actions. The result: in 1917, the names of more than 900 recipients—over a third of the 2,600 that had been awarded up until then—were "stricken from the official Medal of Honor list."[46]

Among the awards rescinded was the one for the only female Medal of Honor recipient. Dr. Mary Walker, a graduate of Syracuse Medical College, served first as a volunteer and later was appointed a War Department surgeon. She was still a civilian but her pay was the equivalent of a junior officer. She cared for patients and the wounded in Washington, DC, and Virginia and later in Tennessee, where she treated casualties from the battle of Chickamauga and was noted for her courage under fire. Remaining behind to care for the wounded as Union forces withdrew in April 1864, she was captured and held as a prisoner of war for four months. Upon her release as part of a prisoner swap for Confederate medical officers, she was then named superintendent of a hospital for women prisoners in Louisville, Kentucky, and an orphanage in Clarksville, Tennessee.

After the war, her request for a military grade promotion was denied and instead, to recognize her service, President Andrew Johnson presented her with the Medal of Honor in January 1866. "She wore it every day for the rest of her life," according to the Association of the United States Army.[47]

Her award was rescinded more than 50 years later, based on the new criteria that the Medal of Honor should be reserved for members of the military who served in combat. Characteristically, the 85-year-old Civil War veteran and suffragist refused to return her medal, as the government requested, and continued to wear it proudly until her death two years later. In 1977, President Jimmy Carter restored her award.[48] A handful of other awards stricken in the early 20th-century review, including for William "Buffalo Bill" Cody, have also been reinstated.[49]

There was no such controversy, or lengthy delay, when it came to the recommendation of the Medal of Honor for Michael J. Crescenz. His selfless heroic actions were universally recognized and applauded. He had even been promoted, posthumously, to corporal.

Within weeks of Wetzel's recommendation, and before 1968 came to a close, approval had already come from the commanding officer of the 196th Brigade and the commanding general of the Americal Division. From there, the packet containing the four eyewitness statements, along with a crudely hand-drawn map of the area of action, a proposed citation, and a summary of the recommendation, worked its way up the chain of command to the deputy commanding general, U.S. Army Vietnam, to the commander, U.S. Military Assistance Command, Vietnam, to commander in chief, U.S. Army Pacific, to commander in chief, Pacific Command, to the Joint Chiefs of Staff at the Pentagon, to the Senior Army Decorations Board. The only glitches, really just a few clerical errors, came in a January 8, 1969, memo bouncing the recommendation back to the commanding general of the Americal

Division because "DA Form 638 is not dated," "Social Security Account Number is omitted," "Items 15 and 16, DA Form 638 are incorrect," and a few similar items needed to be addressed. No detail is too small when it comes to awarding a Medal of Honor.[50]

Approvals from all of the commands involved were noted on a summary sheet dated September 12, 1969, "prepared for the signature of the Secretary of the Army forwarding the necessary documents to the Secretary of Defense for approval and, if he approves, further transmitted to the President for approval." The defense secretary, Melvin Laird, did indeed approve, and wrote in an October 7, 1969, memorandum for the President: "The Secretary of the Army has recommended, and I concur in the award of the Medal of Honor to Corporal Michael J. Crescenz, United States Army, for gallant conduct described in the attached citation and supplementary summary."[51]

The Crescenz family wasn't aware of any of these official proceedings, though months after Michael's burial they had started to receive more details about their beloved son's death and indications that he had exhibited extraordinary gallantry on the battlefield.

"I forget the time frame, months later or the early part of '69, but there were a couple of gentlemen, soldiers from the Army, who came to our house to honor Michael with the Bronze Star and Purple Heart," Joe said. "And I do believe that Mom—Mom was Mom—had dinner for those soldiers so they could have a home-cooked meal. And they honored our brother with the Bronze Star and Purple Heart that night. It was surreal. 'Oh, wow, Mike's getting a couple of medals here. That's pretty cool.' But I still didn't know why. I didn't even really know the significance of the medals, even though I should have with two brothers in the military.

"Probably my mom and dad knew they were coming ahead of time, from a phone call or letter. All I knew is that they wanted the Army guys to come to the house. Mom and Dad didn't want any big to-do. No media. They didn't want anybody to even really know. There had been little articles—in our local neighborhood paper, the *Bulletin*, the *Inquirer*, and even the paper down at Sea Isle City, where we had a Shore house—but just that he had been killed in action. No details. And so, when the Army guys came with the medals, I think Mom and Dad just wanted to keep it within the family. They didn't want to make a big deal of it because they knew how a lot of other parents would have felt, especially those in the neighborhood who lost a son too. They were probably looking out after the other moms and dads, and they didn't want their son to be singled out.

"Mom and Dad were very humble. That's one thing I have to say about them. They didn't want a big to-do about anything, but especially about their son and what he did. Part of it, I think, is that they were still grieving. And grieved, I do believe, probably to the day the good Lord took them both home, over their loss of their son."[52]

Just a week after Defense Secretary Laird's endorsement came this memo, dated October 15, 1969, from the Office of the Secretary of Defense, that states simply, "The attached Proposed Award of the Medal of Honor was forwarded to the White House today."[53]

Tom Gosse was another West Oak Lane kid who wound up in Vietnam. He knew Michael and his family well, having spent time in their home over the years they had all hung out together. He graduated from Dougherty a year ahead of Michael and, after working for a year, enlisted in the Army. He wanted to go to college and decided that the GI Bill would help pay his way after the service. To his surprise, he was pulled aside in basic training and told he qualified for Officer Candidate School. He completed that training, as well as Jungle Warfare School in Panama, and then was shipped off to Vietnam. He served there 11 months, part of that time as a platoon leader with the 9th Infantry Division, which meant four or five months in the boonies chasing the Viet Cong.

"What we did was air assaults, and every day we went out on helicopters—Hueys—and for the entire day rode in and out of landing zones [LZs] until someone shot at us," Gosse said. "When somebody shot at you, you disembarked (a nice gentle word not close to what it actually looked like) from the chopper and then other units flew in and surrounded the area. The ride was always terrifying, especially when you saw the red smoke in your LZ. Charlie waited until you were low and slow, but too high to jump, then opened fire. Inside the helicopter we'd hear the ping of bullets through metal or see cloth fly as rounds tore through our equipment."[54]

After a stint commanding a strike force, he was pulled back to base camp for his last few months, and put in charge of transportation and supplies. He made good use of his downtime by applying for college—until he had second thoughts.

"It dawned on me that I would fly home, land on a Friday and start college on a Monday," he said. "I thought to myself, 'That's nuts. That's not going to happen. You don't leave "this"—Vietnam—without decompressing.' So, I extended for a year and that's when I received my captain's bars."[55]

He was initially assigned to Fort Dix, New Jersey, but pushed back. "The short story is I was assigned to Fort Indiantown Gap, which is a reservist base and where I wanted to go. Close to home." The Gap, as it's known, was about a hundred miles northwest of Philadelphia, not far from Harrisburg.[56]

"I was at 'The Gap' from October '69 until August '70. And the Gap, being where it is geographically and a small base, would get a lot of escort, next-of-kin notifications and other miscellaneous duty, where they needed someone to assist the families going through grief and the ceremony. And I got a few of them. These assignments usually came to you through normal admin channels and landed in your inbox.

"So, it was odd that the base commander asked to see me. He said I have something special for you. You're notifying a family that their son is being awarded the Congressional Medal of Honor posthumously, and then escorting them to the White House for the award ceremony. He handed me the folder. 'Your orders are in here.' He said he chose me because I was the only officer on the base who had been to Vietnam, let alone in combat, with a Combat Infantryman Badge—given only to those who have served in active ground combat, and more important to members of the armed forces than almost any other medal—and a Purple Heart.

"I saluted sharply and went back to my office with the folder under my arm. I was too curious to do anything else once back in my office so I opened it. I remember clearly I tried to absorb the whole thing, then, as I began to focus, I read Michael, then Crescenz. I said it out loud, 'Oh my God, it's Michael.'

"And so, I read that thing from front to back, top to bottom. I don't remember the file being that big. I just wanted to get to the citation itself, and then all that pertained to the duties of calling the family and the subsequent escort to Washington for the presentation.

"I couldn't wait to call Mr. and Mrs. Crescenz, and got a very warm welcome from her when I called. She remembered me and we reminisced but I was anxious to get to the point. I told her I needed to meet with her and Mr. Crescenz because I had more information on Michael's death from the Department of the Army and I wanted to deliver it in person.

"It was a Friday night when I stood on the familiar porch, in full uniform, and rang the bell. Mrs. Crescenz opened the door and we greeted each other, kind of as old friends, but she really hadn't seen me in seven, eight years. Obviously, she had never seen 'Tommy' as a man, nor in full uniform. We went inside. She'd sent the younger brothers upstairs where, I was later told, they sat anxiously at the top of the stairs, listening. They had pulled three dining room chairs into a circle in the living room. We sat almost knee to knee.

"I began, 'By order of the President of the United States and the United States Congress, your son, Michael Crescenz, has been posthumously awarded the Congressional Medal of Honor. You are to be escorted to the White House to receive the Medal from the President on April 7.'

"At the moment I gave them the news they looked at each other and grasped hands. I've often wondered who absorbed it first. Mr. Crescenz said something to Mrs. Crescenz, but I didn't hear it. I gave it a moment to sink in, then I went on about the presentation and trip to the White House. I gave them an envelope containing the orders and citation. I don't remember leaving.

"I went straight to my neighborhood bar to meet friends, but I didn't tell them what I had been doing. Too hard to explain to civilians."[57]

Joe Crescenz remembers the night well. "Me and my two younger brothers were in the living room with Mom and Dad, watching TV," he said. "It was early evening, probably before 8 o'clock. There was a knock on the door and I remember the soldier. Mom and Dad look at me and my two little brothers and say, 'You three, get upstairs right now.' And my dad, in that tone of voice, you didn't argue with that guy. We went on upstairs to our bedrooms but, of course, being nosy kids, especially me, I stayed right at the top of the banister at the top of the landing, upstairs near the bathroom and my parents' bedroom. And I was listening down to what this fella had to say from the Army and I couldn't believe it.

"It didn't sink in until Mom and Dad explained more the next day, that this gentleman was asking my parents to come to the White House to have the Medal of Honor bestowed on our brother Michael for his actions in Vietnam over a year and a half earlier. I couldn't believe my ears. At first, I'll be honest with you, even with two brothers and a father and grandfathers in the military, I didn't really know what the Medal of Honor was. So, it was explained to me that morning and it's like, 'Wow, are you kidding me? This is the highest medal that anybody who serves in uniform can obtain?' And it's like, wow, that's pretty cool. I was 13 and I couldn't believe it.

"When the time came for Mom and Dad to go down to the White House, I was given my orders. Stay at home, watch my two little brothers, and don't give my grandma any lip—and I didn't. Because, well, she was a tough woman anyway, my Irish grandmother. Didn't know what my mom and dad—or my brothers Charlie and Pete, who were going—were going to experience but it must have been a pretty solemn and very special moment. Being in the presence of the President and all the big brass and people from the Pentagon, and all the parents and siblings of all the other men receiving the Medal of Honor that day, that had to be something to see."[58]

Mary Ann Crescenz, holding Joe, poses with her three oldest boys, from left, Charlie, Pete, and Mike, for an Easter picture in the backyard of their Philadelphia home, 1957. (Family photo)

Sea Isle City, New Jersey, from left, Pete, Mike, and Charlie, with Joe in front, circa 1960. (Family photo)

The former Crescenz family home on Thouron Avenue, West Oak Lane neighborhood of Philadelphia. (Larry Kesterson)

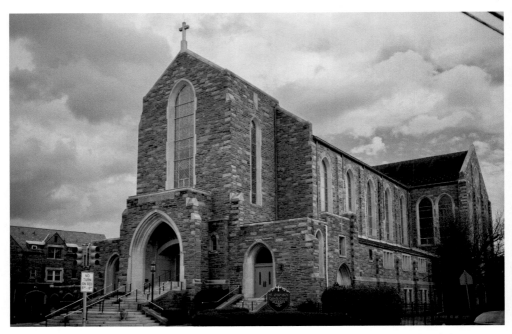

St. Athanasius Roman Catholic Church, Limekiln Pike and Walnut Lane, Philadelphia. (Larry Kesterson)

Graduation from basic training, Fort Bragg, North Carolina. Michael is second from the left, top row. (Family photo)

Michael Crescenz, basic training graduation photo. (Family photo)

Michael Crescenz, South Vietnam. (Family photo)

Michael Crescenz and a fellow soldier, base camp, South Vietnam, 1968. (Family photo)

To Mr. and Mrs. Charles M. Crescenz
With esteem, admiration and deepest appreciation
on behalf of a grateful Nation,

Richard Nixon

President Richard Nixon with Charles and Mary Ann Crescenz at the White House on April 7, 1970. Their son Charlie is behind them. (Family photo)

Camp Crescenz, I Corps, South Vietnam, circa 1970. (Family photo)

The five Crescenz brothers, from left, Joe, Pete, Steve, Chris, and Charlie, at Michael's reburial in Arlington National Cemetery, May 12, 2008. (Family photo)

Soldier placing flag at Michael's grave for Memorial Day, Arlington National Cemetery. (Patrick Hughes)

Corporal Michael J. Crescenz Department of Veterans Affairs Medical Center, Philadelphia. (Patrick Hughes)

Crescenz brothers, from left, Steve, Charlie, Pete, and Chris, at the renaming of the VA Medical Center, May 2, 2015.

Michael's Medal of Honor on display during the VA Medical Center dedication. (Patrick Hughes)

Michael J. Crescenz, M.O.H.–Rising Sun V.F.W. Post 2819 in the Lawndale neighborhood of Philadelphia. (Larry Kesterson)

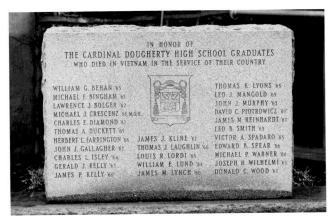

Vietnam memorial stone from Cardinal Dougherty High School. (Larry Kesterson)

Street sign, Lawndale neighborhood of Philadelphia. (Larry Kesterson)

Michael's statue at the Philadelphia Vietnam Veterans Memorial. (Patrick Hughes)

CHAPTER VI

The White House

The ceremony scheduled for the East Room of the White House on April 7, 1970, would honor 21 Vietnam War recipients of the Medal of Honor—all to be presented posthumously to family members by President Richard Nixon. No detail was too small to consider, no contingency was left unexplored.

"There were a corresponding twenty-one escort officers and additional planning staff and officers in charge," said Tom Gosse, the Army captain accompanying the Crescenz family to Washington. "As escorts, we were given preliminary orders and instructions in writing. All attending family members and their escorts arrived in Washington on April 6 and, while the families were checked in to their hotels, the escorts met together for the first time for a briefing, agenda and final instructions: times, travel, dress, etc."[1]

Accompanying Mr. and Mrs. Crescenz were two of their sons, Charlie, the Marine combat veteran who had recently joined the New Jersey State Police, and Peter, who was pulled from the Marine Corps' Parris Island to join his family in Washington to honor his fallen brother.

"The Marines got the orders to release Pete from boot camp to come to the White House and that was from the commander in chief, Richard Nixon," Joe Crescenz said. "So that's the only reason why a Marine got out of boot camp, that's for sure, especially in that time frame with a war going on."[2]

"Obviously, the whole thing is a standout in my memory," Tom continued, "but one incident is worthy of note, if only for humor. Charlie believed that Washington was a dangerous place and it would be his job to protect his parents. So, he insisted on bringing his police service revolver. That created a fuss when we boarded the plane to Washington. The pilot took the gun into the cockpit and returned it in Washington. I suspect Charlie figured out he wouldn't need it in the White House but it was my duty to inform him he was going in without it."[3]

The East Room of the White House is the mansion's largest, at 80 feet long and 37 feet wide, with a 22-foot-high ceiling and windows along three walls almost as tall as the walls. Dominating this massive space is the magnificent life-size portrait of George Washington by Gilbert Stuart, the very one saved by Dolley Madison when the British torched The Executive Mansion during the War of 1812, while her husband, James, was president. That painting, with Washington's hand outstretched forever in welcome, is paired with an accompanying portrait of his wife Martha. It's a grand setting for receptions of all sorts, including the weddings of presidential daughters. But the house's main occupant transacts much official business there as well. Cabinet members and Supreme Court justices take their oaths of office in the East Room, and laws passed by Congress receive executive approval there. Treaties are signed and celebrated. Four short years after presiding over the ceremony honoring Michael Crescenz and 20 other Medal of Honor recipients, Nixon would give his farewell address to the nation from this very same room before resigning. His successor, Gerald R. Ford, took the oath of office under the first president's watchful eye and outstretched hand the very next day. At times the grandeur gives way to solemnity, as presidents who die in office lie in state in the East Room. Among them was Abraham Lincoln, the president who signed the legislation creating the Medal of Honor. Fitting then, that the room hosts these very solemn ceremonies that pay tribute to the ordinary Americans who perform such extraordinary acts of courage during the nation's wars.[4]

On April 7, 1970, more than one hundred family members and loved ones of the 21 soldiers to be honored were given a brief tour of the White House and then arranged in order of medal presentation along the walls of the room facing the Washington portraits and the podium where President Nixon would stand while he spoke to them. After his remarks, he would make his way around the room, presenting the Medals of Honor to family members as Secretary of the Army Stanley Rogers Resor read a portion of each recipient's medal citation—the official record of the actions taken by each soldier who sacrificed his life for comrades in arms and country.[5]

In his welcoming, which lasted about 5 minutes, President Nixon said:

> Ladies and gentlemen, we are gathered in this historic East Room of the White House today for an occasion that is on the one hand a very sad occasion, because we are honoring men who have died for their country. But on the other hand, it's a very proud occasion, because these are men who have given more to their country than any of us have given and have given it in a way that is commemorated by the very highest honor that this nation can provide, the Medal of Honor.
>
> It's quite difficult to find the words to express the gratitude of the nation to these men and to their families and their loved ones on such an occasion. It's difficult to do so because we know the feeling that you have had when you learned of their death, and we know, too, that the pride you will have when you read the citations that they have received.
>
> But I can only say, as one who has been to Vietnam on trips on six different occasions when I was out of office and once since I've been in office, that I've seen those men out there. They're so young, they're so brave, and they make you so proud of this country. And there are those who, I know, critics of this war—as there are critics of all wars—who say, "Why? Why do men have to die? Why do they have to die here particularly?" And, of course, there is an answer. And it's in the history of this country....
>
> Because through the history of this country there have been young men, like your sons, and your husbands, your loved ones, who have, beyond the call of duty, served America, given their lives for this country. We wouldn't be here if it hadn't been for those men.
>
> And so as we look at Vietnam, so far away, a very controversial war, let us just remember, that as we work for, as we are working for, and as we obtain, as we will obtain, a just peace—and what I mean by that, a peace in which the United States is not defeated, but a peace in which the people of South Vietnam have a chance to determine their own future without having it imposed upon them by a foreign power—let us remember that because of what these men and thousands of young Americans like them did, the chance that their younger brothers and that their sons may not have to fight in another war in the future is greatly reduced.
>
> Because of what they did, and their colleagues, this world will be a safer world. It'll be a better world because the forces of aggression will not have won the victory over the forces of freedom and decency.... And so, I simply want to

say, speaking not just as the President of the United States and as commander in chief of the armed forces, but as an American citizen,…there's no prouder moment that I can have in this office than to participate in awarding the Medal of Honor to the next of kin of these men who died in Vietnam.

And I would say, finally, that they wouldn't be the men that they were if they didn't come from good families. We know that. Their mothers, their fathers, those who grew up with them, something came from that family that helped them be the men that they were, that gave them that extra something, which enabled them to do something far beyond the call of duty, which merits the Medal of Honor.

And so, we thank them, and we thank you for what you've done for the country, in helping to give to America such fine young men.[6]

On a recording of the ceremony kept by the Richard Nixon Presidential Library and Museum, at least one child could be heard in the background while the President spoke. As he finished, the commander in chief began making his way around the great hall, to the first of the families who would receive their loved one's Medal of Honor.

Secretary Resor read as Nixon moved from family to family, beginning with the highest-ranking recipient:

The President of the United States of America, authorized by act of Congress March 3, 1863, has posthumously awarded in the name of the Congress, the Medal of Honor to the following individuals for conspicuous gallantry and intrepidity in action at the risk of their lives above and beyond the call of duty.

First Lieutenant Douglas B. Fournet, Infantry, while serving as a rifle platoon leader in Company B, 1st Battalion, 7th Cavalry, 1st Cavalry Division (Airmobile) in the A Shau Valley, Republic of Vietnam, on May 4, 1968.[7]

Lieutenant Fournet's citation reads, in part,

With complete disregard for his safety and realizing the imminent danger to members of his command, he used his body as a shield in front of the mine as he attempted to slash the control wires leading from the enemy positions to the mine. As he reached for the wire the mine was detonated, killing him instantly. Five men nearest the mine were slightly wounded, but First Lieutenant Fournet's heroic and unselfish act spared his men of serious injury or death.[8]

Fournet, of Lake Charles, Louisiana, was three days shy of his 25th birthday when he was killed in action. He was married and his son was born after his death. A statue of him is at the center of the Veterans Memorial Park on the grounds of the Lake Charles Civic Center.[9] The local Douglas Fournet Department of Veterans Affairs Clinic was named for him in 2019,[10] as was a 12.5-mile portion of Interstate 210 that loops around the community.[11] He is buried in Kinder McCrill Memorial Cemetery in Kinder, Louisiana.[12]

Secretary Resor read aloud, "Sergeant First Class Rodney J. T. Yano, while serving with the Air Cavalry Troop, 11th Armored Cavalry Regiment, in the vicinity of Bien Hoa, Republic of Vietnam, on January 1, 1969."[13]

Yano's official Medal of Honor citation states, in part:

> Sergeant First Class Yano was performing the duties of crew chief aboard the troop's command-and-control helicopter during action against enemy forces entrenched in dense jungle. From an exposed position in the face of intense small arms and anti-aircraft fire he delivered suppressive fire upon the enemy forces and marked their positions with smoke and white phosphorus grenades, enabling his troop commander to direct accurate and effective artillery fire against the hostile emplacements.
>
> A grenade, exploding prematurely, covered him with burning phosphorous, and left him severely wounded. Flaming fragments within the helicopter caused supplies and ammunition to detonate. Dense white smoke filled the aircraft obscuring the pilot's vision and causing him to lose control. Although having the use of only one arm and being partially blinded by the initial explosion, Sergeant First Class Yano completely disregarded his welfare and began hurling blazing ammunition from the helicopter. In so doing he inflicted additional wounds upon himself, yet he persisted until the danger was past. Sergeant First Class Yano's indomitable courage and profound concern for his comrades averted loss of life and additional injury to the rest of the crew.[14]

Yano, 25, was born in Hawaii two years after the attack on Pearl Harbor. He left high school before graduating to join the Army in 1961. He was on his second tour of duty in Vietnam and serving as acting crew chief and door gunner when the grenade prematurely exploded aboard his helicopter.[15]

Among the honors he has received, the cargo carrier USNS *Yano* was named for him, along with a helicopter maintenance facility at Fort Rucker, Alabama, and a library at Schofield Barracks in Oahu, Hawaii.[16] He is buried in the National Memorial Cemetery of the Pacific in Honolulu.[17]

Secretary Resor read aloud, "Staff Sergeant Laszlo Rabel, while serving as leader of Team Delta, 74th Infantry Detachment (Long Range Patrol), 173rd Airborne Brigade, in Binh Dinh Province, Republic of Vietnam, on November 13, 1968."[18]

Staff Sergeant Rabel, at 31, was the oldest of the soldiers honored that day at the White House. In 1956, as a teenager, he'd been forced to flee his native Hungary after participating in the failed uprising against Soviet-backed communist rule. He settled in Minneapolis, Minnesota, and joined the Army there in 1965.[19]

Rabel's official Medal of Honor citation states, in part:

> Team Delta was in a defensive perimeter conducting reconnaissance of enemy trail networks when a member of the team detected enemy movement to the front. As Staff Sergeant Rabel and a comrade prepared to clear the area, he heard an incoming grenade as it landed in the midst of the team's perimeter. With complete disregard for his life, Staff Sergeant Rabel threw himself on the grenade and, covering it with his body, received the complete impact of the immediate explosion. Through his indomitable courage, complete disregard for his safety and profound concern for his fellow soldiers, Staff Sergeant Rabel averted the loss of life and injury to the other members of Team Delta.[20]

His wife Eva and daughter Eve were in the East Room to accept Rabel's Medal of Honor from the President. He is buried in Arlington National Cemetery.[21]

Secretary Resor read aloud, "Specialist 5 John J. Kedenburg, while serving as adviser, South Vietnamese long-range reconnaissance team, in the Republic of Vietnam on June 13, 1968."[22]

Kedenburg's official Medal of Honor citation states, in part:

> Prior to reaching the day's objective, the team was attacked and encircled by a battalion-size North Vietnamese Army force. Sp5 Kedenburg assumed immediate command of the team which succeeded, after a fierce fight, in breaking out of the encirclement. As the team moved through thick jungle to a position from which it could be extracted by helicopter, Sp5 Kedenburg conducted a gallant rear guard fight against the pursuing enemy and called for tactical air support and rescue helicopters. His withering fire against the enemy permitted the team to reach a preselected landing zone with the loss of only one man, who was unaccounted for.
> Once in the landing zone, Sp5 Kedenburg deployed the team into a perimeter defense against the numerically superior enemy force. When tactical air support

arrived, he skillfully directed air strikes against the enemy, suppressing their fire so that helicopters could hover over the area and drop slings to be used in the extraction of the team. After half of the team was extracted by helicopter, Sp5 Kedenburg and the remaining three members of the team harnessed themselves to the sling on a second hovering helicopter.

Just as the helicopter was to lift them out of the area, the South Vietnamese team member who had been unaccounted for after the initial encounter with the enemy appeared in the landing zone. Sp5 Kedenburg unhesitatingly gave up his place in the sling to the man and directed the helicopter pilot to leave the area. He then continued to engage the enemy who were swarming into the landing zone, killing six enemy soldiers before he was overpowered. Sp5 Kedenburg's inspiring leadership, consummate courage and willing self-sacrifice permitted his small team to inflict heavy casualties on the enemy and escape almost certain annihilation.[23]

Specialist Kedenburg, from Brooklyn, was 21. Kedenburg Street at Fort Bragg, North Carolina, is named for him and there is a plaque in his honor in the Veterans Memorial Plaza in his hometown of Baldwin, New York.[24] He is buried in Long Island National Cemetery in Farmingdale, New York.[25]

Secretary Resor read aloud, "Corporal Thomas W. Bennett, while serving as a platoon medical aid man, with Company B, 1st Battalion, 14th Infantry, 4th Infantry Division, during a reconnaissance-in-force mission, Pleiku Province, Republic of Vietnam, on February 9, 1969."[26]

Corporal Bennett, 21, a medic from Morgantown, West Virginia, was the second conscientious objector to receive the Medal of Honor. The first was Desmond Doss, a World War II medic whose story was told in the film *Hacksaw Ridge*.[27]

Bennett's citation reads, in part:

> On 9 February…in the initial barrage of fire, three of the point members of the platoon fell wounded. Cpl. Bennett, with complete disregard for his safety, ran through the heavy fire to his fallen comrades, administered life-saving first aid under fire, and then made repeated trips carrying the wounded men to positions of relative safety from which they would be medically evacuated from the battle position. Cpl. Bennett repeatedly braved the intense enemy fire, moving across open areas to give aid and comfort to his wounded comrades. He valiantly exposed himself to the heavy fire in order to retrieve the bodies of several fallen personnel. Throughout the night and following day, Cpl. Bennett moved from position to position treating and comforting several personnel who had suffered shrapnel and gunshot wounds.

On 11 February, Company B again moved in an assault on the well-fortified enemy positions and became heavily engaged with the numerically superior enemy force. Five members of the company fell wounded in the initial assault. Cpl. Bennett ran to their aid without regard to the heavy fire. He treated one wounded comrade and began running toward another seriously wounded man. Although the wounded man was located forward of the company position covered by heavy enemy grazing fire and Cpl. Bennett was warned that it was impossible to reach the position, he leaped forward with complete disregard for his safety to save his comrade's life. In an attempt to save his fellow soldier, he was mortally wounded.[28]

Several places bear Corporal Bennett's name: a youth center at Schofield Barracks in Oahu, a medical clinic at Fort Hood, Texas, a bridge over the Monongahela River in Morgantown, and a residence hall at West Virginia University, where he attended classes before his military service. His family donated his Medal of Honor to the university in 2000. His story was told in *Peaceful Patriot: The Story of Tom Bennett* by Bonni McKeown.

In the last of a series of audiotapes he sent home from Vietnam, Bennett said, "And I want you to understand also that for some reason, right now, I feel—how do I explain it, let's see—I feel that they can't hurt me in any way. I have had and am having such a rich, full, good, exciting life that, well, nobody can take that away from me. It can't be erased or diminished in any way."

He is buried in East Oak Grove Cemetery, Morgantown.[29]

Secretary Resor read aloud, "Staff Sergeant Marvin R. Young, while serving as a squad leader with Company C, 1st Battalion (Mechanized), 5th Infantry, 25th Infantry Division, in the vicinity of Ben Cui, Republic of Vietnam, on October 21, 1968."[30]

Young's citation reads, in part:

As a human wave attack advanced on Staff Sergeant Young's platoon, he moved from position to position, encouraging and directing fire on the hostile insurgents while exposing himself to the hail of enemy bullets. After receiving orders to withdraw to a better defensive position, he remained behind to provide covering fire for the withdrawal. Observing that a small element of the point squad was unable to extract itself from its position, and completely disregarding his personal safety, Staff Sergeant Young began moving toward their position, firing as he maneuvered. When halfway to their position he sustained a critical head injury, yet he continued his mission and ordered the element to withdraw.

Remaining with the squad as it fought its way to the rear, he was twice seriously wounded in the arm and the leg. Although his leg was badly shattered, Staff Sergeant Young refused assistance that would have slowed the retreat of his comrades, and he ordered them to continue their withdrawal while he provided protective covering fire. With indomitable courage and heroic self-sacrifice, he continued his self-assigned mission until the enemy force engulfed his position.[31]

Young, of Alpine, Texas, was 21. A post office in Odessa, Texas, was named in his honor,[32] and the Wilson and Young Medal of Honor VA Clinic in Odessa was named for him and fellow Texas recipient, Marine Pfc. Alfred "Mac" Wilson.[33] Young is buried in Sunset Memorial Gardens in Odessa.[34]

Secretary Resor read aloud, "Sergeant Ray McKibben, while serving as team leader of the point element of a reconnaissance patrol of Troop B, 7th Squadron (Airmobile), 17th Cavalry, 1st Aviation Brigade, near Song Mao, Republic of Vietnam, on December 6, 1968."[35]

McKibben's citation reads:

Sgt. McKibben was leading his point element in a movement to contact along a well-traveled trail when the lead element came under heavy automatic weapons fire from a fortified bunker position, forcing the patrol to take cover. Sgt. McKibben, appraising the situation and without regard for his own safety, charged through bamboo and heavy brush to the fortified position, killed the enemy gunner, secured the weapon and directed his patrol element forward. As the patrol moved out, Sgt. McKibben observed enemy movement to the flank of the patrol. Fire support from helicopter gunships was requested and the area was effectively neutralized. The patrol again continued its mission and as the lead element rounded the bend of a river it came under heavy automatic weapons fire from camouflaged bunkers.

As Sgt. McKibben was deploying his men to covered positions, he observed one of his men fall wounded. Although bullets were hitting all around the wounded man, Sgt. McKibben, with complete disregard for his safety, sprang to his comrade's side and under heavy enemy fire pulled him to safety behind the cover of a rock emplacement where he administered hasty first aid. Sgt. McKibben, seeing that his comrades were pinned down and were unable to deliver effective fire against the enemy bunkers, again undertook a single-handed assault of the enemy defenses.

He charged through the brush and hail of automatic weapons fire closing on the first bunker, killing the enemy with accurate rifle fire and securing the enemy's weapon. He continued his assault against the next bunker, firing his rifle as he charged. As he approached the second bunker his rifle ran out of ammunition;

however, he used the captured enemy weapon until it too was empty, at that time he silenced the bunker with well-placed hand grenades. He reloaded his weapon and covered the advance of his men as they moved forward. Observing the fire of another bunker impeding the patrol's advance, Sgt. McKibben again single-handedly assaulted the new position. As he neared the bunker, he was mortally wounded but was able to fire a final burst from his weapon killing the enemy and enabling the patrol to continue the assault.

McKibben, of Felton, Georgia, was 23. He is buried at the Center Baptist Church Cemetery in Felton.[36]

Secretary Resor read aloud, "Sergeant Anund C. Roark, while serving as a squad leader with Company C, 1st Battalion, 12th Infantry, 4th Infantry Division, in Kontum Province, Republic of Vietnam, on May 16, 1968."[37]

Sergeant Roark, 20, was born in Vallejo, California. His citation reads:

Sgt. Roark was the point squad leader of a small force which had the mission of rescuing 11 men in a hilltop observation post under heavy attack by a company-size force, approximately 1,000 meters from the battalion perimeter. As lead elements of the relief force reached the besieged observation post, intense automatic weapons fire from the enemy occupied bunkers halted their movement. Without hesitation, Sgt. Roark maneuvered his squad, repeatedly exposing himself to withering enemy fire to hurl grenades and direct the fire of his squad to gain fire superiority and cover the withdrawal of the outpost and evacuation of its casualties. Frustrated in their effort to overrun the position, the enemy swept the hilltop with small arms and volleys of grenades. Seeing a grenade land in the midst of his men, Sgt. Roark, with complete disregard for his safety, hurled himself upon the grenade, absorbing its blast with his body. Sgt. Roark's magnificent leadership and dauntless courage saved the lives of many of his comrades and were the inspiration for the successful relief of the outpost.[38]

The Army Reserve Center at Camp Pendleton, California, was named for Roark in 1974.[39] He is buried in Fort Rosecrans National Cemetery in San Diego.[40]

Secretary Resor read aloud, "Sergeant William W. Seay, while serving as a driver with the 62nd Transportation Company (Medium Truck), 7th Transportation Battalion, 48th Transportation Group, on a resupply mission, near Ap Nhi, Republic of Vietnam, on August 25, 1968."[41]

Seay's citation reads:

> The convoy with which he was traveling, carrying critically needed ammunition and supplies from Long Binh to Tay Ninh, was ambushed by a reinforced battalion of the North Vietnamese Army. As the main elements of the convoy entered the ambush killing zone, they were struck by intense rocket, machine gun and automatic weapons fire from the well concealed and entrenched enemy force. When his convoy was forced to stop, Sgt. Seay immediately dismounted and took a defensive position behind the wheels of a vehicle loaded with high-explosive ammunition. As the violent North Vietnamese assault approached to within 10 meters of the road, Sgt. Seay opened fire, killing two of the enemy. He then spotted a sniper in a tree approximately 75 meters to his front and killed him.
>
> When an enemy grenade was thrown under an ammunition trailer near his position, without regard for his own safety he left his protective cover, exposing himself to intense enemy fire, picked up the grenade, and threw it back to the North Vietnamese position, killing four more of the enemy and saving the lives of the men around him. Another enemy grenade landed approximately three meters from Sgt. Seay's position. Again Sgt. Seay left his covered position and threw the armed grenade back upon the assaulting enemy. After returning to his position, he was painfully wounded in the right wrist; however, Sgt. Seay continued to give encouragement and direction to his fellow soldiers. After moving to the relative cover of a shallow ditch, he detected three enemy soldiers who had penetrated the position and were preparing to fire on his comrades.
>
> Although weak from loss of blood and with his right hand immobilized, Sgt. Seay stood up and fired his rifle with his left hand, killing all three and saving the lives of the other men in his location. As a result of his heroic action, Sgt. Seay was mortally wounded by a sniper's bullet.[42]

Seay, of Brewton, Alabama, was 19. A plaza at Fort Eustis, Virginia, was named in his honor in 1970, with a rededication ceremony in 2018, almost 50 years after he was killed in action.[43] Also named for Seay was the Army Reserve Center in Mobile, Alabama, and the vehicle cargo ship USNS *Seay*.[44] He is buried in Weaver Cemetery in Brewton.[45]

Secretary Resor read aloud, "Sergeant Lester R. Stone Jr., while serving as squad leader with Company B, 1st Battalion, 20th Infantry, 11th Infantry Brigade, American Division, near Duc Pho, Republic of Vietnam, on March 3, 1969."[46]

From Stone's citation:

> The 1st Platoon was on a combat patrol mission just west of Landing Zone Liz when it came under intense automatic weapons and grenade fire from a well

concealed company-size force of North Vietnamese regulars. Observing the platoon machine gunner fall critically wounded, Sgt. Stone remained in the exposed
area to provide cover fire for the wounded soldier who was being pulled to safety
by another member of the platoon. With enemy fire impacting all around him,
Sgt. Stone had a malfunction in the machine gun, preventing him from firing the
weapon automatically. Displaying extraordinary courage under the most adverse
conditions, Sgt. Stone repaired the weapon and continued to place on the enemy
positions effective suppressive fire which enabled the rescue to be completed.

In a desperate attempt to overrun his position, an enemy force left its cover
and charged Sgt. Stone. Disregarding the danger involved, Sgt. Stone rose to his
knees and began placing intense fire on the enemy at point blank range, killing
six of the enemy before falling mortally wounded. His actions of unsurpassed
valor were a source of inspiration to his entire unit, and he was responsible for
saving the lives of a number of his fellow soldiers.[47]

Stone, 21, was born in Binghamton, New York, and is buried in that
city's Chenango Valley Cemetery.[48] As a tribute to his fellow Binghamton
native, National Aeronautics and Space Administration astronaut Douglas
Wheelock, with the blessing of Stone's family, took the fallen soldier's
Medal of Honor to the International Space Station with him in 2010.
"We are carrying it as a tribute to all of those who have served and all
of those who love freedom," Wheelock said in a video message from the
orbiting station. "We wanted to send a huge thank you to our veterans
of all services around the globe. We wanted to let you know how much
we appreciate your sacrifice and your years of service for both your
countrymen, your families and for people that you'll never even have a
chance to meet."[49]

Secretary Resor read aloud, "Specialist 4 Nicholas J. Cutinha, while
serving as a machine gunner with Company C, 4th Battalion, 9th Infantry
Regiment, 25th infantry Division, near Gia Dinh, Republic of Vietnam,
on March 2, 1968."[50]

Specialist Cutinha's citation reads:

While serving as a machine gunner with Company C, Sp4 Cutinha accompanied
his unit on a combat mission near Gia Dinh. Suddenly his company came under
small arms, automatic weapons, mortar and rocket propelled grenade fire, from a
battalion size enemy unit. During the initial hostile attack, communication with
the battalion was lost and the company commander and numerous members of
the company became casualties.

When Sp4 Cutinha observed that his company was pinned down and disorganized, he moved to the front with complete disregard for his safety, firing his machine gun at the charging enemy. As he moved forward, he drew fire on his own position and was seriously wounded in the leg. As the hostile fire intensified and half of the company was killed or wounded, Sp4 Cutinha assumed command of all the survivors in his area and initiated a withdrawal while providing covering fire for the evacuation of the wounded.

He killed several enemy soldiers but sustained another leg wound when his machine gun was destroyed by incoming rounds. Undaunted, he crawled through a hail of enemy fire to an operable machine gun in order to continue the defense of his injured comrades who were being administered medical treatment. Sp4 Cutinha maintained this position, refused assistance and provided defensive fire for his comrades until he fell, mortally wounded. He was solely responsible for killing 15 enemy soldiers while saving the lives of at least 9 members of his own unit.[51]

Cutinha, 23, was born in Fernandina Beach in the northeast corner of Florida and is buried in Fort Denaud Cemetery just east of Fort Myers. The Jacksonville chapter of the Vietnam Veterans of America was renamed for Cutinha in 2012.[52] His medal is on display at the nearby American Legion Post 130 in LaBelle. It was presented to the post by his mother, in the hope that all who view it would remember "the price of freedom is often paid with the blood of a nation's youth."[53] Post 130 joined other veteran and civic organizations and the city to memorialize Cutinha with a statue dedicated in LaBelle Veterans Park in 2020.[54]

Secretary Resor read aloud, "Specialist 4 Edward A. Devore Jr., while serving as a machine gunner with Company B, 4th Battalion, 39th Infantry, 9th Infantry Division, near Saigon, Republic of Vietnam, on March 17, 1968."[55]

From Devore's citation:

Sp4c. DeVore's platoon, the company's lead element, abruptly came under intense fire from automatic weapons, Claymore mines, rockets and grenades from well-concealed bunkers in a nipa palm swamp. One man was killed and three wounded about 20 meters from the bunker complex. Sp4c. DeVore raced through a hail of fire to provide a base of fire with his machine gun, enabling the point element to move the wounded back to friendly lines.

After supporting artillery, gunships and air strikes had been employed on the enemy positions, a squad was sent forward to retrieve their fallen comrades. Intense enemy frontal and enfilading automatic weapons fire pinned down this element in the kill zone. With complete disregard for his personal safety, Sp4c.

> DeVore assaulted the enemy positions. Hit in the shoulder and knocked down about 35 meters short of his objectives, Sp4c. DeVore, ignoring his pain and the warnings of his fellow soldiers, jumped to his feet and continued his assault under intense hostile fire.
>
> Although mortally wounded during this advance, he continued to place highly accurate suppressive fire upon the entrenched insurgents. By drawing the enemy fire upon himself, Sp4c. DeVore enabled the trapped squad to rejoin the platoon in safety.[56]

DeVore, 20, grew up in California and joined the Army from there in 1966. He is recognized with a plaque in his hometown of Henryetta, Oklahoma, and there were are plans to name a bridge, along U.S. Highway 75, for him.[57] He has been inducted into the Oklahoma Military Hall of Fame,[58] and a memorial has been "dedicated to the memory and honor of Specialist DeVore and all who have made the ultimate sacrifice in the defense of our Country" in the Green Hills Memorial Park in Rancho Palos Verdes, California, where he is buried.[59]

Secretary Resor read aloud, "Specialist 4 Peter M. Guenette, while serving as a machine gunner with Company D, 2nd Battalion (Airborne), 506th Infantry, 101st Airborne Division (Airmobile), in Quan Tan Uyen, Republic of Vietnam, on May 18, 1968."[60]

This soldier's citation reads:

> While Sp4c. Guenette's platoon was sweeping a suspected enemy base camp, it came under light harassing fire from a well-equipped and firmly entrenched squad of North Vietnamese Army regulars which was serving as a delaying force at the entrance to their base camp. As the platoon moved within 10 meters of the fortified positions, the enemy fire became intense. Sp4c. Guenette and his assistant gunner immediately began to provide a base of suppressive fire, ceasing momentarily to allow the assistant gunner time to throw a grenade into a bunker. Seconds later, an enemy grenade was thrown to Sp4c. Guenette's right flank. Realizing that the grenade would kill or wound at least four men and destroy the machine gun, he shouted a warning and smothered the grenade with his body, absorbing its blast. Through his actions, he prevented loss of life or injury to at least three men and enabled his comrades to maintain their fire superiority.[61]

Guenette, 20, of Troy, New York, left behind a wife, who received his Medal of Honor from President Nixon. During Memorial Day weekend in 2017, an apartment building serving veterans was named in his honor by the Troy Housing Authority.[62] He is buried in St. John's Cemetery in Troy.[63]

Secretary Resor read aloud, "Specialist 4 Kenneth L. Olson, while serving as a team leader with Company A, 5th Battalion, 12th Infantry, 199th Infantry Brigade, near Cho Dien, Republic of Vietnam, on May 13, 1968."[64]

Olson, 22, was born in Willmar, Minnesota, and grew up on a farm. He was the first person in his family to graduate from college, earning a degree in agriculture economics.[65]

Olson's citation reads:

> Spec. Olson was participating in a mission to reinforce a reconnaissance platoon which was heavily engaged with a well-entrenched Viet Cong force. When his platoon moved into the area of contact and had overrun the first line of enemy bunkers, Spec. Olson and a fellow soldier moved forward of the platoon to investigate another suspected line of bunkers. As the two men advanced, they were pinned down by intense automatic weapons fire from an enemy position 10 meters to their front.
>
> With complete disregard for his safety, Spec. Olson exposed himself and hurled a hand grenade into the Viet Cong position. Failing to silence the hostile fire, he again exposed himself to the intense fire in preparation to assault the enemy position. As he prepared to hurl the grenade, he was wounded, causing him to drop the activated device within his own position. Realizing that it would explode immediately, Spec. Olson threw himself upon the grenade and pulled it in to his body to take the full force of the explosion. By this unselfish action Spec. Olson sacrificed his own life to save the lives of his fellow comrades-in-arms. His extraordinary heroism inspired his fellow soldiers to renew their efforts and totally defeat the enemy force.[66]

A portion of a local road, Highway 23, in Paynesville, Minnesota, was renamed in his honor,[67] and he is recognized with identical plaques at the Paynesville American Legion Post 271 and on the St. Paul campus of the University of Minnesota, where he received his bachelor's degree and where a scholarship is endowed in his name.[68] He is buried in Paynesville Cemetery.[69]

Secretary Resor read aloud, "Specialist 4 Hector Santiago-Colon, while serving as a mortar man with Company B, 5th Battalion, 7th Cavalry, 1st Cavalry Division (Airmobile), in Quang Tri, Republic of Vietnam, on June 28, 1968."[70]

Santiago-Colon and his 11 siblings were born in Puerto Rico but the family eventually moved to New York City. He enlisted in the Army from there, hoping one day to join the New York City Police Department.[71] Santiago-Colon's citation reads:

> While serving as a perimeter sentry Sp4c. Santiago-Colon heard distinct move-ment in the heavily wooded area to his front and flanks. Immediately he alerted his fellow sentries in the area to move to their foxholes and remain alert for any enemy probing forces. From the wooded area around his position heavy enemy automatic weapons and small-arms fire suddenly broke out, but extreme darkness rendered difficult the precise location and identification of the hostile force. Only the muzzle flashes from enemy weapons indicated their position.
>
> Sp4c. Santiago-Colon and the other members of his position immediately began to repel the attackers, utilizing hand grenades, antipersonnel mines and small-arms fire. Due to the heavy volume of enemy fire and exploding grenades around them, a North Vietnamese soldier was able to crawl, undetected, to their position. Suddenly, the enemy soldier lobbed a grenade into Sp4c. Santiago-Colon's foxhole. Realizing that there was no time to throw the grenade out of his position, Sp4c. Santiago-Colon retrieved the grenade, tucked it in to his stomach and, turning away from his comrades, absorbed the full impact of the blast. His heroic self-sacrifice saved the lives of those who occupied the foxhole with him, and provided them with the inspiration to continue fighting until they had forced the enemy to retreat from the perimeter.[72]

In 1975, the Puerto Rico National Guard renamed their training base Camp Santiago in honor of Santiago-Colon, 25. Two years later a gym at Fort Benning, Georgia, was named for him. Santiago-Colon's name was also inscribed on the El Monumento de la Recordacion (Monument of Remembrance) in front of the capitol building in San Juan and an oil portrait of him was unveiled in the capitol rotunda in 2008.[73]

Secretary Resor read aloud, "Private First Class James W. Fous, while serving as a rifleman with Company E, 4th Battalion, 47th Infantry, 9th Infantry Division, in Kien Hoa Province, Republic of Vietnam, on May 14, 1968."[74]

From Fous's citation:

> Pfc. Fous was participating in a reconnaissance-in-force mission when his unit formed its perimeter defense for the night. Pfc. Fous, together with three other American soldiers, occupied a position in a thickly vegetated area facing a wood line. Pfc. Fous detected three Viet Cong maneuvering toward his position and,

after alerting the other men, directed accurate fire upon the enemy soldiers, silencing two of them. The third Viet Cong soldier managed to escape in the thick vegetation after throwing a hand grenade into Pfc. Fous' position. Without hesitation, Pfc. Fous shouted a warning to his comrades and leaped upon the lethal explosive, absorbing the blast with his body to save the lives of the three men in the area at the sacrifice of his life.[75]

Fous, 21, was born in Omaha, Nebraska, and is buried at the Fort McPherson National Cemetery, Maxwell, Nebraska.[76]

U.S. Senator Deb Fischer wrote of Fous's sacrifice for a Memorial Day column called *The Ultimate Sacrifice* in 2014: "The bravery Private Fous demonstrated at such a young age by knowingly putting himself in harm's way to protect others is a humbling inspiration to all Americans. His actions exemplify those of a true hero.... Let us reflect on the values for which Private Fous and countless others fought and died as we renew our resolve to honor their legacy."[77]

Secretary Resor read aloud, "Private First Class Garfield M. Langhorn, while serving as a radio operator with Troop C, 7th Squadron (Airmobile), 17th Cavalry, 1st Aviation Brigade, near Plei Djereng, Republic of Vietnam, on January 15, 1969."[78]

"Pfc. Langhorn's platoon was inserted into a landing zone to rescue two pilots of a Cobra helicopter shot down by enemy fire on a heavily timbered slope," his citation reads.

> He provided radio coordination with the command-and-control aircraft overhead while the troops hacked their way through dense undergrowth to the wreckage, where both aviators were found dead. As the men were taking the bodies to a pickup site, they suddenly came under intense fire from North Vietnamese soldiers in camouflaged bunkers to the front and right flank, and within minutes they were surrounded.
>
> Pfc. Langhorn immediately radioed for help from the orbiting gunships, which began to place minigun and rocket fire on the aggressors. He then lay between the platoon leader and another man, operating the radio and providing covering fire for the wounded who had been moved to the center of the small perimeter. Darkness soon fell, making it impossible for the gunships to give accurate support, and the aggressors began to probe the perimeter. An enemy hand grenade landed in front of Pfc. Langhorn and a few feet from personnel who had become casualties. Choosing to protect these wounded, he unhesitatingly threw himself on the grenade, scooped it beneath his body and absorbed the blast. By sacrificing himself, he saved the lives of his comrades.[79]

Langhorn, 20, was born in Virginia but eventually moved to New York. He joined the Army while living in Brooklyn, and was buried in Riverhead Cemetery on eastern Long Island in New York.[80] The post office in Riverhead was named for him in 2010.[81] For years, the PFC Garfield M. Langhorn Memorial Committee and the Pulaski Street Elementary School have sponsored an essay contest where sixth graders answer the question, "How can I emulate and honor PFC Langhorn in my everyday life?" In 2019, one of the winning essayists wrote, "Garfield was like a superhero to me. His actions inspire me to help others.... I am inspired by him and will keep his memory alive."[82]

That same year, on the 50th anniversary of Langhorn's death, there was a push to issue a stamp in his honor that would raise funds to help low-income veterans.[83] That bipartisan legislation was reintroduced in January 2021,[84] and in June of that year Riverhead High School dedicated a Veterans Wall of Honor to the local hero.[85]

Secretary Resor read aloud, "Private First Class Milton A. Lee, while serving as a radio telephone operator with Company B, 2nd Battalion, 502nd Infantry, 1st Brigade, 101st Airborne Division (Airmobile), near Phu Bai, Republic of Vietnam, on April 26, 1968."[86]

From Lee's citation:

> Pfc. Lee was serving as the radio telephone operator with the 3d platoon, Company B. As lead element for the company, the 3d platoon received intense surprise hostile fire from a force of North Vietnamese Army regulars in well-concealed bunkers. With 50 percent casualties, the platoon maneuvered to a position of cover to treat their wounded and reorganize, while Pfc. Lee moved through the heavy enemy fire giving lifesaving first aid to his wounded comrades. During the subsequent assault on the enemy defensive positions, Pfc. Lee continuously kept close radio contact with the company commander, relaying precise and understandable orders to his platoon leader.
>
> While advancing with the front rank toward the objective, Pfc. Lee observed four North Vietnamese soldiers with automatic weapons and a rocket launcher lying in wait for the lead element of the platoon. As the element moved forward, unaware of the concealed danger, Pfc. Lee immediately and with utter disregard for his own personal safety, passed his radio to another soldier and charged through the murderous fire. Without hesitation he continued his assault, overrunning the enemy position, killing all occupants and capturing four automatic weapons and a rocket launcher. Pfc. Lee continued his one-man assault on the second position through a heavy barrage of enemy automatic weapons fire.

> Grievously wounded, he continued to press the attack, crawling forward into a firing position and delivering accurate covering fire to enable his platoon to maneuver and destroy the position. Not until the position was overrun did Pfc. Lee falter in his steady volume of fire and succumb to his wounds. Pfc. Lee's heroic actions saved the lives of the lead element and were instrumental in the destruction of the key position of the enemy defense.[87]

Lee, a native of Louisiana, was 19. He is buried at Fort Sam Houston National Cemetery in San Antonio. In the early 1970s, a recreation center was named for him at Fort Campbell, Kentucky, home of the 101st Airborne Division, and during the War on Terror, in 2013, a center at Campbell dedicated to helping soldiers make a successful transition into civilian life was also named for him.[88]

On an online message board focused on Vietnam veterans, a man identifying himself as Lee's platoon leader wrote, "I want to say that he unselfishly gave his life so others could survive that day. I was very close to Milton during the time he was my Radio Operator, and I was with him when he was shot. I can truly say Milton was the kind of person that everyone liked and respected. He always was willing to help others no matter what the cost."[89]

Secretary Resor read aloud, "Private First Class Phill G. McDonald, while serving as a team leader with Company A, 1st Battalion, 14th Infantry, 4th Infantry Division, near Kontum, Republic of Vietnam, on June 7, 1968."[90]

McDonald's citation reads:

> While on a combat mission his platoon came under heavy barrage of automatic weapons fire from a well concealed company-size enemy force. Volunteering to escort two wounded comrades to an evacuation point, Pfc. McDonald crawled through intense fire to destroy with a grenade an enemy automatic weapon threatening the safety of the evacuation. Returning to his platoon, he again volunteered to provide covering fire for the maneuver of the platoon from its exposed position.
>
> Realizing the threat he posed, enemy gunners concentrated their fire on Pfc. McDonald's position, seriously wounding him. Despite his painful wounds, Pfc. McDonald recovered the weapon of a wounded machine gunner to provide accurate covering fire for the gunner's evacuation. When other soldiers were pinned down by a heavy volume of fire from a hostile machine gun to his front, Pfc. McDonald crawled toward the enemy position to destroy it with grenades.

He was mortally wounded in this intrepid action. Pfc. McDonald's gallantry at the risk of his life…resulted in the saving of the lives of his comrades….[91]

Hailing originally from Avondale, West Virginia, McDonald, 26, the oldest of 12 children, was working in Greensboro, North Carolina, when he was drafted. In his honor, the Glade Creek Bridge in Raleigh County, West Virginia, was renamed the Phill G. McDonald Memorial Bridge. Part of Interstate 64, it is the highest interstate bridge in the country and one of the 10 highest bridges in the United States. In June 2009, McDonald's portrait and Medal of Honor citation were displayed at the McDowell County Courthouse in Welch, West Virginia, about 20 miles from his hometown of Avondale. A lectern-shaped concrete marker with a square bronze tablet describing McDonald's heroism in Vietnam stands in a plaza named for him at the Guilford County Governmental Center in Greensboro. He is buried in Guilford Memorial Park.[92]

Secretary Resor read aloud, "Private First Class David P. Nash, while serving as a grenadier with Company B, 2nd Battalion, 39th Infantry, 9th Infantry Division, in Dinh Tuong Province, Republic of Vietnam, on Dec. 29, 1968."[93]

From Nash's citation:

> When an ambush patrol of which he was a member suddenly came under intense attack before reaching its destination, he was the first to return the enemy fire. Taking an exposed location, Pfc. Nash suppressed the hostile fusillade with a rapid series of rounds from his grenade launcher, enabling artillery fire to be adjusted on the enemy. After the foe had been routed, his small element continued to the ambush site, where he established a position with three fellow soldiers on a narrow dike.
>
> Shortly past midnight, while Pfc. Nash and a comrade kept watch and the two other men took their turn sleeping, an enemy grenade wounded two soldiers in the adjacent position. Seconds later, Pfc. Nash saw another grenade land only a few feet from his own position. Although he could have escaped harm by rolling down the other side of the dike, he shouted a warning to his comrades and leaped upon the lethal explosive. Absorbing the blast with his body, he saved the lives of the three men in the area at the sacrifice of his life.[94]

Nash, 20, was born in Whitesville, Kentucky, and buried in the town's St. Mary of the Woods Cemetery. The portion of Kentucky State Highway 54 that runs through Whitesville is named for him.[95]

As President Nixon, stepped away from the Nash family, Secretary Resor finished his recitation, referring to all the recipients:

> Their conspicuous gallantry, undaunted concern for their comrades, and intrepidity at the cost of their own lives above and beyond the call of duty are in keeping with the highest traditions of the military service and reflect great credit on themselves, their units, and the United States Army.[96]

Returning to the podium, the President said,

> Thank you very much, Mr. Secretary. On this occasion, incidentally, we want you to know that this house belongs to you. And we invite you to, to the extent your schedules will permit, to take a tour of the various rooms in the house and Mrs. Nixon has arranged for some refreshments over in the state dining room and we want you to, to the extent this occasion will permit, we want you to enjoy your visit here and to take away memories that will be pleasant ones of the White House and of all the things that have happened here.
>
> And we want to say again that as we think of this group—as I went around the room, 21 men, and they came from 14 states and from Puerto Rico. This shows you that this is truly one country. When you find brave men, they aren't limited to one state. They come from all of America, from the whole heart of America. And we thank you again for what you have done, as well as for what they have done.[97]

Michael Crescenz was actually the 11th name on the list of recipients that day during the 23-minute, 9-second ceremony in the East Room. A White House photograph shows Mr. Crescenz leaning in toward the commander in chief, looking as if he's saying something in confidence to the President as they shake hands. Mrs. Crescenz, in black, is standing tall and straight, dignified and, though smiling, she seems somewhat uncomfortable—whether with the ceremony itself or the attention is unclear. Charles can be seen behind them. Another shot has them standing patiently waiting while Nixon talks to the group to their right. Peter, in uniform, is behind and between them. (Tom Gosse swears that his ear is clearly identifiable in one of the pictures from the day.[98])

Michael's battalion commander in Vietnam, Sam Wetzel, who had gotten the Medal of Honor process started for the heroic young soldier two years before, attended the ceremony.

"I was working in the Pentagon at the time," he said, "and I got invited to the White House, where President Nixon was going to present the Medal of Honor to Michael's parents. I said, 'Yeah, sure I'd love to meet the parents.' Because I had written to them but hadn't met them. So, you go to the White House and they have a procedure to get everybody into the room and I met Mr. and Mrs. Crescenz, and then there were two brothers, one a Marine veteran of Vietnam and the other one in Marine uniform, on active duty, and I thought, 'Boy, that's quite a family there. You have Michael in the Army and two brothers in the Marine Corps.' Nice guys.

"So, the President welcomed everybody, gave a nice speech, and they had somebody read the citations. And they had a lot of pictures taken as he gave the parents the medal. It was a very nice, very proper ceremony. And he was sincere, the President was very sincere about Michael, which I thought was great.

"And it brought tears to your eyes, really, to mine, because you know I have—I keep in front of my desk—I lost 12 men in six months in Vietnam. I've got their names, addresses, where they are on the Vietnam Wall, and where they're from. It's a little handwritten thing that I keep in front of my desk because I never want to forget these guys, including Michael."[99]

As President Nixon stepped up to the Crescenz family, the Army secretary read, "Corporal Michael J. Crescenz, while serving as a rifleman with Company A, 4th Battalion, 31st Infantry, 196th Infantry Brigade, Americal Division, in the Hiep Duc Valley, Republic of Vietnam, on November 20, 1968."[100]

The family had been grieving for 17 months by that point, the blink of an eye compared to the lifetime of mourning that was still ahead. The Army had used the time since Michael's death to craft the definitive citation for their son, the statement that would forever place him in elite company of heroes. It wasn't read in full that day in the White House—none of the citations were, given the number of honorees—but it captured the courage and sacrifice of Michael, and would forever inspire all those who read it:

Cpl. Crescenz distinguished himself by conspicuous gallantry and intrepidity in action while serving as a rifleman with Company A. In the morning his unit engaged a large, well-entrenched force of the North Vietnamese Army whose initial burst of fire pinned down the lead squad and killed the two point men, halting the advance of Company A.

Immediately, Cpl. Crescenz left the relative safety of his own position, seized a nearby machine gun and, with complete disregard for his safety, charged 100 meters up a slope toward the enemy's bunkers which he effectively silenced, killing the two occupants of each. Undaunted by the withering machine gun fire around him, Cpl. Crescenz courageously moved forward toward a third bunker which he also succeeded in silencing, killing two more of the enemy and momentarily clearing the route of advance for his comrades.

Suddenly, intense machine gun fire erupted from an unseen, camouflaged bunker. Realizing the danger to his fellow soldiers, Cpl. Crescenz disregarded the barrage of hostile fire directed at him and daringly advanced toward the position. Assaulting with his machine gun, Cpl. Crescenz was within five meters of the bunker when he was mortally wounded by the fire from the enemy machine gun.

As a direct result of his heroic actions, his company was able to maneuver freely with minimal danger and to complete its mission, defeating the enemy. Cpl. Crescenz's bravery and extraordinary heroism at the cost of his life are in the highest traditions of the military service and reflect great credit on himself, his unit, and the U.S. Army.[101]

Like most of the other recipients honored that day, Michael was buried close to his family home, in Holy Sepulchre Cemetery, just over the border from Philadelphia in Cheltenham Township, where he could be easily visited by those who loved and missed him most. That day in the East Room, there was no reason to believe the situation would ever change—certainly not as long as Mrs. Crescenz had anything to say about it. But Michael's story would not end there.

CHAPTER VII

Arlington

As much as 13-year-old Joe Crescenz missed his brother, he was equally proud of Michael and the sacrifice he made for his fellow soldiers and for his country. When his mom and dad assembled a picture album of their trip to Washington and the Medal of Honor ceremony, Joe was happy to cram it into his book bag, take it to school, and show it off to his friends. The pictures of Mr. and Mrs. Crescenz at the White House—right there next to the President of the United States—broke right through any adolescent cynicism and poses. "It was a beautiful thick album," Joe's lifelong friend Benjamin Silver wrote to him decades later, "and we just couldn't believe your parents were standing next to President Nixon, and talking to him. It didn't seem real."[1]

What *was* real, besides Joe's pride, was the flat-out fury he couldn't explain or control. So was the fact that the family had to move on.

There were still summer trips to their place down the Shore—where everything had started for Charles and Mary Ann. It was where they met and fell in love, where their boys played in the sand and sea with friends and cousins and then grew to become men.

"The Shore had a very calming effect on her," Mary Ann's niece Mary Lou Allen would say. Another cousin, Kathleen Zippilli, added that at the Shore, her aunt "was more relaxed and enjoyed company more."[2] It was a place to read and let go of her cares and the memories that weighed so heavily on her in their old West Oak Lane neighborhood.

Michael was gone but not far away. Holy Sepulchre Cemetery was only about a mile and a half from where he grew up on Thouron

Avenue—just a 6-minute drive up Cheltenham Avenue, across the city line into Montgomery County. The sprawling Catholic burial ground was the final resting place of tens of thousands, including several congressman and other politicians, Princess Grace Kelly's father and brother, and two other Medal of Honor recipients—Michael McKeever, who received his medal more than 30 years after his heroic actions during the Civil War, and Sgt. John J. McVeigh, who, during World War II, charged the enemy near Brest, France, to save his fellow soldiers. Like Michael, McVeigh was killed in action and awarded his medal posthumously. None of this, of course, was important to Mrs. Crescenz. Only one grave there mattered. Her second boy was close at hand. Just as the pain of his loss always was.

A neighborhood friend, Tom Robinson, came by the house on Thouron Avenue in the spring of 1970 on a rainy, overcast day. He, like Charlie, was a Vietnam vet and the two young men were headed for the Shore.

"I had been discharged from the service in January of 1969 and was into an extended cycle of hanging out in bars, running around like a wild man and so forth," Robinson said. "I had taken to spending time with Charlie and we arranged to head down to the Jersey Shore together on a Saturday afternoon to check out the bars. I was to pick Charlie up at his home and we would be off. Our target was Margate,"[3] a few miles south of Atlantic City.

One of the younger brothers let Tom in when he arrived and, while waiting for Charlie to come downstairs, he was alone for a short time in the living room.

"It was sort of dark due to the lack of sunlight and it took my eyes a bit to adjust," he said. "I saw on the far wall something that took my breath away. I could not believe what I was seeing, which was a case hung on the wall containing the Medal of Honor. I was stunned. I knew what the medal was, what it looked like, and I held it in absolute, total reverence. I didn't know Michael had won the MOH.

"While overseas we used to get copies of a paper called the *Stars and Stripes*. It usually contained a listing of casualties by city and state, which I would peruse, so I was aware that Michael had been killed. Charlie and I never spoke about it. It was not mentioned and I would not bring it up.

"I walked across the room absolutely transfixed on the case and its contents. I recall thinking something like, 'Jesus Christ, Michael won the Medal of Honor.' I remember standing in front of this case and hearing something behind me. I spun around and it was Mrs. Crescenz. My mind was racing. I didn't know what to say and I blurted out, 'Mrs. Crescenz, I didn't know....'

"What I meant was that I knew Michael had been killed but I did not know that he was awarded the Medal of Honor. Mrs. Crescenz then burst into tears and was sobbing, standing just a few feet from me. I wanted not to be there. I felt shame that I had caused this good woman to weep. I wanted to disappear.

"At that moment Charlie came into the room and spoke words of comfort to his mother and Mrs. Crescenz regained her composure and apologized to me. I could not have been more affected.

"Charlie and I then left the house and went off to Margate. Nothing was said of an incident that I have never forgotten."[4]

Fourteen years later, in July 1984, Charles and Mary Ann sold the neat brick twin where they raised a family and settled permanently in Sea Isle, welcoming visits from the boys and their families, especially any of their nine grandchildren. But not long after the move, the retired beer man and proud father of six died, in June 1988. Mary Ann followed her beloved husband four years later. They were laid to rest side by side at the Gerald M. Thornton Veterans' Cemetery in Cape May County, New Jersey. Together at the Shore for eternity.

Michael, with his parents buried about 90 miles from Holy Sepulchre, and his five brothers no longer living in the city of their birth, was alone. Not forgotten, of course, by his loved ones and friends. Some still visited his grave, decorated it for the holidays, cleaned the stone and refreshed the flags as needed. But he was often on his own, and Joe started to worry. Maybe there was something even worse than losing your brother at age 12. Was it possible that all Michael had done, and all that he had sacrificed, could be forgotten?

Joe didn't want that. And, if he could help it, he wasn't about to let that happen to the brother he revered. His first move, after his parents died, was to make a change to the gravesite itself. He wanted to remind all those who visited or went by that they were in the presence of a hero.

When Michael was buried, the tombstone that Charles and Mary Ann placed on his grave made no mention of his Army service. Joe understood their feelings but he didn't think it was right. To correct this, Joe visited the Philadelphia regional office of Veterans Affairs and asked for the flat white marble stone marker that the government for generations has issued to distinguish the graves of veterans. Once installed, it made plain to any passersby—for the first time in decades—that they were in the presence of a Medal of Honor recipient.

After graduating from Cardinal Dougherty in 1974, Joe had headed about 30 miles west of the city to Chester County to continue his education—just as his mother had done decades before. Despite the service of his father and three older brothers, the military had not been an option for Joe. No way was Mary Ann Crescenz risking the possible sacrifice of another of her sons. So he settled into West Chester State College, studying criminal justice and graduating in 1978. In his spare time, he became a passionate rugby player. He'd found a way to keep playing sports and channel his aggression—and through the game his life went in an unexpected but welcome direction.

"I met Joe at a rugby party in a place that could be called a dive bar, in April 1979," said his wife Valerie, who graduated from West Chester the same year as Joe, with a bachelor's degree in music education and piano. "Anyone who knew me at that time would have thought it highly unlikely that I would have been there. But sometimes the wrong place turns out to be the right place. After 42 years of marriage, I can safely say that although it might have been a total fluke for me to be there, it was where I was supposed to be."[5]

When they met, she was working on her master's in piano performance. A little over a year later they were married, on July 26, 1980, and would go on to raise two daughters. Val taught music and Joe directed his considerable energy into a career as a landscaper and groundskeeper.

In the early 1990s, Joe was on staff at Rosemont College and one of his colleagues there was a World War II and Korea combat Seabee named Matt Harkin. Working the grounds, there was always time to share stories, so Matt knew about Joe's family, particularly Michael's tale of heroism. And when the topic came up—especially while Desert Storm dominated the headlines in 1993—Matt always asked, "Why isn't Michael buried in Arlington National Cemetery?" He's a hero, Matt would say, and he deserved to be among his peers.[6]

Joe always demurred. His parents had wanted Michael nearby. Their son couldn't be with them physically, but having him at Holy Sepulchre had been Charles and Mary Ann's way of keeping him close. And, of course, they were devout Catholics. They were born and raised Catholic, as their parents had been and their sons, who'd each done 12 years of Catholic school, from St. A's straight through Cardinal Dougherty. Michael was in a Roman Catholic cemetery and as far as Charles and Mary Ann were concerned, that's where he belonged. Case closed.

Truth be told, Joe didn't necessarily disagree with Matt. The thought that Michael belonged in Arlington, in sacred ground set aside for the nation's veterans and heroes, had crossed his mind before. However, it wasn't something he considered appropriate to raise with his parents, especially his mom. If the family couldn't talk about Michael without upsetting her, having a conversation about moving her beloved son's body wasn't even conceivable. But now that both Charles and Mary Ann were gone? Joe gently pushed back at Matt's suggestion, but it wasn't something he could entirely dismiss from his own mind.

A few years later, Joe was working closer to his Chester County home, as a groundskeeper for the Downingtown Area School District. One day a year he joined a group of volunteers who traveled to Northern Virginia and pitched in to help maintain and beautify the rolling hills of the massive military cemetery in Arlington.

"I belonged to several professional 'green' industry organizations that would get a bunch of us together to pool our talents for a day of 'remembrance' among the tombstones at Arlington," he said. "I saw it as a way to give back to those who sacrificed so much for our freedoms."[7]

Because of his family history, Joe is deeply respectful of those who serve, and when he meets veterans he goes out of his way to thank them for their service. Just as he looked up to Michael, he respects his brother's comrades in arms. That same feeling of respect, even awe, came to him while he worked the grounds of the famous national cemetery. "I was starstruck," he said, "looking at some of the names on the stones. I realized I was in the company of true American heroes. And I thought right then, 'Why not have Mike be among these exceptional Americans?' Shoot, Mike was one of them."[8]

The seed that had been planted by others had taken root and was blossoming into a plan of action. And while it wasn't something he'd been able to express aloud—not even to his brothers—he realized the time had come to do just that. The opportunity arose a few months before one of his annual trips to Arlington. The occasion was a family gathering to say goodbye to one of Joe and Val's daughters, Melanie, who was headed off to California. The extended Crescenz clan came out in force, including all four of Joe's brothers—Charlie, Peter, Steve, and Chris. Joe decided it was time to share his dream for Michael.

"I asked them about moving Michael's body down to Arlington," Joe would later tell Tom Schmidt of the *Philadelphia Daily News*. "I got answers like, 'That would be nice,' and 'Maybe sometime.'

"I took it as a yes."[9]

And so began what would be a two-year odyssey, with Joe encountering a number of people who not only weren't as agreeable to the idea as his brothers appeared to be, but who would also be flat-out hostile to the venture.

He started with Erik Dihle, a horticulturist who was then division chief for grounds, burial operations, and ceremonial support at Arlington. Joe had met Erik while volunteering at the cemetery. How do I go about this? Joe wanted to know. At Dihle's urging, Joe reached out to interment services, the office that can field more than a hundred calls a day from family members trying to find out whether their loved one is eligible for burial in Arlington.

There are about 400,000 veterans and their dependents buried at the 639-acre cemetery, including service members from every major conflict from the Revolutionary War to the wars in Iraq and Afghanistan. Walking its hallowed grounds, visitors are immersed in the history of a nation, as told by grave markers of the generations of patriots who fought and, often, died in the service of their country.

The initial Arlington estate, with its imposing Greek Revival mansion, was seized by the Union Army in 1861 from its inhabitants, Mary Custis Lee, the step-great-granddaughter of George Washington, and her husband, Confederate Gen. Robert E. Lee. The grounds were initially occupied because of their strategic importance. Its hills were just across the Potomac, overlooking the nation's capital, which put the city's streets and inhabitants, not to mention the federal government, in gun range were the property to remain in secessionist hands during the war. While occupied by Union forces, in 1863, part of the land was set aside for a Freedman's Village for freed and escaped slaves. A year later, the first military burial took place.[10]

For decades after, Arlington was just one of several national military cemeteries across the country, though distinguished by its proximity to the nation's capital. But the burial of the young President John F. Kennedy, televised to a grieving world after his assassination in 1963, made Arlington a household name, and requests from veterans and government officials for burial increased dramatically. Kennedy made the cemetery more sought after, but he wasn't the only notable American resting in the revered grounds. President William H. Taft, who also served as chief justice of the United States, is buried there, as are a dozen other Supreme Court justices, including Oliver Wendell Holmes, Thurgood Marshall, and Ruth Bader Ginsburg. Many other historic figures are there as well, including boxer Joe Louis, civil rights activist Medgar Evers, astronauts John Glenn and Charles "Pete" Conrad, Secretary of State John Foster Dulles, polio vaccine inventor Robert Bruce Sabin, explorers Robert Peary and Matthew Henson, author Dashiell Hammett, several of the famed Tuskegee Airmen, and Robert Lincoln, oldest son of Abraham Lincoln.

A long distinguished list of the United States' most renowned military leaders are buried at Arlington, including Gen. Omar N. Bradley, Rear Adm. Richard Byrd, Gen. Benjamin O. Davis Sr., Adm. William Halsey Jr., Rear Adm. Grace Hopper, Gen. George C. Marshall, Gen. John J. Pershing, Gen. Matthew B. Ridgway, and Gen. Philip H. Sheridan. Interspersed among the graves are several monuments and sites that pay tribute to individuals, battles, or generally significant moments in

American history: the Argonne Cross, Chaplains Hill, Korean War Memorial Contemplative Bench, the Nurses Memorial, the Rough Riders Memorial, the Space Shuttles Challenger and Columbia Memorials, McClellan Gate, and the USS *Maine* Memorial.[11]

Among all these reminders of a great nation's storied past are the final resting places of hundreds of thousands of men and women who may not be household names, but whose dedication and selflessness made that great nation possible, and kept it free. And beside these heroes, in many cases, are the family members who also sacrificed while their loved ones wore the uniform. These honored dead include more than four hundred recipients of the Medal of Honor, almost three dozen of them from the Vietnam War. This honor roll of those who received the nation's highest award for valor ranges from heroes who bear easily recognizable names, such as World War II's Audie Murphy, to those known only to God: the three fallen guarded day and night by the Army's 3rd U.S. Infantry Regiment—the Old Guard—at the Tomb of the Unknown Soldier.[12]

Famous or not, most graves at Arlington are designated by the same small, rectangular, white marble marker—24 inches tall, 13 inches wide, and 4 inches thick—that appears on thousands of graves of U.S. service members across the country and in military cemeteries around the world. The graves of many Medal of Honor recipients are no different, except for one important distinction. While most tombstones in military cemeteries have black lettering, a Medal of Honor recipient's name, rank, time of service, birth and death dates, and other information are done in gold leaf. And each bears an etching of the appropriate Medal of Honor for the recipient's branch of service—the Army, Navy, and Air Force each have their own distinct Medal of Honor, with Marines receiving the Navy's version. When members of the military pass these graves and see the medal insignia, they salute. By tradition, Medal of Honor recipients, no matter their rank, are saluted by all who serve, from the newest privates to the most senior general officers.

Because it is seen as such a high honor to be buried at Arlington, and because space is limited despite recent expansions, eligibility is limited. The highest priority goes to "soldiers who die while on active duty, retired members of the Armed Forces, and certain veterans and family members." Also resting there are some government officials or employees, former prisoners of war, and spouses and children of service members. Those who receive certain awards—Purple Heart, Silver Star, Distinguished Service Medal, Air Force Cross, Navy Cross, Distinguished Service Cross—are also eligible. Also on that distinguished list are recipients of the Medal of Honor.[13]

Joe Crescenz may not have known all this history when he volunteered to tend the grounds there, but his gut instinct as he looked around in awe was right. Arlington was home to heroes. Michael belonged there.

By the next spring after the big family gathering, in 2007, Joe was ready to move forward. He first visited the Philadelphia office of the Department of Veterans Affairs on Wissahickon Avenue, hoping they could guide the family through the process of moving Michael. The answer was an unequivocal no. The Army, he was told, had paid for the initial burial in 1968 and would not pay for another. Surprised by the response, Joe pushed back, but the answer remained the same. The VA wouldn't pay for a second funeral, not even for a Medal of Honor recipient.

That same day, an undeterred Joe swung by Holy Sepulchre Cemetery, and explained to the staff what he had in mind. To his surprise, the reception he received wasn't much different from what he'd encountered at the VA. Why would he disturb the remains after 40 years?, they wanted to know. It wasn't normal. A waste of time. Never happen. "You would have thought I was asking for a million bucks," Joe said.[14]

As discouraging as those first two engagements were, that same spring brought a call to the Crescenz family that would ultimately prove fortuitous in Joe's mission. The Archdiocese of Philadelphia wanted to honor Michael with one of the Office of Catholic Education's Distinguished Graduate Awards, enrolling him in the Archdiocesan Hall of Fame, for 2008. The honor was bestowed on those "who have not only achieved professional success in their chosen field but also have demonstrated a commitment to living their lives by the Gospel values that guide and define Catholic education in the Archdiocese." Michael would be in good company, as that year's class of inductees included a cardinal, an astronaut, a university dean emeritus, and the founder of a program to help young actors with disabilities achieve their dreams. The induction wouldn't take place until January 2008, but, as it turned out, the high honor couldn't have come at a more perfect time.[15]

But that was still to come. During the spring and summer, Joe was discouraged by his lack of progress in properly honoring Michael. Frustrated, he finally reached out in August 2007 to his congressman, Joe Pitts, who represented the 16th Congressional District, which covered parts of Chester and Lancaster Counties. Pitts was a U.S. Air Force veteran who had completed more than a hundred combat missions during his three tours of duty in Vietnam. He turned out to be just the right man to contact on a matter concerning a hero from that war.

"I think Pitts himself had to contact the superintendent of Arlington cemetery to inform that gentleman of the situation, that Mike was a Medal of Honor recipient and that he deserved to be there with his brothers in arms," Joe said. "The superintendent, John Metzler, contacted me directly. Metzler was a Nam vet and had a son who was a police officer nearby in Norristown, Pennsylvania. And he confirmed that Mike indeed qualified for an Arlington burial. All I had to do was forward Mike's Medal of Honor certificate, coupled with his honorable discharge papers, to Vicki Tanner, who was the point person for all interments at Arlington."[16]

By the fall, the paperwork for Mike's transfer was complete, and it was time to schedule a burial date—something that has to be done months in advance for Arlington, which can see two dozen burials, each with full military honors, a day. Complicating matters, at the time the Crescenz family wanted to move Michael, the surge of troops ordered by President George W. Bush to stabilize the American position in Iraq was in full swing, resulting in a spike in casualties among the military and, sadly, a greater need for services in Arlington.

Joe called his oldest brother for advice. Charlie suggested a date in the spring and cemetery officials okayed the request. Corporal Michael J. Crescenz would be laid to rest in Arlington National Cemetery at 1300 hours on May 12, 2008.

In January, the archdiocese presented its 2008 Distinguished Graduate Awards at a reception in the famed Crystal Tea Room, an elegant venue known for its crystal chandeliers and carved columns on the ninth floor of the Wanamaker Building, just across the street from city hall in Center City Philadelphia and four short blocks from the old armed forces induction center where Michael had begun his military career.

The Crescenz brothers and their families were dressed to the nines and out in force, and also on hand were many old friends from West Oak Lane. Among them was Jack Osborne, who had known Mike and Charlie since their days at St. Athanasius school. He was also close to Bishop Joseph P. McFadden, who was in charge of that night's ceremony. As kids, the two had put in a lot of time on the basketball courts together and the Hall of Fame event gave them a chance to catch up. When Jack introduced the bishop to the Crescenzes, Joe took the opportunity to ask for advice about moving Michael from an archdiocese cemetery.

"I approached the bishop regarding my dilemma, and the lack of response from the cemetery office in Philly," Joe said, "and he assured me the archdiocese would take care of it. Two days later, a nice lady from downtown called me to confirm Holy Sepulchre would exhume the remains, in conjunction with the undertaker, and would make the appropriate arrangements with Arlington."[17]

Just like that, the pieces had fallen into place—but with the good news came the realization that it was time to figure out how to pay for it all.

"Now we had to raise funds for both the removal of Mike's remains—the undertaker fees—and the final burial in Virginia," Joe said.[18]

It wasn't going to be cheap, but it was a burden the Crescenzes would not have to bear alone. Word of the family's efforts to honor their heroic brother, four decades gone, spread quickly. Many people—especially those in the tight-knit, take care of our own world of the veteran and military community—were eager to help.

"John Getz, another Nam vet, and the Pennsylvania state commander of the Veterans of Foreign Wars, heard about moving Mike," Joe said, "and he had me contact Carmen DeSanti, another combat vet from World War II. Carmen was tied in with the Disabled American Veterans and the VFW at the state level, and he's the one who suggested setting up a temporary checking account at my bank. Susan Hernandez, at Willow Financial Bank, set things up so it would be used solely to pay the James J. Terry Funeral Home in Downingtown. Hernandez's husband was a two-tour Iraq vet."[19]

That was just the start. Joe and his family were soon overwhelmed by the outpouring from people who wanted to pitch in, both financially and emotionally.

"It may not have happened if not for all the support received from the Medal of Honor Society, and many VFWs and American Legion posts throughout Pennsylvania and New Jersey," Joe said, "and veterans' groups like the Gathering of Eagles, Patriot Guard, Rolling Thunder, Second Brigade, Leathernecks, Philly Motorcycle Clubs, and the Vietnam Marines Corps Brigade, to name a few. All these groups raised money to move Michael down to Arlington.

"People started coming out of the woodwork to help, and I began to realize that this meant a whole lot to the Nam vets, who never got their 'welcome home.' This was the funeral they couldn't attend when they were overseas, the respect they didn't get when they came home."[20]

The effort was so successful that later, after all bills had been paid, there was money left, which Joe donated to veterans' organizations.

To handle the arrangements, Joe reached out to a trusted friend from his parish, St. Joseph's in Downingtown, Pennsylvania. Denny Luminella had been part of the Terry Funeral Home since it had opened 10 years before. "Denny said it would be an honor since one of his boyhood friends had been killed in Vietnam," Joe said. It was Denny who persuaded a casket supplier to donate a new coffin, and his son, a Navy vet of Desert Storm, would drive the hearse that took Michael to Arlington.[21]

Michael's body was exhumed in late April, and placed in the new donated casket. After almost 40 years since that cold December day when he'd been buried, the original coffin couldn't be reused. The funeral home prepared Michael's remains for reburial and his return to Holy Sepulchre for a brief graveside disinterment service on May 2—appropriately enough the feast day of the family's old parish saint, Athanasius, whose courage, like Michael's, "never falters."[22]

On May 2, a beautiful sunny day, at the gate of Holy Sepulchre Cemetery, Michael's two families came together. There were four of his five brothers from West Oak Lane—Charlie, Peter, Joe, and Steve—and their families and friends. And there were Michael's other brothers, the guys he served with in Vietnam, men who'd been able to grow old, raise families, have long lives because Michael grabbed that M60 on the slopes of Nui Chom Mountain. Among them were several combat medics from the 196th, including Bill Stafford, who Michael had loomed over in the last seconds of his short life. "I got this, Doc, no problem," he'd told him.

"He definitely stood up that day and broke the logjam we were in," Stafford, wearing a blue suit with a Purple Heart pin on his lapel, told a reporter watching the scene unfold at Holy Sepulchre. "Things happen so quickly in a war, and you wonder why certain things happen to some but not others. I figured out after many years that it just wasn't my time.

"But Michael's day was that day—to help his comrades—and that was it. I got to have a family and kids thanks to him."[23]

That day, Michael's old comrades were his pallbearers, grasping the handles of the flag-draped casket as it rolled from the hearse, and carrying it to the grave whose nearness had comforted Mary Ann Crescenz during her decades of grief. As they placed their brother gently upon the catafalque, Michael's world gathered round. Brothers, cousins, sisters-in-law he never got a chance to meet, nieces and nephews who only knew him from stories and the family photographs of the big kid with the wide smile. His classmates from St. A's, and buddies from that schoolyard, from the Rec Center, and from the ball fields and basketball courts at Dougherty. So many who had gone on from West Oak Lane, blessed in ways Michael's selflessness prevented him from ever experiencing.

"I got an email from someone that said Michael was going to be moved to Arlington National Cemetery," said his close friend Ron Burke, who was in basic training when he heard what happened to Michael and couldn't get home to say goodbye. "I knew that no matter how busy I was going to be that day—I was a sales manager at the time—but I just knew I had to stop everything I was doing. The reason, of course, was that I never got to have closure with Mike. I never got to his funeral. When I got home, I was able to see his parents and at least acknowledge that I certainly missed being at his funeral, but I would remember him as a friend for life. So, I knew I wanted to be there at Holy Sepulchre that day.

"I made it a point to go, and saw his brother Joe. I called him aside and mentioned to him that I knew I had to be there that day. And I took out a picture from my wallet, which is the prom picture of me and Mike. And I said, 'This is how I'll always remember Mike.' He was stunned that I still had the picture. He was only 12 or 13 when Michael was killed so I don't know if he really knew what kind of relationships Mike had with his friends. So, he was absolutely stunned that I still had that. And I said, 'Well, I wanted to make it a point that you and your family knew that, again, Mike is still dear to my heart.' And I had it actually in the top pocket of my suit coat, and I tapped my heart and said, 'That's where he's at.'

"And then he called Charlie over and his brother Pete, who was a year behind me in school, and I hadn't seen him in years either, and just made it a point, as I said, that the whole family knew where Mike stood with me."[24]

Bill Stafford had only found out about Michael's Medal of Honor a half dozen years before his body was moved. Just the year before, after he'd posted a thank-you to Michael on the Vietnam Veterans Memorial's online "wall," one of the Crescenz brothers reached out to him. And through them he learned of the reburial efforts. May 2 was his first time meeting Michael's family, though he'd often thought about the young man who'd saved his life. He'd even considered reaching out to them in the years after returning to the States.

"Twice I was going to Philly to meet his parents but I couldn't do it," he said. "I've thought about it for a long time and this brings closure for me."[25]

It was a reunion on many levels.

"I thought in general it was a great idea to move Mike's body to a place such as Arlington, where so many U.S. veterans who made the ultimate sacrifice were buried," said Jim Engler. "I thought it was great that he was going to get this tribute and it certainly made me feel very proud of knowing Mike, and growing up with him and sharing my younger days with him. I have to congratulate Joe Crescenz, and his efforts, that he wouldn't let that die. Mike's memory is ongoing because of Joe and his efforts.

"And thank God, Joe brought us all together to embrace the idea of moving Mike's body from Holy Sepulchre down to Arlington. Certainly, a lot of other people who grew up in the neighborhood showed their respect, and showed their support for that effort. Because at the cemetery, there was a pretty large crowd there. People you hadn't seen in awhile, from our childhood days, were there, as well as people representing Cardinal Dougherty and the alumni association from there. People from all eras, from Joe's age, through the older kids in our neighborhood. I know I was very proud and I wouldn't have missed both the reinterment and Mike's burial, again, in Arlington."[26]

At Holy Sepulchre on that spring day, veterans' groups had established a perimeter of flags around the tent over the grave. Many of the vets were clad in jeans and the leather vests and colors of their motorcycle clubs, while others were dressed in olive drab or camouflage fatigue uniforms. They stood at attention, holding 3-by-5-foot American flags. The Vietnam Veterans of America Chapter 590 set up an honor guard and "field cross"—M16 in the ground, bayonet first, helmet atop the weapon, boots in front and dog tags hanging from the trigger guard.

Four of Michael's brothers—Charlie, Stephen, Peter, and Joe—stood together at graveside, just as they'd once done as young men and children.

Father Carl F. Janicki, president of Michael's alma mater, Cardinal Dougherty, prayed, "Our brother Michael has gone to his rest in Jesus Christ. May the Lord now welcome him to the table of God's children in heaven. With faith and hope in the eternal light, we assist him with our prayers and we pray also to the Lord for ourselves. May we who mourn be reunited one day with our brother. Together may we meet Christ Jesus, when he who is our light, appears in glory."[27]

Mike Prendergast, the longtime alumni director at Dougherty who graduated just a few years after Michael, read from the New Testament. "Brothers and sisters," he said, "listen to the words of the first letter of Paul to the Thessalonians. 'We do not want to be unaware, brothers and sisters, about those who have fallen asleep, so that you may not grieve like the rest who have no hope. For if we believe that Jesus died and rose, so too will God, through Jesus, bring him with those who have fallen asleep. Indeed, we tell you this on the word of the Lord that we who are alive, who are left until the coming of the Lord, will surely not precede those who have fallen asleep. For the Lord himself, with the word of command, with the voice of an archangel and the trumpet of God, will come down from heaven and the dead in Christ will rise first. Then we who are alive, who are left, will be called up together with them in the clouds to meet the Lord in the air. Thus, we shall always be with the Lord. Therefore console one another with these words."[28]

After the reading, Father Janicki, again addressed the assembled:

> On Wednesday at Cardinal Dougherty we had our annual Mass of Commitment, where we celebrate the commitment of teachers for their time at Cardinal Dougherty, for married couples and the years of fidelity to the vows they made, and we recognize the commitment of so many Dougherty graduates at that Mass. We mentioned Michael and the commitment he made, in Vietnam, for us. Right over the hill—we mentioned another Dougherty graduate, who is buried in this cemetery and who died in October, officer Chuck Cassidy.
>
> And commitment on our part is about remembering, and that's what we do as we gather here today. We remember the sacrifice of Michael. We remember the sacrifice of so many of our brothers and sisters who have fought and given their lives for our country. Part of remembering is a virtue, an act of virtue that we all celebrate so that we do not forget the sacrifices that have been made so that we may enjoy living in this country.
>
> We gather on this feast of St. Athanasius and part of the commitment that Cardinal Dougherty is making to keep Michael's memory alive is that today we announce a scholarship for a St. Athanasius student who has financial need and will continue to live the virtues that we celebrate here—sacrifice, honor, commitment. Those things which Michael did on the ground in Vietnam. We pause today, we commend all of our departed brothers and sisters to almighty God and in particular we remember and express our honor for Michael's sacrifice.
>
> We now make these intercessions for our brother Michael and we pray to our Lord Jesus Christ, who has told us, "I am the way, the truth, and the life. Whoever believes in me shall live even in death and whoever lives and believes should never die."[29]

A student, wearing a sweater in Dougherty's trademark garnet red that Michael surely would have recognized, then recited the intercession prayers, closing with, "Comfort us in our sorrow for the loss of Michael. Let our faith be our consolation and eternal life our hope."

"Lord, hear our prayer," the congregation replied.

Father Janicki closed the intercessions by leading those gathered in saying the Hail Mary and then the Lord's Prayer.

A boyhood friend of Joe's, Father Mike Kelly, led one of the concluding prayers:

> Almighty God, through the death of your son on the cross you destroyed our death, through his rest in the tomb, you hallowed all of the graves of all who believe in you, and through his rising again you restored all of us to eternal life. God of the living and of the dead, accept now our prayers for those who have died in Christ and are buried with him in the hope of rising again. Since they were true to your name on earth, let them praise you forever in the joys of heaven. We ask this through Christ our Lord.[30]

"Amen."

After the final graveside prayers from Father Janicki, urging all to go in the "peace of Christ," a representative from the city stepped forward. Edgar Howard, director of the Philadelphia Veterans Advisory Commission, read a letter from Mayor Michael Nutter:

> It is with mixed emotions that I write to you on this extremely solemn occasion. My initial feelings of sorrow and loss are slowly giving way to ones of relief and happiness. I feel the deep sadness and loss of a young man in a faraway land yet I also sense a strong sentiment of relief that his family will finally find a resting place and a home as he will be in a place of peace with his fellow fallen soldiers.
>
> From what I have read, Michael's life, although much too brief, was unquestionably not given in vain. Even now, forty years after his passing, his memory and his noble sacrifices live on and are an inspiration. Moreover, at this time, Michael's family and friends can take comfort in knowing that he will forever rest in America's most sacred and honored resting place, Arlington National Cemetery. I encourage you to carry on and dedicate a portion of each day, either by sacrifice or good deed, to the memory and legacy of Michael. By doing this, you will truly pay homage to an American hero.

Howard ended with his own message: "To the family, I say God bless Michael for all his sacrifices and may he live forever in our lives."[31]

Members of the 111th Air Force Honor Guard, based out of nearby Willow Grove Naval Air Station, played "Taps," and Michael's pallbearers lifted their brother once more and carried him back to the waiting hearse.

The good wishes, the reminiscing, and the reunions continued though, lasting as long as, if not longer than, the actual service. The decades melted away as friends and family caught up, exchanged stories about the old days on West Oak Lane and remembered Michael. Finally, as the crowd thinned and some were preparing for the trip to Downingtown, one of the women from the funeral home approached Joe.

"As the procession from Holy Sep began to move, a young female undertaker presented me with a button that had popped off Mike's uniform during the initial disinterment in April," Joe said. "It was from the one put on him 40 years ago at Dover Air Force Base when they first brought him home. She wanted me to have it. I spoke to Marie—Charlie's wife—later and told her when the time came, it would be appropriate to have the button buried with Charlie, reuniting the two oldest Crescenz brothers."[32]

Charlie's time would come in another spring, 11 years later. He died peacefully at home, age 71, leaving behind a wife, two children and their spouses, and five grandchildren (a sixth would be born a few years later). The combat veteran's ashes were interred not far from Michael in Arlington.

"He changed after Mike was exhumed and reburied at Arlington," Joe said, though he never talked to his big brother about it. "Charlie kept it all inside for 40 years, but after Arlington he just seemed as if a big burden had been lifted from him. He seemed more jovial and at peace."[33]

Reflecting on the brother he lost in Vietnam, and what he would think about all the ceremony and attention surrounding the move, Charlie commented, "Michael would say, 'What's the big deal? I did what I had to do.' But he's being taken to where he really belongs, with the rest of the heroes."[34]

His brother Stephen echoed those sentiments in the video, *Honoring Corporal Michael J. Crescenz*: "He's a hero to the country and at this time we need our heroes to be together rather than apart."[35]

The procession from the cemetery to the Downingtown funeral home, where Michael would stay until the day of the Arlington burial, had been meticulously arranged. Several veterans, among them Frank Tacey, Chris

Hill and Charlie Becker—another alum of St. A's and Dougherty—along with Tony Boyle of the Philadelphia Police Department, had arranged the escort by veterans' groups and local police for the almost 40-mile journey. First, they would travel 2 miles up Route 309 to the Pennsylvania Turnpike, where local police blocked off every ramp for 28 miles heading west so the funeral procession could speed by unimpeded, taking exit 312 and then Route 100 south into Downingtown.

People witnessing the motorcade found their own ways to honor Michael.

"As we passed through the Downingtown toll plaza, the toll operator stood, saluting Mike's remains," Joe said. "It is indescribable how proud I felt to see normal, everyday working people paying their respects to a fallen soldier."[36]

Between that May 2 service and the trip to Arlington for the reburial, Michael's remains were in a private room at the funeral home in Downingtown. "They allowed me to visit every day from May 2 to May 12—*every day*—so I could spend time with Mike," Joe said.

His visits lasted 30 to 45 minutes. At times he stood by the casket and prayed. Sometimes he talked to the big brother and protector he'd lost when he was just a boy.

"It was a very tranquil time for me," Joe said. "It was the closest I felt to Mike in over 40 years."[37]

Burial at Arlington was scheduled for 1300 hours on May 12. Ceremonies there are precise and exact, as are all things related to the 3rd Infantry.

Senator Tom Cotton, once a member of the Old Guard, wrote about the legendary unit in his book *Sacred Duty: A Soldier's Tour at Arlington National Cemetery*:

> Our standard was nothing short of perfection. The Old Guard can conduct more than twenty funerals per day. But for the fallen and their families, each funeral is unique, a once-in-a-lifetime moment. As Old Guard soldiers, we viewed the funerals through their eyes as we trained, prepared our uniforms, and performed the rituals of Arlington. We held ourselves to the standard of perfection in sweltering heat, frigid cold, and driving rain. Every funeral was a no-fail, zero-defect mission, whether we honored a famous general in front of hundreds of mourners or a humble private at an unattended funeral.[38]

Of the soldiers who carry out this sacred responsibility, Cotton wrote that they "embody the meaning of words such as *patriotism, duty, honor,* and *respect*. These soldiers are the most prominent public face of our Army, perform the sacred last rites for our fallen heroes, and watch over them into eternity. The Old Guard represents to the public what is best in our military, which itself represents what is best in us as a nation."[39]

The procession from the Terry Funeral Home to Arlington was being coordinated by the Vietnam Vets Motorcycle Club and numerous police departments. Their advice to anyone who wanted to participate was to be in Downingtown, ready to roll, at 7 a.m., sharp. No excuses.

Before departure, Bishop McFadden led the gathered in prayer inside the funeral home, with Michael's five brothers behind him. "May God be with us today as we make this last journey with our brother Michael," he said. "Eternal rest grant unto him, O Lord."

"And let perpetual light shine upon him," those gathered intoned.

"May his soul and the souls of all the faithful departed in the mercy of God, rest in peace."

"Amen."

"In the name of the Father, and the Son, and the Holy Spirit."[40]

People blessed themselves with the sign of the cross upon those words. And now it was time to prepare Michael for one more ride.

First, Army vet Chris Hill gently picked up Michael's Medal of Honor and reverently carried it out the door and down the sidewalk toward the hearse, flanked on either side by his fellow veterans, some holding flags.

"Detail," he called after he'd passed the vets. "Ten-hut."

The men came to attention.

"Present arms."

Their right hands went up in salute as Michael's flag-draped casket was borne down the steps and along the sidewalk, his brothers among the eight pallbearers. Once he was inside the hearse, a staff member ensured the flag was properly in place over the casket, and Joe gave his brother's coffin one final pat.[41]

Charlie's friend Ray Miller had designed a sign for the rear window of the hearse. It displayed a Medal of Honor with its traditional light blue ribbon and white stars. "Cpl. Michael J. Crescenz" was emblazoned along the top and the bottom featured the words "U.S. Army."

The weather gods were not fair that spring day. It was cold, high in the low 40s, overcast, windy, and rainy. In other words, just plain miserable.

And yet, people were not deterred from sharing this final journey with Mike. Dozens of them, hundreds of them. Boyle, again the lead motorcycle, coordinated the entire route south with local and state police. The first leg of the journey would take a little over an hour, to the Maryland House rest area along Interstate 95. There the motorcade from Downingtown pulled in to hook up with another procession—50 cars strong, as well as the Rolling Thunder and Patriot Guard motorcycle groups—that had left early in the morning from the Philadelphia Vietnam Veterans Memorial along the Delaware River. The Philly gang arrived at Maryland House first and they were ready for their fellow travelers. As the Downingtown contingent rolled in, Joe remembers seeing a huge banner honoring Mike, posted proudly by veterans from the Philly tristate area. Joe was overwhelmed by the many well-wishers who were braving the rain, most without umbrellas, ready with a wave or a salute.

From there, the massive combined motorcade made its way south through the downpour for the final 70 miles to Arlington. Each time they crossed a state line, a new contingent of state troopers took over escort duty. For the last stretch into the cemetery itself, the Virginia and District of Columbia officers left the formation, leaving lead biker Tony Boyle to guide the procession into Arlington. Inside the cemetery gates, even more veterans and civilians were awaiting Michael's arrival. Among them were not just longtime friends, like Matt Kuehn, who had been the best man at Joe and Val's wedding, but also two of Michael's peers, veterans of Vietnam who had also been awarded a Medal of Honor. Brian Thacker served as an Army first lieutenant in the war and Harvey "Barney" Barnum was a Marine officer there who retired as a colonel after 27 years with the Corps.

The procession now entered Arlington, slowly snaking its way along the roadways to the McClellan Arch, where it was directed to a site close to where the ceremony would take place. Soon, the narrow road to the gravesite in Section 59 was lined with hundreds of people. Service members in their camouflage fatigues were intermingled with those in Class A uniforms, and civilians were clad in everything from suits and ties to motorcycle club colors.

A horse-drawn caisson awaited. It would carry Michael the last few yards to his final resting place. The rain continued, but the soldiers of the Old Guard, intent on the business of honoring one of their own, neither flinched nor faltered. Video of the event shows the heavy winds and rain inverting a number of umbrellas of onlookers but the faces and demeanor of the soldiers betrayed nothing.[42]

The casket already had a plastic cover to protect it and the flag as the eight soldiers from the Old Guard prepared to remove it from the hearse. First, they lined up in two rows facing the back of the vehicle, four on each side. On command, the two lines turned smartly to face each other. The soldier on the end marched to the casket. He drew it out slowly from the hearse, with the men on either side grasping the handles as they came within reach. Once they had their brother securely in hand, the Old Guard soldiers carried Michael to the waiting horse-drawn caisson. Onlookers stood at attention, soldiers and veterans saluting, others with their hand over their heart. Charlie, clad in a trench coat and Marine Corps baseball cap, rendered a perfect salute, eyes intently focused on his brother's remains. Once Michael was on the caisson, the plastic was rearranged to provide maximum protection and the casket was secured to its carrier.

As the caisson moved forward, the soldiers marched along on either side. Behind, on foot, were, first, the five Crescenz brothers, then their family members, then a host of supporters. Family, friends, veterans, police.

At Section 59, the caisson was halted and the casket ceremoniously removed from it. The Old Guard pallbearers began the short, solemn walk to the gravesite. Once Michael had been carefully set down, under a tent, the soldiers rolled up and then neatly folded the plastic covering.

Next, the soldiers, four on each side, lifted the flag, holding it over Michael one last time.

Bishop McFadden called the congregation to order.

"In the name of the Father, and of the Son, and of the Holy Spirit. Amen.

"We gather here to commend our brother Michael to God, our father, and to commit his body to the earth. In the spirit of faith in the resurrection of Jesus Christ from the dead, let us offer our prayers for Michael.

"Lord Jesus Christ, by your own three days in the tomb, you hallowed the graves of all who believe in you, and so made the grave a sign of hope that promises resurrection, even as it claims our mortal bodies.

"Grant that our brother Michael may sleep here in peace, until you awaken him to glory. For you are the resurrection and the light, that he will see you face to face, and in your light will see light and know the splendor of God, for you live and reign forever and ever. Amen.

"Before we go our separate ways, let us take leave of our brother Michael. May our prayer well express our affection for him. May it ease our sadness and strengthen our hope. Merciful Lord...listen to our prayers. Open the gates of paradise to your servant Michael. Merciful lord... you are attendant to the prayers of the humble. Hear your people who cry out for their needs and strengthen their hope. We ask this through Christ our Lord."

"Amen."

"Eternal rest grant unto him, O Lord."

"And let perpetual light shine upon him."

"May he rest in peace and may his soul, and the souls of all the faithful departed, in the mercy of God, rest in peace."

"Amen."

"May the love of God, and the peace of the Lord Jesus Christ, bless and console you and wipe the tears from your eyes. In the name of the Father, and of the Son, and of the Holy Spirit."[43]

"Amen."

The bishop sprinkled holy water on the silver casket and then the drums of the Old Guard were heard.

"Present...arms."

Arms snapped up in salute.

Off to one side, was a seven-man detail. After the commands "Ready. Aim. Fire," they fired three volleys in quick succession. The salute complete, they too moved to stand at attention as a bugler with the Old Guard, somewhere off in the distance, began the poignant and mournful 24 notes of "Taps." As the last note was still fading away, the command "Order arms" was given.

The white-gloved soldiers of the Old Guard who had been holding the flag over Michael during these final prayers snapped it taut at the command, and then folded it in half. Another snap. And in half again. Snap. Then the triangle folds were begun, one over the other, until only a square remained. Half that square was tucked into the other folded portion, forming a triangle. Once secured into one solid triangle, a soldier on the end took the folded flag, pressed it flat into his chest, checked the corners and handed it to the soldier across the casket from him. That soldier reached over the top to receive the flag, and then handed it off to the soldier on his left. This continued man to man until it reached the soldier at the head of the casket. He received the flag, one hand atop, one underneath. The soldier who had made the final handoff saluted, and the detail marched off, leaving only the soldier bearing the flag behind with the assembled mourners.

As the rituals had proceeded, the five Crescenz brothers were seated nearest the casket, directly behind one row of the soldiers holding Michael's flag. Joe on the end, Charlie to his left, then Chris, Peter, and Stephen.

Traditionally at the funerals of veterans and service members, the folded flag is presented to a family member in that first row, often a widow, or parent, and the presenter says, "On behalf of the President of the United States, the United States Army, and a grateful nation, please accept this flag as a symbol of our appreciation for your loved one's honorable and faithful service."

Almost 40 years before, Charlie and Mary Ann Crescenz had accepted the flag that had covered their son's coffin. This time, Joe thought it should go to their oldest brother, the Marine combat veteran who served in Vietnam, just as Michael had done. Charlie wouldn't hear of it. He credited Joe for making Arlington a reality for their family's hero, and insisted that his younger brother accept the flag. Joe did, and teared up while doing so. The soldier saluted and returned to standing at attention at the head of the casket.

Then those who had stood quietly in the rain during the ceremony slowly started filing by the grave, offering condolences to the five sons of Charles and Mary Ann Crescenz, and thanking them for honoring their brother—and, in the process, recognizing the honorable service and sacrifices of all Vietnam veterans. A bagpipe duo, one of them without rain gear and thoroughly soaked through, played "Amazing Grace." The pair were from the New Jersey State Police, a salute to Charlie who had served there for 21 years. During the playing of the hymn, while some of the brothers looked toward the pipers, Charlie kept his eyes on Mike and at one point teared up.

"You were in the company of the greatest, humbling," Timothy Brooks, a Dougherty grad and a detective with the Philadelphia Police Department who had made it a point to be there to honor his fellow alum, said of the ceremony at Arlington. "I had heard stories about Mike as a kid. Now, I was honored to be a part of it."[44]

"The reception line included all the Crescenz boys—Charlie, Peter, Steve, Chris, and me—and we thanked all those who came to pay their respects and honor Mike," Joe said.[45] Charlie rose and saluted smartly when Vietnam veterans Brian Thacker and Barney Barnum, the two Medal of Honor recipients present, came up to the brothers.

Hundreds had turned out to honor this hero of the Vietnam War, including retired Lieutenant General Sam Wetzel, who had been the first to recognize that Michael's actions were worthy of the Medal of Honor. Now here were Michael's brothers greeting Wetzel and all those who took the time to join them in Arlington, moved by the kindness and good wishes of so many and doing their best to express their deepest appreciation to all who had helped them bring their brother home.

The notion that had been in the back of Joe's mind for so long, to have his brother Michael among his fellow heroes, had become a reality. There had been many obstacles along the way, but also an army of supporters. And now the long, seemingly endless process was over. Michael was where he belonged. His younger brother, forever haunted by the memory of answering the door when the Army came knocking to tell the family of their loss, never lost faith.

"I was determined that this was going to happen, getting Michael to Arlington," he said. "I didn't entertain the thought that it wasn't going to happen."[46]

CHAPTER VIII

Renaming the VA Medical Center

Frank Tacey was visiting Holy Sepulchre Cemetery a month before the graveside service for Michael Crescenz on May 2, 2008, that would start the Medal of Honor recipient on his journey to Arlington. Frank was part of the Patriot Guard Riders, a national organization formed just three years before to provide a voluntary honor guard at military funerals—and sometimes shield mourners from anti-war protesters and other activists who would use memorial services to air their grievances.

The Patriot Guard planned to be on hand for Michael's graveside service and Frank, an Air Force veteran of Vietnam, was there to do some reconnaissance. The riders wanted to be present, but were always careful that they were seen as a help, not an intrusion.

"I wanted to ensure the motorcycles were out of the way of the gravesite," Frank said, "so I go to Holy Sep by myself, and after speaking to the caretaker, they assisted me in finding Mike's grave. It was a flat gravestone, Medal of Honor recipient noted on it. I am looking around, looking around, to see where we can place people. So, I get down on one knee—suddenly—*everything* turned to black and white. No color anymore. It was spring. But it got cold. Like a blast of winter had suddenly come through. I say, 'What is happening?'"[1]

It was as if he'd been transported back 40 years, to that bleak December day the Crescenz family said goodbye to Michael at Holy Sepulchre. Tacey could see the freshly dug grave, the mourners, the string of cars lining the cemetery roads. He could actually feel the chill of the coming-of-winter cold.

Just weeks later, after Michael had been laid to rest in Arlington, Joe Crescenz invited family, friends, and supporters to his house for a barbecue. Frank was there and he made a point of taking Joe aside. He had to tell him what he'd experienced at Michael's gravesite at Holy Sepulchre.

"I told him my vision," Frank said, "how many cars were there, how many people, what the weather was like. Joe responds, 'No way.' I say, 'Joe, this was *before* Michael was disinterred. I saw all this in a vision.'"

Joe told Frank that there wasn't much coverage of Michael's funeral in 1968, so he couldn't have seen pictures of what occurred that day. "There was no way you could ever know that," Joe said, "other than Michael coming down and telling you."

"I swear to God, that is the day Michael got into my soul and in my heart," Frank says. "And from that point on, knowing we were dealing with a Medal of Honor recipient, from that point on I *knew* I had to do something. I had to get Michael's story out."[2]

That firm belief was solidified by all he saw and experienced at Arlington. He met the men who served with Michael, including Doc Stafford, Jim Willard, Jack Bisbee, and his commanding officer, Sam Wetzel, by then a long-retired three-star general.

"Michael really got into my brain," Frank said, "and subsequently has done so multiple times since then. For people who say visions do not happen, I believe they do. So again, I knew I had to get Michael's story out. Honestly, it was the only thing I ever did that started from an idea to finish in my entire life."[3]

Frank wasn't the only one inspired to honor Michael after the Vietnam war hero was laid to rest among his peers at Arlington. In fact, as more and more Philadelphians learned about the sacrifice Michael had made to save others, there was dismay, particularly in veteran circles, that more had never been done by the city to honor the valor of its native son. Had it not been for the recognition and retelling of Michael's story as his body was being moved, the young soldier from West Oak Lane might well have continued to be neglected by his hometown.

Due to the nature of Michael's award, his place was always secure in the annals of Medal of Honor recipients, from recognition by the

Congressional Medal of Honor Society to being included among medal recipients named and honored in the Pennsylvania section of the 42-acre Medal of Honor Grove just north of Philadelphia in Valley Forge, Pennsylvania, a site renowned for its own acts of heroism, sacrifice, and endurance during the Revolutionary War. The sprawling grove, an arboretum and bird sanctuary, pays tribute to the more than 3,500 recipients, individually and by the state or territory each hailed from. Each state's honor roll of heroes is engraved upon an 8-foot obelisk, and recipients also have a plaque on their respective state grounds that provides details of their service and the act of valor that earned the Medal of Honor.[4]

His fellow Vietnam veterans didn't wait for Michael to become a Medal of Honor recipient before honoring him. Not long after his heroic actions at Nui Chom, his brothers in Vietnam stepped up, naming a small, 450-man base Camp Crescenz, in Quang Province, about 4.5 miles west of I Corps's Da Nang Air Base.[5]

Michael also held a special place in the heart of his old commanding officer, Sam Wetzel, who nominated the young infantryman for the Medal of Honor, and then joined the family in the White House when the president of the United States presented them with the nation's highest award for valor. He saw them again a dozen years later when Fort Benning, Georgia—the renowned home of the infantry—named a weapons storage facility for Michael. At that time, Wetzel, a two-star general and a cancer survivor, was the commander of the post where Michael had done his advanced infantry training before he was deployed to Vietnam. Crescenz family members spent three days there as special guests of the U.S. Army in November 1982. They toured the massive base, home to armor and infantry units, visited with top brass, observed airborne training, and were given places of honor during the dedication ceremony. On November 20, the 14th anniversary of Michael's death, they headed home to Philadelphia.

And Wetzel was there for the family again when Michael was brought to Arlington.

"They had a 60-car convoy in the pouring rain, escorted by Vietnam veterans on motorcycles, all the way from Philadelphia right into the Arlington cemetery," Wetzel said, almost in disbelief. "I was there with my wife and a number of soldiers, guys who had been in the outfit, who had come from all over the country.

"The Old Guard did a magnificent job for Michael in this pouring rain, with the horse-drawn carriage, everything, just like you would see it in the movies or any films. It was pouring rain, but it didn't matter. They did a terrific job."[6]

It wasn't too long after that memorable day in Arlington that Ray Miller, a great friend of Charlie Crescenz, asked, "Why wasn't anything ever done in Philly to honor Michael?" Ray, like Charlie, was a veteran. He'd spent four years in the Air Force—from 1963 to '67—stationed in Germany, most of the time serving as a military policeman. Then he and Charlie spent decades together as New Jersey state troopers. Off duty, they golfed all up and down the East Coast and were known to truly appreciate a good cigar. From 2005, their families had lived across the street from each other in Island Heights, New Jersey, and they often went on cruises together.

"Charlie was probably the best friend you could ever want," Ray said. "If he told you something, he meant it. Never hesitated to help out with anything."[7]

Not long after the reburial, Ray was commander of the George Vandeveer American Legion Post 129 in Toms River, New Jersey. He'd witnessed all the Crescenz family had done for their fallen brother, and couldn't help but wonder why Michael's hometown had never properly honored him. Well, he finally decided, if Philly wouldn't act, Post 129 would.

"I had my vice commander contact Toms River High School East to speak with the art teacher, whom he knew," Ray said. "Soon after, two 11th graders come over to the post, along with their teacher, Bill Dishon. After being told how much room they had to operate…and what their purpose would be, they worked two hours a day, every day, after school. For almost five weeks. The area was cordoned off in the post the whole time. It was hand-painted. It was just a blank wall originally. The students laid out the mural—and it was then hand drawn in its entirety, all 12 feet by 12 feet."[8]

That space was transformed into a wall-size picture of an American flag that included the American Legion seal as well as the seals of each branch of the military. Quotes from Michael's Medal of Honor citation are inscribed at the bottom left. His medals, a photo of him, and other items hold a place of honor above the mural. The names of the student artists, Lauren Marion and Armando Ramirez, and their teacher are in the bottom right.

"You can read the printing on the medals," Ray said of the details in the mural. "Wow. Amazing. The kids were totally committed and honored to do it. They were dedicated."[9]

The post presented each student with a $1,000 scholarship to be used at the college of his or her choice. Dishon and his wife were treated to a full weekend at a bed and breakfast in Cape May.

When the mural was complete, Ray and his vice commander were discussing whether it needed a frame. One post member, Tom King, overheard the discussion and vetoed the idea. "A frame?" he asked. "That is not going to look good." King was a cabinet maker and set about creating a beautiful wood encasement for the mural—all labor and materials donated.

Art teacher Bill Dishon was honored to participate in the project and touched by the dedication ceremony.

"Armando, Lauren and I were invited to a dedication ceremony that was truly moving," Dishon said. "I will never forget sitting in the hall with my father, my two students, and their parents when the Legion Riders and Honor Guard arrived with Mr. Crescenz's medal and flag. The reverence displayed by the men escorting those two objects into the hall was something I will take with me for the rest of my life. Even while typing this email, all these years later, there is a lump in my throat thinking of that solemn event, as I watched those veterans honor the life and heroic actions of Mr. Crescenz."[10]

Six years later, the other town where the Crescenz brothers grew up, the one on the Jersey Shore—Sea Isle City—stepped up to honor its adopted son. The boys' grandparents, Charles and Cecilia Crescenz, had bought a summer home near 46th Street and Landis Avenue shortly after World War II.

On Veterans Day 2014, a portion of 46th Street was renamed for the local hero, and a green street sign adorned with white lettering and an American flag was hung, officially proclaiming: "Cpl. Michael J. Crescenz, Medal of Honor—Vietnam." An exact replica of the sign was presented to Michael's brothers, which they donated to VFW Post 2819 in Northeast Philadelphia.

The effort had been championed by Vietnam veteran Joe Griffies, director of veterans' affairs at Ocean City's WIBG (1020 AM, 101.3 FM) and host of the weekly "Welcome Home" veterans radio show. "His memory and his legend will live on forever," Joe said of Michael to the *CMC Digest*, based in Jersey's Cape May County.[11]

Michael, of course, was remembered that day for his actions in combat, but his brothers were on hand to ensure that the person they knew growing up would also be remembered.

Chris Crescenz, who was seven when Michael died, told the *Press of Atlantic City*, "I remember Mike, one time my parents didn't want him to go out of the house on a date when he was sixteen, was so mad he punched a wall and broke his hand. There was always a dent in the wall after that."[12]

Charlie recalled, "Me being the oldest and him being the next down, we were always battling. It was always a competition. I was faster and he was stronger."[13]

"He was my best friend," brother Peter told the *Press*. "He used to take care of me all the time, any kind of trouble I got in."[14] Peter passed away in 2022, leaving a wife, a daughter, a son named for his best friend, and a grandson.

The Philly VFW post that received the copy of the street sign was so thrilled to be a small part of Michael's story that they decided to return the honor by renaming themselves the Michael J. Crescenz Rising Sun VFW Post 2819.

"We were all shocked," Joe Crescenz told the *Inquirer*'s Edward Colimore. "My brothers and I never expected anything like this. It will be forty-six years this November 20 that Michael saved his brothers in Vietnam, and now they're trying to save his memory. These guys are a great bunch."[15]

"Philadelphia, as big as it is, has never done anything for this Medal of Honor winner and he's the only one from the city during the Vietnam

War," the post's commander, Navy veteran Frank DeFranco, told the *Inquirer*. "You can put up a statue to Rocky Balboa and you can't do anything for a Medal of Honor winner?

"I spent thirty-one years in the military. I am a transplant from Ohio, and I have never seen anything like it," said DeFranco. "In other cities, there would be library, a street, or building named after him."[16]

DeFranco told the *Inquirer* that Michael deserved to have a post named after him. "He thought about his comrades first," DeFranco said.

Tom Roberts, an Air Force veteran of Vietnam, pushed for the name change. Michael, he said, "was a typical Philadelphia boy who fought in an unpopular war."

"He paid the ultimate price—his life," Roberts told *Inquirer* staff writer Ed Colimore. "He was from the City of Brotherly Love, and maybe he was showing that when he left a safe position" to save his fellow soldiers on Nui Chom Mountain that fateful day in November 1968.

"Those who came home will never forget those who could not," Roberts said.[17]

As a reminder of the sacrifices made by so many who served and never made it back, a replica of Michael's Medal of Honor has a special place of honor at Post 2819.

Roberts' commitment to Michael's legacy didn't stop with renaming his post. He had a much grander vision about how the city of Philadelphia should honor its hero. Subsequently, he led a group of veterans, including those in the Philadelphia Vietnam Veterans Memorial Society, in raising $60,000 to fund a larger-than-life statue of Michael to be placed near the Philadelphia Vietnam Veterans Memorial, at Penn's Landing along the Delaware River. The memorial honors the 648 Philadelphians who gave their lives while in service to their country during the Vietnam War. The site bears witness to this enormous sacrifice by having the name of each fallen warrior engraved in its granite walls. The plaza also offers visitors a fuller story of the conflict, with giant reproductions of photographs from the war etched into 7-foot-tall slabs of granite, and three separate monuments dedicated to Purple Heart recipients, the South Vietnamese forces that fought and died alongside their American allies, and prisoners of war and those still missing in action. Into this mix, Roberts and his fellow veterans wanted to add one more story.

The result is an 8-foot bronze statue that rests atop a 2-foot-tall granite base, and has Michael towering over visitors. It depicts the young soldier in the last moments of his life, in full combat gear, M60 in hand, preparing to face the enemy on Nui Chom Mountain on November 20, 1968. The statue was dedicated on April 24, 2016, with hundreds of veterans and others from the Philadelphia area in attendance.

"Michael is the only Medal of Honor recipient from Philadelphia during the Vietnam War and we need to honor this young man for his heroic deeds," Roberts said.[18]

Sculptor Chad Fisher told the *Inquirer* while the statue was still in progress, "I always thought when I started doing sculpture how great it would be to make a monument to a person who really did something with their life, someone who exemplifies the virtues of society—honor, courage, loyalty, commitment and discipline."[19]

Michael was all that and more.

It was those very virtues exhibited by Michael that had inspired Frank Tacey. And from the day of his vision at Holy Sepulchre Cemetery, Frank believed with his heart and soul that it was more than past time for Michael to be recognized—in such a way that he would never be forgotten. In December 2010, he and Joe Crescenz were again at Arlington, paying their respects to Michael but also as participants in the Wreaths Across America campaign. The annual tribute places wreaths on each of the more than 400,000 graves at Arlington—as well as at national military cemeteries throughout the United States and around the world. While they walked among the final resting places of the nation's heroes, Frank had a surprise request for Joe.

"I asked him if I could pursue my goal of renaming the Veterans Affairs hospital in Philly after Michael," Frank said. "Joe, after a discussion with his brothers, gave me the green light."[20]

What Frank may not have seen in his vision was just how monumental a task he had given himself. If Joe's quest to have Michael's body moved to Arlington seemed long on bureaucracy and other obstacles, it was nothing compared to the challenges Frank would face in pursuit of his goal. But Joe had set a high bar when it comes to determination, and Frank would prove equally formidable.

Among the protocols for a VA hospital name change is getting the approval of a state's entire congressional delegation—no easy task in a state where the people range from extremely liberal to extremely conservative, and whose U.S. House districts reflect that ideological diversity when electing their representatives. But among the earliest supporters of the hospital name change were Republican Congressman Mike Fitzpatrick of Bucks County, Philadelphia's neighbor to the north, and the city's own Representative Bob Brady, the longtime chairman of Philadelphia's Democratic Party. They set a bipartisan tone that continued throughout the process. The Vietnam veteran Joe Pitts, who had provided crucial aid to Joe Crescenz in moving Michael to Arlington, was once again more than willing to help. As one congressional staffer, a wounded warrior from Iraq, put it, "This is a no-brainer. I don't know why this wasn't done before." Staff members in the various congressional offices all made one thing clear though: Philadelphia Congressman Chaka Fattah had to be on board. Fattah's district included Michael's old Thouron Avenue home, so Fattah would have to be the initial sponsor of a bill to rename the hospital.

In addition to all 19 of the commonwealth's U.S. House members approving, both of the state's U.S. senators—Democrat Bob Casey and Republican Pat Toomey—had to agree. State chapters of veterans' organizations such as the American Legion would also have to give their okay.

That's a daunting amount of outreach and lobbying, enough for an office full of staff. Frank Tacey was, initially, doing all this on his own. And the case was made slightly more difficult by the fact that Frank wasn't, at that time, a Pennsylvanian. Yes, he'd grown up in the Bridesburg section of Philadelphia and graduated from one of the city's Catholic high schools, Father Judge. But that was long ago. During the hospital campaign, he lived in Florida. It would be no easy task to get the attention of Pennsylvania politicians whose understandable instinct was to put their own constituents first. Fortunately for Frank, just as individuals and organizations had jumped in when Joe needed their aid so he could properly honor his brother, even more were prepared to make Frank's vision a reality.

General Wetzel became an early supporter of the effort. Just as he'd been willing to work through the military bureaucracy to ensure Michael was awarded the Medal of Honor, he was once again happy to put in the time and effort necessary to make this case. As he told *Inquirer* journalist Bob Moran after a bill for the renaming had been submitted for consideration in Congress: "Michael is a Medal of Honor winner. He's the only Vietnam Medal of Honor winner from Philadelphia. It's an honor to perpetuate his name on a veterans' hospital. It was a hospital for veterans and here is a veteran who won the Medal of Honor, who was a Philadelphia native. They named a lot of buildings for different people for different reasons, and Mike, in this case, I think it's very important that if you're going to name this for a soldier, then why not for the only Medal of Honor winner from Philadelphia from the Vietnam War?"

"I think it will go through, frankly. All your Pennsylvania guys in the congressional delegation, both Republicans and Democrats, are for it. Why not? But if not, we'll go back and fight again for another bill. That's what we've been doing, fighting for this bill. So, we'd go at it again."[21]

There is never a clear, straight path for legislation, and the Corporal Michael J. Crescenz Act of 2013 was no exception. Some lawmakers held back their support, weighing their options, and others debated whether to make the VA name change an amendment to bigger pieces of legislation, leaving this tribute to Michael subject to issues and partisan disputes unrelated to honoring a veteran. But once Congressman Fattah was fully on board, it was only a matter of time before a way forward was cleared. Finally, on December 16, 2014, Michael's bill was signed into law by President Barack Obama. It stated, "The medical center of the Department of Veterans Affairs located at 3900 Woodland Avenue in Philadelphia, Pennsylvania, shall after the date of the enactment of this Act be known and designated as the 'Corporal Michael J. Crescenz Department of Veterans Affairs Medical Center.'"

The renaming ceremony was set—appropriately enough—for May 2, 2015. Once again, a day honoring Michael would also be the feast day of St. Athanasius.

And like the spring day at Holy Sepulchre when the community came together for the short graveside service that started Michael on the road to Arlington seven years before, this May 2 had picture-perfect weather. Hundreds gathered. Family, friends, veterans, elected and other government officials. On stage for the ceremony, under a huge tent, were the dignitaries, including the recently retired Pennsylvania Supreme Court Chief Justice Ron Castille, a Marine Corps veteran who had lost a leg in Vietnam and who had also served as Philadelphia district attorney; Sen. Pat Toomey, an early and staunch supporter of the hospital renaming; Congressman Chaka Fattah, the prime sponsor of the bill; retired Lieutenant General Sam Wetzel, Michael's commanding officer in Vietnam; and Father Edmond Speitel, an 89-year-old veteran of World War II who had served as a chaplain in Vietnam and later in a number of Philadelphia area parishes. With them, representing the family, was Charlie Crescenz, who wasn't big on public speaking but agreed to step up because Joe was too ill to attend.

Castille served as master of ceremonies, at one point quoting remarks given by President Calvin Coolidge at Arlington to drive home why they were gathering in Philadelphia. "He said, and I quote, 'The nation which forgets its defenders will itself be soon forgotten.' Today we again remember the bravery of one of our nation's defenders, who gave his life in service to our nation in Vietnam. Everyone who now enters this VA facility will now remember Medal of Honor recipient Corporal Michael J. Crescenz."[22]

Castille asked the audience to rise for the presentation of the colors by the retired 82nd Airborne Honor Guard—the home base of the 82nd Airborne Division is Fort Benning, where Michael had trained—and the presentation of the unit flag of the 4th Battalion, 31st Infantry Division, Honor Guard, representing Michael's old unit.

After the singing of the national anthem, Castille called forward Frank Tacey, who had worked so hard to make the day possible, and Jim Willard, U.S. Army retired, who was Michael's squad leader in Vietnam, to lead the assembly in the Pledge of Allegiance.

Chaplain Fredi P. Eckhardt, of the VA Medical Center, prefaced the invocation by noting that the Latin root of Crescenz has to do with the idea of thriving, of growing, of flourishing. To my mind, this renaming, was not just serendipity, but somehow aligned by the stars because what we always want to do here is to flourish, and to thrive, and to always increase, to build and to grow in service to our veterans. And for those with eyes to see and ears to hear, our new name—which I admit will take some time to get used to, but that we are also very proud of—highlights our mission. The name itself highlights our mission.

Let us pray.

Gracious and eternal one, we give thanks this day for Michael J. Crescenz, who so many of us did not know but would love to have known. We recognize in him all the qualities that we see time and time again and appreciate in the many veterans that we meet. Commitment to comrades, to country, to family, friends, to you, O God. Also, strength, courage, honor, and selflessness. He went above and beyond, no doubt about that. But it is probably true that like many brave and heroic individuals, he would not want to be singled out as special but rather as loyal and dedicated. Nevertheless, it is a privilege to honor him, and we take on his name in gratitude and so we do that this day. And in doing so we honor all veterans who have given so much of themselves.

We trust that as we make the shift to his name it will coincide with an increase of our work here, that the care we provide will continue to grow, to thrive, to blossom and flourish as we do our best to provide for those who serve. So, we ask you, O God, to bless Michael's memory and the things you continue to inspire. Bless the Crescenz family and close friends, those who are present today as well as those who are with us in spirit. They would be proud, as always, of their beloved Michael. Bless us all. May we honor the name of Michael J. Crescenz and your support, O God, by the work that we do, the kindness and generosity that we offer, and the peace and good will that we share with others. Amen.[23]

Castille noted that the gathering that day was taking place approximately 40 years since the fall of the capital of South Vietnam, Saigon, to North Vietnamese forces, and that questions and debates about the controversial war continued to this day. But, he emphasized, there should be no controversy about those who served in that conflict.

There is no doubt that over a million brave Americans answered our nation's call to service in that war, whether by the draft or volunteering or by professional military service. Over 58,000 Americans—soldiers, sailors, Marines, airmen and Coast Guardsmen—lost their lives while serving in Vietnam. Their names are now indelibly etched in the national Vietnam Veterans Memorial in Washington, DC, and even closer on our own Vietnam Veterans Memorial honoring the 648 Philadelphians who died in the Vietnam War. It is often stated that some who serve gave their all, all who served gave something. So today we memorialize, with this dedication ceremony renaming the Philadelphia Department of Veterans Affairs Medical Center, one of our own Philadelphians, who gave his all in service to our nation, U.S. Corporal Michael J. Crescenz, a recipient of the United States' highest military honor, the Medal of Honor.

Castille noted that of the hundreds of VA medical centers, only two others were named for Medal of Honor recipients: one for World War I hero Alvin C. York, in Murfreesboro, Tennessee, and the other, in San Antonio, Texas, for Audie L. Murphy, one of the most decorated soldiers of the Second World War. (In five years, another Medal of Honor recipient would join those ranks, with the renaming of the Hershel Woody Williams VA Medical Center in Huntington, West Virginia. At the time of that renaming in 2018, Williams was one of only a handful of surviving Medal of Honor recipients from World War II. Four years later, he was the only one.)

"And to that distinguished list of heroes, today we add Corporal Michael J. Crescenz, Medal of Honor recipient," Castille said to thunderous applause.[24]

Daniel Hendee, director and CEO of the VA Medical Center, pledged that he and his staff would strive to live up to Michael's memory and example.

> It is truly an honor for this facility to be renamed for a hometown Philadelphia hero. Michael Crescenz received the Medal of Honor for the bravery and courage he displayed years ago fighting for freedom on the battlefields of Vietnam. Today our facility becomes only the third VA Medical Center to be named after a Medal of Honor recipient. As director I assure you that we will take that responsibility very seriously—the responsibility to follow in Michael's footsteps and serve all vets with compassion, dignity, and honor, providing excellence each and every day; the responsibility to the veteran community to live up to the example Michael set of selfless bravery and dedication to others; and the responsibility to honor Michael's memory each and every day that our staff walks through these doors.... I pledge to you today that our staff will work hard to live up to our new name and be worthy of the legacy left by Corporal Michael J. Crescenz.[25]

When Congressman Fattah rose to speak, he, too, spoke of the impact Michael had even 45 years after his death.

> This is a young man, who, while others were seeking deferments, he enlisted. This is someone when the opportunity may have been to be something less than,

he was brave, time and time again in defense of his fellow soldiers in a far-off land.... He was someone who could have just been ordinary, but he provided an extraordinary lesson for others to follow, which is that he took it upon himself to serve his country and to do it in a remarkable way. And so, it's appropriate that we would dedicate and memorialize this brave young man in this way. It's probably one of the greatest things that I've been involved in. Because we're not talking about someone who was chasing headlines. This is someone who saw his responsibility and met it.... I don't think any of us who have not been in those shoes know what it would be like to have to knowingly risk your life on behalf of your country and your fellow man.... We're going to make sure that every day this facility lives up to the great name that's being bestowed upon it.[26]

Senator Toomey spoke to the challenge lawmakers often faced when trying to accomplish things in Congress. "Sometimes it's difficult to get Democrats and Republicans to agree that today is Saturday," he joked, "but this is something we were able to get done." He applauded his Senate colleague, Democrat Bob Casey, and then Congressman Fattah for leading a bipartisan effort in the House. "Most of all," he added, "this would not have happened without you, without your input, without your reminding all of us how important this is for this family, for the memory of Michael, for Philadelphia. You put this on our radar, you encouraged this process and you helped to make the system work. So, thank you for doing that."

While the day was about saluting the courage and sacrifice of one man, Toomey said he was sure that Michael would want to share this important day.

He lived in the great city of Philadelphia, a city that paid a huge price in lost sons in the war in Vietnam. Philadelphia lost 648 brave citizens during that war. And, of course, there were thousands of others who served courageously and made big sacrifices themselves. So, while today is rightfully a celebration of the great heroism and patriotism of a great American, Michael Crescenz, we also salute all of his brothers in arms—those who returned and those who were not able to return. I think Michael would have wanted this recognition to be a broader one so let me just suggest that at that time there were too many men who were coming back from Vietnam and they were not treated with the appreciation and respect that they deserved, and that they had earned. And so, while we are rightfully naming this facility after Michael today, this is also a recognition and a celebration to all those who served in Vietnam. And we celebrate and express our gratitude to all of you as well.[27]

Castille next introduced Michael's former commanding officer, Lt. Gen. Sam Wetzel, to thunderous applause and a standing ovation. The old soldier was taken aback. "My God," he joked, "you'd think the Pope had arrived here." (Not quite. Pope Francis wasn't scheduled to visit the city until later that year, for the World Meeting of Families.) He recovered quickly though and singled out those responsible for the day, first mentioning the members of Congress who introduced the bill and saw to its passage. And then this honorable mention.

"There's a guy somewhere here in the audience named Frank Tacey, who made the push. I don't know where Frank is." But Frank was quickly identified and stood to his own round of applause. "If it hadn't been for him, this would not ever have happened," the general said.

Then he asked the Vietnam veterans to stand, and they too received an ovation, and the standing Charlie Crescenz saluted his fellow vets from the stage. Next, Wetzel called for recognition for the members of the unit he once led, the 4/31, specifically mentioning William "Doc" Stafford by name.

He then recounted the days that claimed the life of Michael Crescenz and others.

It was a historic seven-day battle on Nui Chom Mountain, and we destroyed the 21st NVA Regiment. The days were from 17 to 23 November 1968. We were attacking 37 miles from the South China Sea, out in the mountains toward Laos. We'd just had heavy rains and monsoon season so the mountain was slippery, steep, rocky. We had to practically crawl up the mountain.

We were looking for the 21st NVA Regiment. Delta Company located the enemy first and Lieutenant John Dolan had the first firefight. John, where are you? Stand up. I instructed Delta Company to set up a defensive position and to keep in close contact with us, the regiment, at the base of the hill. I moved Alpha Company, Michael's company, up the left ridge, Charlie Company up the center ridge, and Bravo Company up the right ridge.... My plan was to use lots of artillery, lots of mortars, lots of gunships, and constant airstrikes so our troops would have as much protection as possible as they crawled up that mountain. At one time we were even supported by the battleship New Jersey.

Now, listen very closely. After the battle, when we get to the top, we had counted 250 two-man bunkers, dug in. Three-fourths of these bunkers were dug in, so you couldn't see the bunkers until you were right on them. Let me say that again: 250 two-man dug-in bunkers on a tall steep mountain, about the same size as well-publicized Hamburger Hill. Do the math, 250 two-man bunkers, lots of troops. Now on top of the mountain we captured a doctor and a nurse and a dug-in hospital. That sets the stage. I'm going to talk about Michael now.

Alpha Company was pinned down. They couldn't move. For some reason, as Jack Bisbee, his squad leader told me, Michael picked up the machine gun of another man, not his weapon. He charged the first bunker, and killed two. He charged the second bunker, and killed two. He charged the third bunker, and killed two. And then Doc Stafford over here was tending a wounded man in no-man's-land and Michael ran right past Doc and said, "I'll take care of you." He charged the last bunker, the fourth bunker, and he was mortally hit.

Doc immediately got up, ran over, and checked Michael. Unfortunately, he was gone.

Michael did this on his own, with wounds on his right side and without hesitation. As a result of Michael's actions, they were able to move up the hill. The part that isn't recognized or talked about very much is that Michael's actions saved many more lives by permitting Alpha Company to continue on up the mountain, taking out more bunkers and more of the enemy. So, as a result of this action, we recommended Michael for the Medal of Honor.

I was fortunate to be in the White House when President Nixon presented the Medal of Honor to Michael's parents and two of his brothers, who had both worn the uniform, incidentally. They are both here.

We lost five good men in that seven-day battle. I carry a list in my pocket. This list contains the names of all the men I lost in Vietnam and where they are on the Vietnam Veterans Memorial wall. Corporal Michael Crescenz you know about. A Company, Medal of Honor, 38W, 016. That's his place on the Vietnam Wall.

Lieutenant Kevin Burke, A Company, Distinguished Service Cross, a Notre Dame graduate, from Anita, Iowa. Matter of fact they named an airfield in Anita, Iowa, for Kevin Burke.

Sergeant Danny Hudson, A Company, from Chadron, Nebraska.

Specialist Thomas Dickerson, from B Company, Thomaston, Georgia.

Corporal Harold Glover, Bravo Company, from Siler City, North Carolina.

And seven more good men killed in separate actions during the time I commanded the 4th Battalion, 31st Infantry. All never to be forgotten and God bless them all.

During that seven-day battle, 33 of our men were also wounded and evacuated, mostly to Da Nang. And then off to the States.

You may ask, what about the enemy? We actually counted 66 bodies. The doctor and the nurse on top of the mountain told us that they had evacuated many more dead and many more wounded before we got to the top.

We focused our remarks and our attention today on the actions of Alpha Company, Michael's company. But there are many more stories of brave young soldiers...stories yet to be told...

It's said that there is combat and there's close combat, combat up close and personal. It's also said that every soldier fights for his buddies in his squad. Veterans of Nui Chom Mountain fought in close combat, fought for their buddies. Why did Michael decide to pick up that machine gun and charge alone up the mountain? He charged up the mountain to protect his buddies, and in the course of that action he saved the life of Doc Stafford, who is sitting here. There's no nobler man than a close combat infantryman. Michael Crescenz is that noble man. That noble man who should never be forgotten.

Now I hope here today that this Veterans Medical Center does its job properly and timely to take care of our veterans. Remember [at this point, the general pointed up with his right hand], Michael will be watching. Thanks for inviting us to the ceremony. We really appreciate it. God bless Michael Crescenz...and God bless America. Thank you.[28]

As Hendee, Charlie Crescenz, and General Wetzel prepared to unveil the plaque that would hang in the medical center, Michael's Medal of Honor citation was read aloud by Castille. Upon completion, the audience rose to its feet, cheering and applauding. A smaller version of the hospital's plaque was presented to the Crescenzes. The family was also awarded a Legion of Honor gold medallion to "honor the brave sacrifice of Michael in service to his country" from the Chapel of the Four Chaplains, a Philadelphia nonprofit organization that promotes "interfaith cooperation and selfless service."

Congressmen Brady and Fitzpatrick were called upon to offer impromptu remarks and Philadelphia's Democratic Party chair talked about what it was like to be on the receiving end of the relentless lobbying to rename the VA hospital.

This guy Frank Tacey calls me. What a pain in the.... And he calls me and calls me, "We gotta get this done. We gotta get this done. We gotta get this done." For five years, imagine, once a week, twice a week, getting a phone call from him. And then another guy, Joe Griffies, calls me. Joe Griffies has a radio show and he's calling me every week. I go down the Shore for a couple days, he calls me to be on the show and wants to know, "When are you gonna get this medical center named after Michael?" So let me tell you something, Justice Seamus McCaffery, Frank Tacey and Joe Griffies are why we're here today.[29]

Brady had a U.S. flag flown over the Capitol in honor of Michael and he presented it to the Crescenz family.

Congressman Fitzpatrick noted how Sam Wetzel had pointed up when referring to Michael.

> When the lieutenant general mentioned Michael at the very end of his remarks, he pointed up to heaven and we know that's where Michael is. God has given us a beautiful day to celebrate today. And Michael and his comrades, brothers and sisters who served and died for our nation, they gave us the freedom to enjoy today. And I know that he's up there praying for us today because I know that he was taught the tenets of our faith when he attended Cardinal Dougherty High School. He was taught the power and importance of intercessionary prayer, and Michael is praying to the great saints today for us. But as Representative Brady said, he's praying for the men and women who followed him into service and continue to serve us in harm's way, in very dangerous places today. And I'm sure that he'll be praying for every man and woman that walks into the Corporal Michael J. Crescenz VA Medical Center for the care that they have earned and that they deserve, and that will be delivered because, as Dan said at the beginning of the ceremony, this is a new day for the VA today.[30]

The next speaker introduced by Castille was a fellow Marine.

> It is now my distinct pleasure to introduce to all of us, Charlie Crescenz, U.S. Marine Corps veteran. Mr. Crescenz is Michael's older brother, a Marine Corps combat veteran who served in Vietnam himself. You will note that the program identifies Joe Crescenz as the family spokesman. Unfortunately, Joe could not be with us today. We thank Charlie for stepping in to accept this award and this renaming and to speak on behalf of the Crescenz family. Charlie Crescenz, please come forward.[31]

Again, there was thunderous applause, whistles, yells and a standing ovation, which Charlie quietly and humbly acknowledged as he put on his reading glasses once at the podium. Only after he had saluted the crowd, and someone yelled "semper fi," did people start to quiet down and take their seats.

> Good morning and thank you for being here today to honor my brother Michael. My family and I would especially like to thank Frank Tacey, who you've heard so much about. He was the driving force in having the VA hospital named in Mike's memory. Frank was assisted in that effort by various veterans' organizations and it took Frank probably about five years to do it. I hope that having Michael's name on the hospital will inspire those who work here, who have the honor and responsibility to serve our veterans, to give our vets the very best that they can. I would now like to recognize some of the men Mike served with who are

with us today: Lieutenant General Sam Wetzel, Bill "Doc" Stafford, John Dolan, and Jim Willard. As we know, Mike was one of 648 men from Philadelphia who gave their lives in Vietnam and the naming of this veterans' hospital honors all of them. In conclusion I want to thank all who put their lives on the line each day to protect us around the world and in this city. Thank you very much.

Before leaving the podium, amid applause and cheers, he said above the din, "And to my Marine brothers, semper fi."[32]

"Thank you, Charlie," Castille said once he returned to the podium, while behind him each person onstage walked over to shake Charlie's hand and congratulate him, "and once again thanks to the Crescenz family for the honor they have bestowed upon our city by allowing this building to be named after Corporal Michael J. Crescenz."

With the crowd once again settled, Castille said, "Please stand again, if you are able, for a benediction by the Reverend Edmond Speitel, a retired U.S. Army colonel and former chaplain at Cardinal Dougherty High School, which Michael and all of his brothers attended in Philadelphia. Chaplain Speitel."[33]

The 89-year-old combat veteran of World War II, who later served as a chaplain during Vietnam, walked slowly to the podium and then said softly,

> I am both proud and humbled to be here today for this occasion. We had a great day. The congressman from Bucks County, Mike Fitzpatrick, pretty much did my job in invoking God's blessings upon us and thanking him for the graces he's given us and the nation and the people and the family.
>
> Beloved God, we ask you to continue to be gracious to us. Help us to be brave and humble and courageous and aware of your presence among us. We ask this Lord in your holy name. Amen.

When the audience responded, "Amen," Chaplain Speitel replied softly, "God bless."[34]

Six long years after his visit to Holy Sepulchre Cemetery, the tribute Frank Tacey's vision had inspired had come to fruition.

For those who had known Michael, some as far back as elementary school, it was a recognition both long overdue and well deserved.

"Every time I drive by the VA center that now carries Michael's name, I say to myself, 'I grew up with that kid. I was part of his life. I can tell a

---

story,'" said Ron Burke, who still remembers Michael coming to his aid when he was threatened by opposing players during a basketball game. "His actions didn't surprise me in the least. I served in the military, so I know exactly how hard it was for him to take those steps. He never knew he was going to lose his life. He never knew he was going to lose his family. But what didn't happen is people haven't forgotten Michael. And the end result is that by putting his name up there, it is something to say, 'Hey, this is somebody good and decent that I grew up with and who did something great for his country.' And the very fact that we can put his name up there means a lot to all those who supported him. I knew him. It was a privilege."[35]

And from the close circle of friends from West Oak Lane privileged to have known Michael and grown up with him, there is one more honor worth noting.

"As a lasting tribute and in memory of Mike, my wife Anna and I named our first son Michael," Jim Engler said. "That was how highly I felt about Mike and our friendship."[36]

CHAPTER IX

No Greater Love

When it comes to remembering Michael J. Crescenz, first and foremost for many will always be his heroic actions on the steep, steamy jungle hillside of Nui Chom Mountain on November 20, 1968. It's why the veterans' hospital in his hometown bears his name. It's why there is a larger-than-life statue of him at the Philadelphia Vietnam Veterans Memorial, showing him clad in full combat gear, facing the enemy, M60 in hand. It's why his parents were called to the White House to accept the nation's highest military honor from the President of the United States, who praised their gallant son and thanked them for making Michael the man he was.

It's why he is among a select group of about 3,500 U.S. service members, out of millions who have served, to be awarded the Medal of Honor. A tribute so revered that all those who wear the medal are saluted by members of the military—everyone, from the newest privates, sailors, and airmen to the most senior generals and admirals. It's not a requirement, simply a sign of respect to those who have been recognized for having gone above and beyond the call of duty, for putting their very lives at risk to save their comrades in arms. The recipients themselves almost universally do not see their actions as anything extraordinary, or more than they saw others doing every single day.

Peter Collier interviewed more than a hundred recipients for his book *Medal of Honor: Portraits of Valor Beyond the Call of Duty*. He came away in awe of not just their heroism, but also their humility. In his author's note he wrote,

In talking to the men profiled in this book, I asked them how they were capable of acts of heroism that seem unfathomable to an average person. They all replied in so many words that it was no big deal, that they were just doing their duty. This was no foot-scuffling, aw-shucks false modesty. They truly believe that they are ordinary men called upon to do something extraordinary on a given day—just as firmly as they believe that they merely hold this medal in trust for all those they served with in our time of need, many of whom never came home.[1]

Historian Victor Davis Hanson, who wrote one of the forewords for Collier's book, says the men were aware of the dangers they faced. "They knew exactly what they were doing in risking their lives," he wrote, adding,

there is something carnal, physical, sudden about the battlefield heroics of those who have received the Medal of Honor, where there is no time for careful deliberation, and when thought and weighted language count little against a grenade or bullet. Speed, instant reflex, and physical strength in all these accounts make the difference between saving lives and failure. So, these men were not just brave and principled, but both brave and principled as second nature in a moment's flash and equipped with the necessary poise, speed, and power to see their instant decision to fruition. They were athletes of a sort, the prize not being fame and money, but honor—with death, not defeat, the risk.[2]

Collier writes that the men

who fell on grenades to save their buddies, single-handedly charged enemy machine guns, or fought on long after ordinary bravery should have been exhausted would not have suffered in the eyes of their comrades if they had decided to live to fight another day. But for reasons that are beyond our understanding—reasons having much to do with duty, country, and honor, and little to do with fame and glory—they made a different decision: to look unflinchingly into the face of death.[3]

Michael Crescenz's battalion commander, Sam Wetzel, would serve 34 years in the Army, starting as a young officer in the Korean War and rising to the rank of lieutenant general. Decades after the battle of Nui Chom, he was still in awe of Michael's actions.

"What he did to save his buddies by going up to four bunkers to take them out so they could move up the hill, was the most heroic thing I have ever seen in combat," Wetzel told the *Ledger-Enquirer* for its series on the 50th anniversary of the battle.[4]

"Why did he do this? I don't know," he said to Bob Moran of the *Philadelphia Inquirer,* as he described the firefight.

> His squad and platoon were pinned down, they couldn't move. The enemy's firing and we're firing. You could see the bunkers up ahead, you could see where they were, but you didn't dare stick your head up. And for some reason, I guess Michael got frustrated and decided, "I gotta do something about it." And he picked up the machine gun off his buddy—cause he was just a rifleman, he didn't have a machine gun—picked up the machine gun and charged the first bunker, killed two, second, killed two, third, killed two. And then went past Sergeant Stafford on up to kill the guys in the fourth bunker and they shot him in the process. Why did he do it? Soldiers do…in battle, for some reason, I don't know whether they snap or they say, "We just can't sit here, I'm gonna help us go on up the mountain." What was his thought process that day? I don't know. But he did it, and he did it on his own. It wasn't the squad leader telling him to do anything, it wasn't the platoon leader telling him to do it. It was Michael Crescenz alone who took that action to help A Company then move on up the hill.[5]

And, of course, beyond giving his life to ensure the success of the mission of the 4th Battalion, 31st Infantry, that day beneath the triple canopy, he saved the lives of the soldiers around him.

"They used to say if a bullet has your name on it, that's it," Doc Stafford said. "I think that day, Michael Crescenz altered the name on my bullet."[6]

Stafford would add in another interview, "When you willingly give up your life so that others might live, that's about the highest sacrifice you can make."[7]

His words echo the well-known Bible verse from the Book of John, 15:13: "Greater love has no one than this, than to lay down one's life for his friends."

It's a verse that Michael, the veteran of 12 years of Catholic school, would have known well. And on November 20, 1968, in Vietnam, knowingly or not, he was following the way of the cross, in the footsteps of Jesus of Nazareth, who sacrificed himself that others might live. How many times had Michael heard that verse in his life? At home, in school, or at Mass? And when he wasn't hearing it, there were reminders all about. Naturally at his parish, St. Athanasius. At school, a crucifix looked down on him from above the blackboards of every classroom he entered as a boy and young man. His mom and dad also had one hanging in their bedroom.

No greater love.

At the root of Jesus' crucifixion, and Michael's sacrifice, was love. For his family. For his friends. For his fellow soldiers. For his country. An instinctive, deeply ingrained love that comes with the profoundest responsibilities.

"We should not be surprised that all true love requires sacrifice," Pope John Paul II told the thousands of young people who flocked to see and hear him during his pilgrimage to New Zealand in 1986. "Do not be afraid, then, when love makes demands. Do not be afraid when love requires sacrifice. Do not be afraid of the Cross of Christ. The Cross is the Tree of Life. It is the source of all joy and peace. It was the only way for Jesus to reach resurrection and triumph. It is the only way for us to share in his life, now and forever."[8]

No greater love.

So often in his heartbreakingly short life, Michael Crescenz didn't seem to be afraid when called on to demonstrate his love. At home where he looked after his brothers. On the schoolyard when defending his friends from bullies. In battle, saving the lives of his fellow soldiers from enemy machine gun fire. His friends speak of his strength, not just physically, but marrow deep in his character as well. Backed by the support and example of his family, Michael seemed to know, even so very young, who he was, and he wasn't afraid to stand up for what was right, no matter the cost.

And being who he was, he no doubt would have demurred, almost to the point of being embarrassed, at being singled out for his actions in Vietnam. It was the job. His duty. He was merely doing his part, just as so many others were doing every minute of every day. Consider the 20 other men posthumously honored that day in the White House when Michael's parents received his Medal of Honor from the President of the United States. Those 20 men from all across the United States, of varying faiths and different races, also sacrificed their lives for others. Seven of them—seven—threw themselves on a grenade in the hope of saving the soldiers around them. Others, like Michael, charged entrenched enemy positions until fatally wounded. A young officer put himself between his troops and a mine before it was detonated. A medic, a conscientious objector, braved hostile fire to save and care for the wounded. A noncommissioned officer, his unit outnumbered by the advancing enemy, gave up his place on the last chopper out to another, staying behind to fight until overwhelmed and mortally wounded, but ensuring the safety of his soldiers.

No greater love. The Book of John may not be referenced in official military medal citations, but it is the very heart and soul of the Medal of Honor.

"Love is demanding. It draws us outside ourselves," said Archbishop Charles Chaput, who led the Archdiocese of Philadelphia long after Michael's time in the city. "The greater the love, the greater our willingness to sacrifice. So, when we know, honestly, what we're willing to sacrifice for, even to die for, we're able to see the true nature of our loves. And that will tell us who we really are."[9]

He may not have been able to put it into words, but Michael appeared to know who he really was that day on Nui Chom Mountain. As did his friends back home. To them, the news of his Medal of Honor and the valor he demonstrated in Vietnam, coming almost two years after his death, brought back both painful memories of his loss and pride in his selflessness and gallantry.

"When I learned the details and saw the content of the citation, none of it surprised me," Ron Burke said. "It reminded me of the incident on the basketball court where he stood up for me, and, you know, Mike would step up for anybody. And it wasn't part of his training or his military command, but the citation stating how he reacted, and how quickly he reacted, that to me was Mike Crescenz. And, obviously, he paid the ultimate price for our country and the family lost a great son and a brother and we all lost a good friend that day. But the end result is, that was Michael. He was one who would step up and none of what was in the citation surprised me. It was troubling to read, troubling to know that he passed away, but looking at it, it was special and he was a special guy."[10]

He says of the two oldest Crescenz brothers he knew best. "Charlie came home from Vietnam. Michael gave his life so others could come home. Neither one is forgotten.

"I have stated this many times over the years: I knew a hero. I grew up with a hero. I miss that hero terribly. I loved that hero. I loved Michael like a brother."

Jim Engler echoed Ron's moving words. "It was one of the saddest days of my life when I received news in a letter from my parents of Mike's death," he said. "It brought immediate tears to my eyes. I couldn't believe it. We would all find out later just how heroic his actions were on that fatal day. It certainly came as no surprise that he faced that danger and certain death with the same unabashed courage that he demonstrated often as he was growing up.

"You know, when I first read the account of Mike's heroic deeds, I just thought this was not out of character. I heard later that when Mike left for Vietnam, maybe his mom had some kind of portent and she said to him, 'No heroic business.' Well, he didn't heed that. He put his life on the line. It was tremendous what he did, and I'm sure those guys in his company were really grateful and thankful and amazed at what he did as well. I can say I wasn't surprised at his gallantry. When it came to overcoming challenges, he could be fearless."[11]

Another friend from St. A's and Cardinal Dougherty, Bill Peglow, said, "What Mike did for his country and the way he died will live with me forever. Only two months away from his twentieth birthday when he died. As a parent, I can only imagine how his parents must have felt."[12]

John Norton told Joe Crescenz, "I watch Mike's disinterment and reinterment video over and over. It keeps me in touch with Mike and Charlie. I've had my son and daughter watch it so Mike and Charlie's memory will not be forgotten."[13]

Ben Silver wrote to Joe, "I remember when you got off the bus from high school and showed me and my twin the photo album of your parents receiving the Medal of Honor from President Nixon at the White House. It was a beautiful, thick album, and we just couldn't believe your parents were standing next to President Nixon and talking to him. It didn't seem real.

"I also remember the last time I saw Mike. He was coming out of the drug store on the corner with Charlie. I was standing right outside the store and I said hi to them. One of them gave me a playful pop on the back of my head—and then they turned around and chuckled at me. It was a 'love tap'—all meant in fun."[14]

"The very first time we met, Joe told me about his brother Mike," Valerie Crescenz said. "I remember how proud Joe was of his brother, and what an amazing story it was. It took me a very long time to understand the devastating impact that Mike's loss had on Joe, his family, and pretty much everyone who knew him. I heard so many stories about Mike's life, and it seemed that there were several threads that weaved their way through almost all of them: he was devoted to his family and friends, he did not tolerate bullies, and he was a fierce competitor. All of these made him the person who could do what he did on November 20, 1968, the day he died.

"Over the years, Joe and his older brother Charlie kept in touch with many of Mike's old friends from the neighborhood in Philly. We've also met a lot of new friends, some of whom were with Mike when he was killed. Some of them are like brothers to Joe. Some of them have expressed guilt that they survived when Mike didn't. When their minds torment them with the question 'Why him and not me?,' they know there is no answer. It's a deep and troubling question. I wonder what Mike would think about that.

"Mike must have forged some very close relationships in the short time he was in Vietnam. When he and his unit found themselves in serious trouble, Mike did what he always did—he took care of his friends. And although his family and friends back home would have never wanted him to be there, maybe it was exactly where he was supposed to be."[15]

Working to keep Mike's memory alive is exactly where Joe Crescenz is supposed to be. He has dedicated a good part of his life to the effort and is in his element when spending time with the men who served with Michael in Vietnam and old neighborhood friends. One of the latter group is Manny Silver, twin brother to Ben, who lives in South Florida. Joe and Manny are in touch regularly despite the distance between them. Joe and his brother Michael are often in Manny's thoughts, and they inspired him to write a piece about the Crescenz family for his synagogue, Temple Beth El, of Hollywood, Florida, on May 1, 2019:

> One of the childhood memories seared into my soul is the shock and sadness that swept over our neighborhood when Mike was killed in Vietnam many years ago. Every time I walked by the Crescenz home, I could feel the immense sadness and the pain coming from their house.
>
> As I delivered my paper route every morning in the predawn darkness, I would see Mike's mother headed to church for daily Mass. Sometimes our eyes would meet and I would very respectfully say, "Good morning, Mrs. Crescenz."
>
> That was all I could say to my friend's mom. What could a young boy say to a grieving mother whose son died in war? But all these years later, I can never forget.
>
> Neither can the people of Philadelphia or the Vietnam vets all across America. Mike was awarded the Congressional Medal of Honor for his heroic actions on the battlefield and there is a statue of him in downtown Philadelphia at the Vietnam Veterans Memorial. I was there last year and I placed a stone there, my own way of following Jewish custom of placing stones at the graves of those who live on in our hearts....
>
> My Dad fought in World War II and hardly ever talked about it. But he used to lecture me and my brothers, "Thank God you were born in this country!" He gave us that speech a few times and it made such an impression on me that I can recite the rest of it by heart.
>
> "Do you know where my mother was born? Do you know what they did to Jews there? Thank God you were born in America."[16]

Such tributes move Joe to tears. He is understandably still in awe of the big brother he lost so many years ago. He never told Michael how proud he was to be his little brother, but why would a kid risk the teasing and likely knuckles across his head by telling his big brother such a thing? Besides, Mike would always be around, wouldn't he? In a sense, Michael is. Joe sees Michael and his impact all around him.

"What his actions and that medal have done, not just for this family, but for a lot of the guys that Michael grew up with in the neighborhood, the guys who survived the battle, including his commanding officer, it's uncanny. The lives he has touched from the day he died, it's indescribable. I've gotten to know so many soldiers who served with Mike, and some of them are grandfathers now and they see their own sons or grandsons fighting these wars on terror in Iraq and Afghanistan. And those who served with Mike, what they must feel right now, that angst, that anxiousness until their sons or daughters get the hell on home and hit the soil in America again. You know, life kept going on but Mike in his short 19 years had an impact on these people.

"His actions remind me of what we were taught as kids, that you fend for the weak, defend against bullies in life. He took that to heart. Mike was, he was unique. My brothers, Charlie and Pete, Steve and Chris, and myself are proud of what he did. But I think more proud and happier that his own buddies to this day still remember Mike, still remember his birthday, still remember the day he died, still remember the good times they had at their junior and senior proms in high school. Good people."[17]

Michael Crescenz was a hero, no question, and much, more more. As was written about another warrior centuries ago, "The most glorious exploits do not always furnish us with the clearest of discoveries of virtue or vice in men; sometimes a matter of less moment, an expression or a jest, informs us better of their characters and inclinations than the most famous sieges, the greatest armament, or the bloodiest battles."[18]

No one knew Michael's virtues and moments, his expressions and jests, better than the parents who adored him. How heartened they must have been then, almost 18 years after his death, to receive a letter from one of his many cousins, Denise McLaughlin, and know that others held him in such high esteem. Heartened, even as reading her thoughts may have caused them to mourn anew. Denise wrote:

> Dear Aunt Mary and Uncle Charlie,
>
> Hope all is well with you both. We are all fine here. Michael is in good health and working hard. Anna at six has just mastered swimming in deep water. And Natanya at two and a half is learning to yell back and not be manipulated so easily by her big sister.
>
> I'm fine. I just turned thirty-eight, which is so incredible to me. Whoever thought I would really grow up?
>
> Have been thinking of your son Michael regularly since Memorial Day, when a shower of tears and warm memories overcame me. I wanted to share a few of them with you both.
>
> When Michael was killed in Vietnam, I had just turned twenty the previous summer and was still attending nursing school. Someone called to tell me the devastating news about Michael. I remember most clearly the numbness I felt, as I couldn't fathom the death of this healthy, much-loved cousin. In the weeks that followed, I made small steps toward processing the finality of his death.

The only positive thing I could conjure up was that to us all, Michael would always be that well liked, loving, optimistic, good looking young man. This memory would be imprinted in our minds.

He would never know the despair of failure in business, friendship or love. He would never get flabby, settle for less, or be boring. In my naivety, I saw this all as a meager, yes, but nevertheless positive point in all this sadness. I desperately needed something positive to hang on to.

Almost eighteen years later, I'm writing to tell you that I've changed my mind. This even small rationalization doesn't any longer help me accept his death. True, his memory is a shiny, glorious youthful one. But my life and the lives of everyone else who knew him are diminished by his death. I still miss him and wish he too would turn thirty-eight soon, be flabby, have gray hair and share in both the despair and joy that come with relationships that fail and/or succeed; in short, I wanted that we should all grow up and old together.

He was always my favorite cousin, sharing in the shadows of being second born children, following flashier big brothers. He was always fun, warm and considerate. I never knew him to be selfish or mean spirited. As I look back to pinpoint his uniqueness, I falter for words and imagery. However, an image emerges that surprises me as I put it in perspective.

I don't know how many people Michael did this with but he always made me feel special and fully accepted by him. I never had to brag, show off or hit a home run to impress him or get his attention. He always made me feel liked, loved and accepted—me with scrapes, adolescent awkwardness, scraggly hair and all! What a remarkable feat for a young man! What a gift you both, as his parents, gave him—the ability to accept and delight in people just as they are.

I'm sure I'm not alone in receiving these good vibes from Michael. Others have surely told you this over the years. I just wanted to tell you that for me his gift lives on. I still feel it and try to emulate this style of his.

I hope this letter doesn't hit you like a bolt of painful memories. I only wanted to share with you, these many years later, what a remarkable legacy you gave your son, Michael. I wanted to let you know that you aren't alone in remembering him. As you count the many whose lives Michael touched in a good way and remember him fondly, don't forget me.

Much love,
Denise[19]

Endnotes

Prologue: Fortress in the Clouds

1   Sgt. George Hawkins, "Nui Chom Mountain," *Americal*, May 1969, 2, https://www.americalfoundation.org/cmsalf/images/AMCAL-Mags/Ammag_6905_Small.pdf.
2   William "Doc" Stafford, video interview by Bob Moran, *Philadelphia Inquirer*, March 2, 2013.
3   Hawkins, "Nui Chom Mountain," 5.
4   William "Doc" Stafford, email to Joe Crescenz, January 30, 2021.

Chapter I: Family

1   Joe Crescenz, cell-phone and in-person interviews by John A. Siegfried, various dates, 2017.
2   Kathleen Zippilli and Mary Lou Allen, email to Joe Crescenz, June 21, 2021.
3   Joe Crescenz, video interview by Bob Moran, *Philadelphia Inquirer*, February 24, 2013.
4   Joe Crescenz, video interview by Bob Moran, February 24, 2013.
5   Samantha Crawford, "Michael Crescenz: Never Forgotten," video, December 3, 2015, 50:41, https://www.youtube.com/watch?v=dpC97Q9m-oA.
6   Joe Crescenz, video interview by Bob Moran, February 24, 2013.
7   Joe Crescenz, video interview by Bob Moran, February 24, 2013.
8   Ron Burke, email to Joe Crescenz, January 8, 2020.
9   Ron Burke, email to Joe Crescenz, January 8, 2020.
10   Joe Crescenz, video interview by Bob Moran, February 24, 2013.
11   Crawford, "Michael Crescenz."
12   Joe Crescenz, video interview by Bob Moran, February 24, 2013.
13   James Engler, email to Joe Crescenz, January 25, 2020.
14   Joe Crescenz, video interview by Bob Moran, February 24, 2013.
15   James Engler, video interview by Bob Moran, *Philadelphia Inquirer*, March 16, 2013.
16   Steve Cronin, "Sea Isle City honors Medal of Honor recipient," *Press of Atlantic City*, November 11, 2014, https://pressofatlanticcity.com/news/sea-isle-city-honors-medal-of-honor-recipient/article_3e26f438-69f6-11e4-9cad-8304fd873da5.html.

17 Joe Crescenz, video interview by Bob Moran, February 24, 2013.
18 Crawford, "Michael Crescenz."
19 Ron Burke, video interview by Bob Moran, *Philadelphia Inquirer*, March 24, 2013.
20 John Norton, email to Joe Crescenz, March 27, 2020.
21 Joe Crescenz, video interview by Bob Moran, February 24, 2013.

Chapter II: Community

1   Senator John McCain with Mark Salter, *Character Is Destiny: Inspiring Stories Every Young Person Should Know and Every Adult Should Remember* (New York: Random House, 2005), 55.
2   Crawford, "Michael Crescenz."
3   James Engler, video interview by Bob Moran, March 16, 2013.
4   James Engler, email to Joe Crescenz, January 25, 2020.
5   James Engler, video interview by Bob Moran, March 16, 2013.
6   Ron Burke, video interview by Bob Moran, March 24, 2013.
7   Ron Burke, video interview by Bob Moran, March 24, 2013.
8   Ron Burke, email to Joe Crescenz, January 8, 2020.
9   Ron Burke, video interview by Bob Moran, March 24, 2013.
10 Tom Stanton, email to Joe Crescenz, January 5, 2020.
11 Joseph Lynch, email to Joe Crescenz, February 2, 2020.
12 Tom Corcoran, email to Joe Crescenz, January 8, 2020.
13 Ron Burke, video interview by Bob Moran, March 24, 2013.
14 James Engler, video interview by Bob Moran, March 16, 2013.
15 Ron Burke, video interview by Bob Moran, March 24, 2013.
16 James Engler, email to Joe Crescenz, January 25, 2020.
17 Ron Burke, email to Joe Crescenz, January 8, 2020.
18 William Peglow, email to Joe Crescenz, January 23, 2020.
19 Rick Gallagher, email to Joe Crescenz, January 24, 2020.
20 Rick Gallagher, email to Joe Crescenz, January 24, 2020.
21 Jeff Jacobs, email to Joe Crescenz, January 26, 2020.
22 Joe Crescenz, video interview by Bob Moran, February 24, 2013.
23 James Engler, video interview by Bob Moran, March 16, 2013.
24 James Engler, video interview by Bob Moran, March 16, 2013.
25 James Engler, email to Joe Crescenz, January 25, 2020.
26 Ron Burke, video interview by Bob Moran, March 24, 2013.
27 James Engler, email to Joe Crescenz, January 25, 2020.
28 James Engler, video interview by Bob Moran, March 16, 2013.
29 Ron Burke, email to Joe Crescenz, January 8, 2020.
30 Ron Burke, email to Joe Crescenz, January 26, 2020.
31 Ron Burke, email to Joe Crescenz, January 8, 2020.

32 Maria Panaritis, "VA Hospital to bear war hero's name," *Philadelphia Inquirer*, May 1, 2015, https://www.inquirer.com/news/va-hospital-be-renamed-vietnam-war-hero-michael-crescenz-20150430.html.

33 Ron Burke, email to Joe Crescenz, January 8, 2020.

34 Ron Burke, video interview by Bob Moran, March 24, 2013.

35 James Engler, email to Joe Crescenz, January 25, 2020.

36 Ron Burke, email to Joe Crescenz, January 8, 2020.

37 Ron Burke, email to Joe Crescenz, January 26, 2020.

38 Ron Burke, email to Joe Crescenz, January 8, 2020; Ron Burke, video interview by Bob Moran, March 24, 2013.

Chapter III: Call to Service

1 James Engler, video interview by Bob Moran, March 16, 2013.

2 James Engler, email to Joe Crescenz, January 25, 2020.

3 James Engler, email to Joe Crescenz, January 25, 2020.

4 Ron Burke, email to Joe Crescenz, January 26, 2020.

5 Crawford, "Michael Crescenz."

6 Joe Crescenz, video interview by Bob Moran, February 24, 2013.

7 Joe Crescenz, video interview by Bob Moran, February 24, 2013.

8 Joe Crescenz, video interview by Bob Moran, February 24, 2013.

9 Joe Crescenz, video interview by Bob Moran, February 24, 2013.

10 Joe Crescenz, video interview by Bob Moran, February 24, 2013.

11 Ron Burke, video interview by Bob Moran, March 24, 2013.

12 Joe Crescenz, video interview by Bob Moran, February 24, 2013.

13 Crawford, "Michael Crescenz."

14 Joe Crescenz, video interview by Bob Moran, February 24, 2013.

15 Joe Crescenz, video interview by Bob Moran, February 24, 2013.

16 James Engler, video interview by Bob Moran, March 16, 2013.

17 James Engler, email to Joe Crescenz, January 25, 2020.

18 Bob Gleason, cell-phone interview by John A. Siegfried, May 27, 2017.

19 Bob Gleason, cell-phone interview by John A. Siegfried, May 27, 2017.

20 Bob Gleason, cell-phone interview by John A. Siegfried, May 27, 2017.

21 Joe Rosato Jr., "Former Vietnam War Flight Attendants Reunite in Sacramento," NBC Bay Area, February 25, 2014, https://www.nbcbayarea.com/news/local/former-vietnam-war-flight-attendants-reunite-in-sacramento/74765/.

22 Bob Gleason, cell-phone interview by John A. Siegfried, May 27, 2017.

23 Bob Gleason, cell-phone interview by John A. Siegfried, May 27, 2017.

24 Rosato, "Flight Attendants."

25 Bob Gleason, cell-phone interview by John A. Siegfried, May 27, 2017.

26 Jim Willard, cell-phone interviews by John A. Siegfried, June 13 and 19, 2017.

27 William "Doc" Stafford, interview by Bob Moran, March 2, 2013.

28 William "Doc" Stafford, interview by Bob Moran, March 2, 2013.

29 William "Doc" Stafford, interview by Bob Moran, March 2, 2013.

30 William "Doc" Stafford, interview by Bob Moran, March 2, 2013.

31 William "Doc" Stafford, interview by Bob Moran, March 2, 2013.

32 William "Doc" Stafford, interview by Bob Moran, March 2, 2013.

33 Jim Willard, cell-phone interviews by John A. Siegfried, June 13 and 19, 2017.

34 Chuck Williams, "Retired Lt. Gen. Wetzel's career spanned 34 years, but he vividly recalls one hellish week 50 years ago," Columbus *Ledger-Enquirer*, November 26, 2018, https://www.ledger-enquirer.com/news/local/military/article221702910.html.

35 Lt. Gen. Sam Wetzel, retired, video interview by Bob Moran, *Philadelphia Inquirer*, February 11, 2013.

36 Joe Crescenz, video interview by Bob Moran, February 24, 2013.

37 Joe Crescenz, video interview by Bob Moran, February 24, 2013.

38 Joe Crescenz, video interview by Bob Moran, February 24, 2013.

39 Joe Crescenz, video interview by Bob Moran, February 24, 2013.

40 Michael Crescenz, letter home from Vietnam, October 31, 1968.

41 Michael Crescenz, letter home from Vietnam, November 19, 1968.

42 Kevin Ferris, "A letter home from a fallen Vietnam soldier," *Philadelphia Inquirer*, May 25, 2008, http://www.arlingtoncemetery.net/jfcochrane.htm.

43 Kevin Ferris, "A letter home from a fallen Vietnam soldier."

Chapter IV: The Battle of Nui Chom Mountain

1 Members of the 31st Infantry Regiment Association, *The 31st Infantry Regiment: A History of America's Foreign Legion in Peace and War* (Jefferson, NC: McFarland, 2018), 279, https://www.amazon.com/31st-Infantry-Regiment-History-Americas-ebook/dp/B07KQDKWR1.

2 Members of the 31st Infantry Regiment Association, *The 31st Infantry Regiment: A History of America's Foreign Legion in Peace and War*, 279, https://www.amazon.com/31st-Infantry-Regiment-History-Americas-ebook/dp/B07KQDKWR1.

3 Chuck Williams, "'We moved closer and got behind a large rock. Then all hell broke loose': Lt. remembers Nui Chom," Columbus *Ledger-Enquirer*, November 23, 2018, https://www.ledger-enquirer.com/news/local/military/article221764560.html.

4 Members of the 31st, *The 31st Infantry Regiment: A History of America's Foreign Legion in Peace and War*, 279, https://www.amazon.com/31st-Infantry-Regiment-History-Americas-ebook/dp/B07KQDKWR1.

5 Williams, "Lt. remembers Nui Chom."

6 Members of the 31st Infantry Regiment Association, *The 31st Infantry Regiment: A History of America's Foreign Legion in Peace and War*, 279.

7 Williams, "Lt. remembers Nui Chom."

8 Lt. Gen. Sam Wetzel, retired, video interview by Bob Moran, February 11, 2013.

9 Hawkins, "Nui Chom Mountain," 3.

10 Williams, "Lt. remembers Nui Chom."

11 Williams, "Lt. remembers Nui Chom."

12 Hawkins, "Nui Chom Mountain," 3, 4.

13 Williams, "Lt. remembers Nui Chom."

14 Williams, "Lt. remembers Nui Chom."

15 Chuck Williams, "Lt. Col. Wetzel pulled his plan to attack Nui Chom right out of the history books, WWII," Columbus *Ledger-Enquirer*, November 23, 2018, https://www.ledger-enquirer.com/news/local/military/article221774370.html.

16 Williams, "Lt. Col. Wetzel pulled his plan."

17 Lt. Gen. Sam Wetzel, retired, video interview by Bob Moran, February 11, 2013.

18 Hawkins, "Nui Chom Mountain," 4.

19 Hawkins, "Nui Chom Mountain," 4.

20 William "Doc" Stafford, interview by Bob Moran, March 2, 2013.

21 Jack Bisbee, email to Joe Crescenz, April 1, 2013.

22 Chuck Williams, "Doc Stafford on Nui Chom: 'I think that day, Michael Crescenz altered the name on my bullet," Columbus *Ledger-Enquirer*, November 26, 2018, https://www.ledger-enquirer.com/news/local/military/article221777575.html.

23 William "Doc" Stafford, interview by Bob Moran, March 2, 2013.

24 Williams, "Doc Stafford on Nui Chom."

25 William "Doc" Stafford, interview by Bob Moran, March 2, 2013.

26 William "Doc" Stafford, interview by Bob Moran, March 2, 2013.

27 William "Doc" Stafford, email to Joe Crescenz, January 30, 2021.

28 Hawkins, "Nui Chom Mountain," 5.

29 William "Doc" Stafford, interview by Bob Moran, March 2, 2013.

30 William "Doc" Stafford, interview by Bob Moran, March 2, 2013.

31 William "Doc" Stafford, interview by Bob Moran, March 2, 2013.

32 Williams, "Doc Stafford on Nui Chom."

33 Lt. Gen. Sam Wetzel, retired, video interview by Bob Moran, February 11, 2013.

34 Williams, "Doc Stafford on Nui Chom."

35 William "Doc" Stafford, interview by Bob Moran, March 2, 2013.

36 Williams, "Doc Stafford on Nui Chom."

37 Chuck Williams, "During recovery of dead American soldiers, Alpha Company finds life amid the carnage," Columbus *Ledger-Enquirer*, November 26, 2018, https://www.ledger-enquirer.com/latest-news/article221781950.html.

38 Williams, "During recovery."

39 Hawkins, "Nui Chom Mountain," 7.

40 Hawkins, "Nui Chom Mountain," 7.

41 Chuck Williams, "Sam Wetzel: 'You were the most gallant fighting soldiers I saw in my entire 34 years in the Army," Columbus *Ledger-Enquirer*, November 26, 2018, https://www.ledger-enquirer.com/news/local/military/article221785175.html.

42 Williams, "Sam Wetzel."

43 Williams, "Sam Wetzel."

44 Williams, "Sam Wetzel."

45 Kevin Ferris, "Long-awaited honor for vet," *Philadelphia Inquirer*, May 9, 2008, https://www.inquirer.com/philly/opinion/inquirer/20080509_Back_Channels__Long-awaited_honor_for_vet.html.

46 William "Doc" Stafford, interview by Bob Moran, March 2, 2013.

Chapter V: Medal of Honor

1 Joe Crescenz, video interview by Bob Moran, February 24, 2013.

2 Crawford, "Michael Crescenz."

3 Joe Crescenz, video interview by Bob Moran, February 24, 2013.

4 Crawford, "Michael Crescenz."

5 Joe Crescenz, video interview by Bob Moran, February 24, 2013.

6 Ron Burke, video interview by Bob Moran, March 24, 2013; Joe Crescenz, email from Ron Burke, January 8, 2020

7 Ron Burke, video interview by Bob Moran, March 24, 2013; Ron Burke, email to Joe Crescenz, January 8, 2020.

8 James Engler, video interview by Bob Moran, March 16, 2013.

9 John Norton, email to Joe Crescenz, March 26, 2020.

10 Rick Gallagher, email to Joe Crescenz, January 24, 2020.

11 Tom Corcoran, email to Joe Crescenz, January 8, 2020.

12 Nikki Wentling, "High school with highest death rate in Vietnam embraces its legacy," *Stars and Stripes*, September 21, 2017, https://www.stripes.com/special-reports/vietnam-stories/1967/high-school-with-highest-death-rate-in-vietnam-embraces-its-legacy-1.488823; Lou Baldwin, "Bringing Our Brothers Home," CatholicPhilly.com, November 10, 2010, https://catholicphilly.com/2010/11/news/bringing-our-brothers-home/.

13 Joe Crescenz, video interview by Bob Moran, February 24, 2013.

14 Charles B. Herbermann et al., eds., *The Catholic Encyclopedia* (New York: Robert Appleton, 1907), https://books.google.com/books?id=m8xJAQAAMAAJ&pg=PA36&lpg=PA36&dq=His+courage+was+of+the+sort+that+never+falters.&source=bl&ots=mmhS4dGTnM&sig=ACfU3U2d_d6wtTyv5GrcOKRre3LEmrum1w&hl=en&sa=X&ved=2ahUKEwjqqvzhmOn1AhUMkWoFHeDvBlwQ6AF6BAgOEAM#v=onepage&q=His%20courage%20was%20of%20the%20sort%20that%20never%20falters.&f=false.

15 "History of the Parish," St. Athanasius Parish (website) About Us page, http://www.stathanasiuschurch.us/index.php/homepage/about-us.

16 Joe Crescenz, video interview by Bob Moran, February 24, 2013.

17 Joe Crescenz, video interview by Bob Moran, February 24, 2013.

18 Joe Crescenz, video interview by Bob Moran, February 24, 2013.

19 Joe Crescenz, video interview by Bob Moran, February 24, 2013.

20 Joe Crescenz, video interview by Bob Moran, February 24, 2013.

21 Kathleen Zippilli and Mary Lou Allen, email to Joe Crescenz, June 21, 2021.

22 Crawford, "Michael Crescenz."

23 Cantor Emanuel Silver, bulletin of Temple Beth El of Hollywood, Florida, May 1, 2019.

24 John Cardinal Krol, letter to Crescenz family, November 26, 1968.

25 President Lyndon B. Johnson, letter to Crescenz family, November 29, 1968.

26 Mayor James J. Tate, Philadelphia, letter to Crescenz family, January 1969.

27 Lt. Col. Sam Wetzel, letter to Crescenz family, January 9, 196.

28 "Highest Ranking U.S. Military Medals," Veteran.com, https://militarybenefits. info/ranking-military-medals/.

29 "The Medal of Honor," Congressional Medal of Honor Society (website), https://www.cmohs.org/medal.

30 "What Is a Bronze Star?" Medals of America – Military Blog (website), https://www.medalsofamerica.com/blog/what-is-a-bronze-star/

31 Fred L. Borch and Robert F. Dorr, "For Gallantry in Action: The Silver Star," militarytrader.com, July 14, 2008, https://www.militarytrader.com/ militaria-collectibles/for-gallantry-in-action-the-silver-star

32 "Vietnam War – Service Cross," Home of Heroes (website), https://homeofheroes. com/distinguished-service-cross/vietnam-war/#:~:text=There%20are%20over%20 1%2C700%20recipients,Cross%20during%20the%20Vietnam%20War.

33 Congressional Medal of Honor Society (website), Statistics and FAQs page, https://www.cmohs.org/medal/faqs.

34 Lt. Gen. Sam Wetzel, retired, video interview by Bob Moran, February 11, 2013.

35 Captain Billie J. Braswell, statement in packet recommending Michael J. Crescenz for the Medal of Honor.

36 Spc. 4 Donald L. Phelps, statement in packet recommending Michael J. Crescenz for the Medal of Honor.

37 Summary of Recommendation for Award of Medal of Honor in packet recommending Michael Crescenz for the Medal of Honor.

38 Lt. Gen. Sam Wetzel, retired, video interview by Bob Moran, February 11, 2013.

39 "Stories of Sacrifice: Theodore Roosevelt," Congressional Medal of Honor Society (website), https://www.cmohs.org/recipients/theodore-roosevelt.

40 "Stories of Sacrifice: Theodore Roosevelt," Congressional Medal of Honor Society (website).

41 Nicholas Fandos, "Medal of Honor Goes to Vietnam Medic Who Ran through 'Hell on Earth,'" New York Times, July 31, 2017, https://www.nytimes.com/2017/07/31/ us/politics/medal-of-honor-trump-james-mccloughan.html.

42 Frank Miles, "Marine veteran, 80, receives Medal of Honor for Vietnam bravery," Fox News Digital, October 17, 2018, https://www.foxnews.com/us/ marine-veteran-80-receives-medal-of-honor-for-vietnam-bravery.

43 Dan Lamothe, "'I had to react': The Army's David Bellavia becomes first living Medal of Honor recipient from the Iraq War," *Washington Post*, June 25, 2019, https://www.washingtonpost.com/national-security/2019/06/25/i-had-react-armys-david-bellavia-becomes-first-living-medal-honor-recipient-iraq-war/.

44 Mark C. Mollan, "The Army Medal of Honor: The First Fifty-five Years," *Prologue*, Summer 2001, https://www.archives.gov/publications/prologue/2001/summer/medal-of-honor-1.html.

45 Mollan, "Army Medal of Honor."

46 Mollan, "Army Medal of Honor."

47 "Dr. Mary E. Walker," Association of the United States Army (website), https://www.ausa.org/dr-mary-e-walker

48 "Dr. Mary E. Walker," Association of the United States Army (website), https://www.ausa.org/dr-mary-e-walker

49 Lew Freedman, "Buffalo Bill was awarded Medal of Honor," Cody Enterprise, July 3, 2017, https://www.codyenterprise.com/news/local/article_1f6fd238-6031-11e7-8c35-8febb429e32b.html.

50 Joe Crescenz, family collection of Michael Crescenz military records.

51 Joe Crescenz, family collection.

52 Joe Crescenz, video interview by Bob Moran, February 24, 2013.

53 Joe Crescenz, family collection.

54 Tom Gosse, email to Kevin Ferris, April 30, 2020.

55 Tom Gosse, email to Kevin Ferris, April 30, 2020.

56 Tom Gosse, email to Kevin Ferris, April 30, 2020.

57 Tom Gosse, email to Kevin Ferris, April 30, 2020.

58 Joe Crescenz, video interview by Bob Moran, February 24, 2013.

Chapter VI: The White House

1 Tom Gosse, email to Kevin Ferris, April 30, 2020.

2 Joe Crescenz, video interview by Bob Moran, February 24, 2013.

3 Tom Gosse, email to Kevin Ferris, April 30, 2020.

4 "The East Room," White House Historical Association (website), https://www.whitehousehistory.org/white-house-tour/the-east-room.

5 Audio Recording of Medal of Honor Ceremonies, Richard Nixon Presidential Library and Museum, National Archives, April 7, 1970, https://www.nixonlibrary.gov/media/14778.

6 Nixon Library recording, https://www.nixonlibrary.gov/media/14778.

7 Nixon Library recording, https://www.nixonlibrary.gov/media/14778.

8 "Douglas Bernard Fournet," Congressional Medal of Honor Society (website), https://www.cmohs.org/recipients/douglas-b-fournet.

9 "Veterans Memorial Park," Visit Lake Charles (website), https://www.visitlakecharles.org/listing/veterans-memorial-park/148869/.

10 "Lake Charles VA clinic renamed after local Medal of Honor recipient," KPLC, November 6, 2019, https://www.kplctv.com/2019/11/06/lake-charles-va-clinic-renamed-after-local-veteran/.

11 Eric Cormier, "I-210 stretch to be named for hero from Vietnam War," *American Press*, June 8, 2001, https://www.mishalov.com/Fournet.html.

12 "Fournet," Congressional Medal of Honor Society (website).

13 Nixon Library recording, https://www.nixonlibrary.gov/media/14778.

14 "Rodney James Tadashi Yano," Congressional Medal of Honor Society (website), https://www.cmohs.org/recipients/rodney-j-yano.

15 Duane Vachon, "Into the Breach," *Hawaii Reporter*, August 4, 2012, https://www.hawaiireporter.com/into-the-breach-sergeant-first-class-rodney-james-tadashi-yano-u-s-army-vietnam-war-medal-of-honor-1943-1969/.

16 Katie Lange, "Meet Rodney Yano, one of 33 Asian-American Medal of Honor recipients," Department of Defense News, May 22, 2018, https://www.army.mil/article/187417/meet_rodney_yano_one_of_33_asian_american_medal_of_honor_recipients.

17 "Rodney James Tadashi Yano," Congressional Medal of Honor Society (website).

18 Nixon Library, https://www.nixonlibrary.gov/media/14778.

19 June Gossler Anderson, "Laszlo Rabel," https://www.minnesotamedalofhonormemorial.org/wp-content/uploads/2017/12/Rabel-Laszlo-Bio-July-16.pdf.

20 "Laszlo Rabel," Congressional Medal of Honor Society (website), https://www.cmohs.org/recipients/laszlo-rabel.

21 Anderson, "Laszlo Rabel."

22 Nixon Library recording, https://www.nixonlibrary.gov/media/14778.

23 "John James Kedenburg," Congressional Medal of Honor Society (website), https://www.cmohs.org/recipients/john-j-kedenburg.

24 Mike Russo, "Baldwin was home to two Medal of Honor recipients," *Baldwin Herald*, May 30, 2010, https://www.liherald.com/baldwin/stories/baldwin-was-home-to-two-medal-of-honor-recipients,25347.

25 "John James Kedenburg," Congressional Medal of Honor Society (website).

26 Nixon Library recording, https://www.nixonlibrary.gov/media/14778.

27 Duane Allen Vachon, "A Passive Patriot," *Hawaii Reporter*, March 9, 2014, https://www.hawaiireporter.com/thomas-w-bennett-corporal-usa-a-passive-patriot/.

28 "Thomas William Bennett," Congressional Medal of Honor Society (website), https://www.cmohs.org/recipients/thomas-w-bennett.

29 "Remember...Thomas William Bennett," West Virginia Veterans Memorial (website), http://129.71.204.160/history///wvmemory/vets/bennettthomas/bennettthomas.html.

30 Nixon Library recording, https://www.nixonlibrary.gov/media/14778.

31 "Marvin Rex Young," Congressional Medal of Honor Society (website), https://www.cmohs.org/recipients/marvin-r-young.

32 "President Bush Signs Legislation to Rename Postal Facilities," American Presidency Project, August 9, 2007, https://www.presidency.ucsb.edu/documents/statement-the-press-secretary-president-bush-signs-legislation-rename-postal-facilities.

33 "Local VA clinic renamed to honor Wilson and Young," CBS7, October 17, 2019, https://www.cbs7.com/content/news/Local-VA-clinic-renamed-to-honor-Wilson--Young-563292061.html.

34 "Marvin Rex Young," Congressional Medal of Honor Society (website).

35 Nixon Library recording, https://www.nixonlibrary.gov/media/14778.

36 "Ray McKibben," Congressional Medal of Honor Society (website), https://www.cmohs.org/recipients/ray-mckibben.

37 Nixon Library recording, https://www.nixonlibrary.gov/media/14778.

38 "Anund Charles Roark," Congressional Medal of Honor Society (website), https://www.cmohs.org/recipients/anund-c-roark.

39 Grace Marshall, "Army sergeant had lifelong desire to protect, serve," *San Diego Union-Tribune*, May 26, 2016, https://www.sandiegouniontribune.com/military/sdut-anund-roark-hero-2016may26-story.html.

40 "Anund Charles Roark," Congressional Medal of Honor Society (website).

41 Nixon Library recording, https://www.nixonlibrary.gov/media/14778.

42 "William Wayne Seay," Congressional Medal of Honor Society (website), https://www.cmohs.org/recipients/william-w-seay.

43 Airman 1st Class Monica Roybal, "JBLE hosts rededication, time capsule ceremony," Joint Base Langley-Eustis (website), May 11, 2018, https://www.jble.af.mil/News/Article-Display/Article/1519318/jble-hosts-rededication-time-capsule-ceremony/.

44 John Vick, "Ambush at Ap Nhi," *Andalusia Star-News*, April 2, 2021, https://www.andalusiastarnews.com/2021/04/02/ambush-at-ap-nhi-the-heroism-of-sergeant-william-w-seay-u-s-army-vietnam-war-medal-of-honor-conclusion/.

45 "William Wayne Seay," Congressional Medal of Honor Society (website).

46 Nixon Library recording, https://www.nixonlibrary.gov/media/14778.

47 "Lester Raymond Stone Jr.," Congressional Medal of Honor Society (website), https://www.cmohs.org/recipients/lester-r-stone-jr.

48 "Lester R. Stone Jr.," Congressional Medal of Honor Society (website).

49 Tariq Malik, "Veterans Day in space: Space Station astronauts pay tribute to fallen hero," November 11, 2010, https://www.csmonitor.com/Science/2010/1111/Veterans-Day-in-space-Space-Station-astronauts-pay-tribute-to-a-fallen-hero.

50 Nixon Library recording, https://www.nixonlibrary.gov/media/14778.

51 "Nicholas Joseph Cutinha," Congressional Medal of Honor Society (website), https://www.cmohs.org/recipients/nicholas-j-cutinha.

52 Khristopher J. Brooks, "Vietnam veterans chapter renamed in honor of Fernandina Beach native," *Florida Times-Union*, November 18, 2012, https://www.jacksonville.com/story/news/military/2012/11/19/vietnam-veterans-chapter-renamed-honor-fernandina-beach-native/15847202007/.

53 "Nicholas J. Cutinha," Wikipedia, https://en.wikipedia.org/wiki/ Nicholas_J._Cutinha#cite_note-4.

54 Patty Brant, "'Nickie' Cutinha honored with statue," South Central Florida Life, April 2, 2020, https://www.southcentralfloridalife.com/stories/ nickie-cutinha-honored-with-statue,8353.

55 Nixon Library recording, https://www.nixonlibrary.gov/media/14778.

56 "Edward Allen Devore Jr.," Congressional Medal of Honor Society (website), https://www.cmohs.org/recipients/edward-a-devore-jr.

57 "Edward DeVore to be remembered by state," thehenryettan.com, 2022, https:// thehenryettan.com/index.php?option=com_content&view=article&id=5336:edw ard-devore-to-be-remembered-by-state&catid=8&lang=en&Itemid=367

58 "Edward Allen Devore Jr.," Oklahoma History Center (website), https://www. okhistory.org/historycenter/militaryhof/inductee.php?id=322.

59 "Edward A. Devore Jr.," Medal of Honor, Historical Marker Database, https://www.hmdb.org/m.asp?m=109065.

60 Nixon Library recording, https://www.nixonlibrary.gov/media/14778.

61 "Peter Mathew Guenette," Congressional Medal of Honor Society (website), https://www.cmohs.org/recipients/peter-m-guenette.

62 Chris Bragg, "New Troy apartments dedicated to Vietnam hero," *Albany Times Union*, May 27, 2017, https://www.timesunion.com/local/article/New-Troy- apartments-dedicated-to-Vietnam-hero-11178430.php.

63 "Peter Mathew Guenette," Congressional Medal of Honor Society (website).

64 Nixon Library recording, https://www.nixonlibrary.gov/media/14778.

65 Karrie Louise-Norenberg Blees, "Kenneth Lee Olson," Minnesota Medal of Honor Memorial, July 21, 2016, https://www.minnesotamedalofhonormemorial.org/ wp-content/uploads/2017/12/Olson-Kenneth-Bio-July-16.pdf.

66 "Kenneth Lee Olson," Congressional Medal of Honor Society (website), https://www.cmohs.org/recipients/kenneth-l-olson.

67 Chrissy Gaetke, "Portion of Highway 23 in Paynesville dedicated to Medal of Honor recipient," WJON-AM, May 15, 2017, https://wjon.com/portion- of-highway-23-in-paynesville-dedicated-to-medal-of-honor-recipient/#:~:text= PAYNESVILLE%20%2D%2D%20A%20portion%20of,graduate%20of%20 Paynesville%20High%20School.

68 Blees, "Kenneth Lee Olson."

69 "Kenneth Lee Olson," Congressional Medal of Honor Society (website).

70 Nixon Library recording, https://www.nixonlibrary.gov/media/14778.

71 Allan Bourdius, "SP4 Hector Santiago-Colon, USA," Their Finest Hour blog, June 28, 2012, https://theirfinesthour.blogspot.com/2012/06/tfh-628-sp4-hector- santiago-colon-usa.html?m=0.

72 "Hector Santiago-Colon," Congressional Medal of Honor Society (website), https://www.cmohs.org/recipients/hector-santiago-colon.

73 Allan Bourdius, "SP4 Hector Santiago-Colon, USA."

74 Nixon Library recording, https://www.nixonlibrary.gov/media/14778.

75 "James William Fous," Congressional Medal of Honor Society (website), https://www.cmohs.org/recipients/james-w-fous.

76 "James William Fous," Congressional Medal of Honor Society (website).

77 U.S. Senator Deb Fischer, "The Ultimate Sacrifice," Deb Fischer, United States Senator for Nebraska (website), May 15, 2014, https://www.fischer.senate.gov/public/index.cfm/2014/5/the-ultimate-sacrifice.

78 Nixon Library recording, https://www.nixonlibrary.gov/media/14778.

79 "Garfield McConnell Langhorn," Congressional Medal of Honor Society (website). https://www.cmohs.org/recipients/garfield-m-langhorn.

80 "Garfield McConnell Langhorn," Congressional Medal of Honor Society (website).

81 "Winners announced for 15th annual Pfc. Garfield Langhorn essay contest," *Riverhead News-Review*, October 25, 2019, https://riverheadnewsreview.timesreview.com/2019/10/96166/winners-announced-15th-annual-pfc-garfield-langhorn-essay-contest/.

82 Denise Civiletti, "Remembering—and being inspired by—a Riverhead hero, PFC Garfield McConnell Langhorn Jr.," *Riverhead Local*, October 22, 2019, https://riverheadlocal.com/2019/10/22/remembering-and-being-inspired-by-a-riverhead-hero-pfc-garfield-m-langhorn-jr/.

83 Joe Werkmeister, "A legacy that never fades: Remembering Pfc. Garfield Langhorn," *Riverhead News-Review*, January 21, 2019, https://riverheadnewsreview.timesreview.com/2019/01/91574/a-legacy-that-never-fades-remembering-pfc-garfield-langhorn/.

84 Denise Civiletti, "PFC Garfield Langhorn stamp will raise funds for program assisting low-income veteran families," *Riverhead Local*, January 16, 2021, https://riverheadlocal.com/2021/01/16/pfc-garfield-langhorn-stamp-will-raise-funds-for-program-assisting-low-income-veteran-families/.

85 Tara Smith, "Veterans Wall of Honor, dedicated to Pfc. Garfield Langhorn, unveiled at Riverhead High School," *Riverhead News-Review*, June 4, 2021, https://riverheadnewsreview.timesreview.com/2021/06/105433/veterans-wall-of-honor-dedicated-to-pfc-garfield-langhorn-unveiled-at-riverhead-high-school/.

86 Nixon Library recording, https://www.nixonlibrary.gov/media/14778.

87 "Milton Arthur Lee," Congressional Medal of Honor Society (website), https://www.cmohs.org/recipients/milton-a-lee.

88 Katie Lange, "Medal of Honor Monday: Army Pfc. Milton A. Lee," defense.gov, April 26, 2021, https://www.defense.gov/News/Feature-Stories/story/Article/2577725/medal-of-honor-monday-army-pfc-milton-a-lee/.

89 Neil Mishalov, "Medal of Honor: Milton A. Lee," Mishalov.com, September, 10, 2001, https://www.mishalov.com/LeeMilton.html.

90 Nixon Library recording, https://www.nixonlibrary.gov/media/14778.

91 "Phill Gene McDonald," Congressional Medal of Honor Society (website), https://www.cmohs.org/recipients/phill-g-mcdonald.

92 "Remember...Phill Gene McDonald," West Virginia Veterans Memorial (website), http://129.71.204.160/history/wvmemory/vets/mcdonaldphill/mcdonaldphill.html.
93 Nixon Library recording, https://www.nixonlibrary.gov/media/14778.
94 "David Paul Nash," Congressional Medal of Honor Society (website), https://www.cmohs.org/recipients/david-p-nash.
95 Becky Riddle, "Medal of Honor Winners," Explore Kentucky History, https://explorekyhistory.ky.gov/items/show/283?tour=17&index=5.
96 Nixon Library recording, https://www.nixonlibrary.gov/media/14778.
97 Nixon Library recording, https://www.nixonlibrary.gov/media/14778.
98 Tom Gosse, email to Kevin Ferris, April 30, 2020.
99 Lt. Gen. Sam Wetzel, retired, video interview by Bob Moran, February 11, 2013.
100 Nixon Library recording, https://www.nixonlibrary.gov/media/14778.
101 "Michael Joseph Crescenz," Congressional Medal of Honor Society (website), https://www.cmohs.org/recipients/michael-j-crescenz.

Chapter VII: Arlington

1 Benjamin Silver, email to Joe Crescenz, January 24, 2020.
2 Kathleen Zippilli and Mary Lou Allen, email to Joe Crescenz, June 21, 2021.
3 Tom Robinson, email to Joe Crescenz, April 17, 2021.
4 Tom Robinson, email to Joe Crescenz, April 17, 2021.
5 Valerie Crescenz, email to Kevin Ferris, February 22, 2022.
6 Joe Crescenz, email to Kevin Ferris, March 30, 2021.
7 Joe Crescenz, email to Kevin Ferris, March 30, 2021.
8 Joe Crescenz, email to Kevin Ferris, March 30, 2021.
9 Tom Schmidt, "A hero's final journey to rest among heroes," *Philadelphia Daily News*, April 29, 2008, http://www.arlingtoncemetery.net/mjcrescenz.htm.
10 National Park Service (website), Arlington House, the Robert E. Lee Memorial page, https://www.nps.gov/arho/learn/management/national-memorial-to-robert-e-lee.htm.
11 Arlington National Cemetery (website), https://www.arlingtoncemetery.mil/Explore
12 Arlington National Cemetery (website), https://www.arlingtoncemetery.mil/Explore
13 Arlington National Cemetery (website), https://www.arlingtoncemetery.mil/Explore
14 Joe Crescenz, video interview by Bob Moran, February 24, 2013.
15 Meredith Wilson, "Archdiocese of Philadelphia inducts six honorees into Hall of Fame," Archdiocese of Philadelphia press releases for 2008, https://archphila.org/wp-content/uploads/2016/05/2008.html.
16 Joe Crescenz, video interview by Bob Moran, February 24, 2013.

17 Joe Crescenz, video interview by Bob Moran, February 24, 2013.

18 Joe Crescenz, video interview by Bob Moran, February 24, 2013.

19 Joe Crescenz, video interview by Bob Moran, February 24, 2013.

20 Joe Crescenz, video interview by Bob Moran, February 24, 2013.

21 Joe Crescenz, video interview by Bob Moran, February 24, 2013.

22 Charles B. Herbermann et al., eds., *The Catholic Encyclopedia* (New York: Robert Appleton, 1907), https://books.google.com/books?id=m8xJAQAAMAAJ&pg=PA36&lpg=PA36&dq=His+courage+was+of+the+sort+that+never+falters.&source=bl&ots=mmhS4dGTnM&sig=ACfU3U2d_d6wtTyv5GrcOKRre3LEmrum1w&hl=en&sa=X&ved=2ahUKEwjqqvzhmOn1AhUMkWoFHeDvBlwQ6AF6BAgOEAM#v=onepage&q=His%20courage%20was%20of%20the%20sort%20that%20never%20falters.&f=false.

23 Kevin Ferris, "Long-awaited honor for vet," *Philadelphia Inquirer*, May 9, 2008, http://www.arlingtoncemetery.net/mjcrescenz.htm.

24 Ron Burke, video interview by Bob Moran, March 24, 2013.

25 Ferris, "Long-awaited honor."

26 James Engler, video interview by Bob Moran, March 16, 2013.

27 Tom Johnson, "Honoring Corporal Michael J. Crescenz," Alliance Video Productions, 2008.

28 Tom Johnson, "Honoring Corporal Michael J. Crescenz."

29 Tom Johnson, "Honoring Corporal Michael J. Crescenz."

30 Tom Johnson, "Honoring Corporal Michael J. Crescenz."

31 Tom Johnson, "Honoring Corporal Michael J. Crescenz."

32 Joe Crescenz, video interview by Bob Moran, February 24, 2013.

33 Joe Crescenz, video interview by Bob Moran, February 24, 2013.

34 Crawford, "Michael Crescenz."

35 Tom Johnson, "Honoring Corporal Michael J. Crescenz."

36 Joe Crescenz, video interview by Bob Moran, February 24, 2013.

37 Joe Crescenz, video interview by Bob Moran, February 24, 2013.

38 Senator Tom Cotton, *Sacred Duty: A Soldier's Tour at Arlington National Cemetery* (New York: William Morrow, 2109), 7, 8, https://www.amazon.com/Sacred-Duty-Soldiers-Arlington-National/dp/0062863150#detailBullets_feature_div.

39 Cotton, *Sacred Duty*, 6.

40 Tom Johnson, "Honoring Corporal Michael J. Crescenz."

41 Tom Johnson, "Honoring Corporal Michael J. Crescenz."

42 Tom Johnson, "Honoring Corporal Michael J. Crescenz."

43 Tom Johnson, "Honoring Corporal Michael J. Crescenz."

44 Timothy Brooks, email to Joe Crescenz, 2021.

45 Joe Crescenz, video interview by Bob Moran, February 24, 2013.

46 Joe Crescenz, email to Kevin Ferris, spring 2021.

Chapter VIII: Renaming the VA Medical Center

1 Frank Tacey, interviews by John A. Siegfried via cell phone July 16–17, 2017, and in person March 10, 2020.
2 Frank Tacey, interviews by John A. Siegfried via cell phone July 16–17, 2017, and in person March 10, 2020.
3 Frank Tacey, interviews by John A. Siegfried via cell phone July 16–17, 2017, and in person March 10, 2020.
4 Friends of the Medal of Honor Grove (website), https://friendsmohgrove.org/.
5 MSgt. Ray Bows and Pia Bows, "In Honor and Memory: Installations and Facilities of the Vietnam War," (New Smyrna, Florida: Bows Military Books, 2015).
6 Lt. Gen. Sam Wetzel, retired, video interview by Bob Moran, February 11, 2013.
7 Ray Miller, in-person interview by John A. Siegfried, May 2020.
8 Ray Miller, in-person interview by John A. Siegfried, May 2020.
9 Ray Miller, in-person interview by John A. Siegfried, May 2020.
10 William Dishon, email to Kevin Ferris, February 1, 2022.
11 Beau Weisman, "VA Medical Center in Phila. Renamed for Medal of Honor Recipient Michael J Crescenz," *CMC Digest*, April 26, 2015, http://cmcdigest.com/va-medical-center-in-phila-renamed-for-medal-of-honor-recipient-michael-j-crescenz/.
12 Steve Cronin, "Sea Isle City honors Medal of Honor recipient," *Press of Atlantic City*, November 11, 2014, https://pressofatlanticcity.com/news/sea-isle-city-honors-medal-of-honor-recipient/article_3e26f438-69f6-11e4-9cad-8304fd873da5.html#tncms-source=login.
13 Cronin, "Sea Isle City."
14 Cronin, "Sea Isle City."
15 Edward Colimore, "Honoring Phila.'s Vietnam War Medal of Honor Winner," *Philadelphia Inquirer*, October 31, 2014, https://www.inquirer.com/philly/news/local/20141031_Honoring_Phila__s_Vietnam_War_medal_of_honor_winner.html.
16 Colimore, "Honoring Phila.'s Vietnam War Medal of Honor Winner."
17 Colimore, "Honoring Phila.'s Vietnam War Medal of Honor Winner."
18 Edward Colimore, "Three Phila. war veterans will be honored in bronze," *Philadelphia Inquirer*, April 19, 2015, https://www.inquirer.com/philly/news/20150419_Three_Phila__war_veterans_will_be_honored_in_bronze.html.
19 Colimore, "Phila. war veterans."
20 Frank Tacey, interviews by John A. Siegfried via cell phone July 16–17, 2017, and in person March 10, 2020.
21 Lt. Gen. Sam Wetzel, retired, video interview by Bob Moran, February 11, 2013.
22 Frank Tacey, "Renaming of Corporal Michael J. Crescenz Philadelphia VAMC," video, https://www.youtube.com/watch?v=0F9RJytKrRI.
23 Tacey, "Renaming of Corporal Michael J. Crescenz Philadelphia VAMC."
24 Tacey, "Renaming of Corporal Michael J. Crescenz Philadelphia VAMC."
25 Tacey, "Renaming of Corporal Michael J. Crescenz Philadelphia VAMC."

26 Tacey, "Renaming of Corporal Michael J. Crescenz Philadelphia VAMC."
27 Tacey, "Renaming of Corporal Michael J. Crescenz Philadelphia VAMC."
28 Tacey, "Renaming of Corporal Michael J. Crescenz Philadelphia VAMC."
29 Tacey, "Renaming of Corporal Michael J. Crescenz Philadelphia VAMC."
30 Tacey, "Renaming of Corporal Michael J. Crescenz Philadelphia VAMC."
31 Tacey, "Renaming of Corporal Michael J. Crescenz Philadelphia VAMC."
32 Tacey, "Renaming of Corporal Michael J. Crescenz Philadelphia VAMC."
33 Tacey, "Renaming of Corporal Michael J. Crescenz Philadelphia VAMC."
34 Tacey, "Renaming of Corporal Michael J. Crescenz Philadelphia VAMC."
35 Ron Burke, video interview by Bob Moran, March 24, 2013.
36 James Engler, video interview by Bob Moran, March 16, 2013.

Chapter IX: No Greater Love

1   Peter Collier, *Medal of Honor: Portraits of Valor Beyond the Call of Duty*, 3rd edition (New York: Artisan, 2011), xxiii.
2   Collier, *Medal of Honor*, xviii.
3   Collier, *Medal of Honor*, xx.
4   Williams, "Doc Stafford."
5   Lt. Gen. Sam Wetzel, retired, video interview by Bob Moran, February 11, 2013.
6   Williams, "Doc Stafford."l
7   Michael Miller, "Philadelphia VA to be renamed for soldier who died saving others," *Press of Atlantic City*, April 26, 2015, https://pressofatlanticcity.com/news/breaking/philadelphia-va-to-be-renamed-for-soldier-who-died-saving-others/article_2eccc4ee-ec83-11e4-90e6-53819b665028.html.
8   Pope John Paul II, "Address of John Paul II to the Young People," Domain Park, Auckland, New Zealand, November 22, 1986, https://www.vatican.va/content/john-paul-ii/en/speeches/1986/november/documents/hf_jp-ii_spe_19861122_giovani-auckland-nuova-zelanda.html.
9   Archbishop Charles J. Chaput, "Things Worth Dying For: The Nature of a Life Worth Living," University of Notre Dame, October, 11, 2019.
10 Ron Burke, video interview by Bob Moran, March 24, 2013.
11 James Engler, video interview by Bob Moran, March 16, 2013.
12 William Peglow, email to Joe Crescenz, January 23, 2020.
13 John Norton, email to Joe Crescenz, March 27, 2020.
14 Benjamin Silver, email to Joe Crescenz, January 24, 2020.
15 Valerie Crescenz, email to Kevin Ferris, February 22, 2022.
16 Cantor Emanuel Silver, bulletin of Temple Beth El.
17 Joe Crescenz, video interview by Bob Moran, *Philadelphia Inquirer*, February 24, 2013.
18 Joseph Epstein, "Plutarch Without Parallel: The ancient world's first man of letters," *Claremont Review of Books*, Fall 2021, 78.
19 Denise McLaughlin, letter to Charles and Mary Ann Crescenz, July 6, 1986.

Acknowledgements

It was Tom Roberts, U.S. Air Force crew chief and Vietnam veteran, who finally pushed me to see the light and write this book about the Philly kid. It was Bob Moran from the *Philadelphia Inquirer*, who after many months of gleaning Michael's life from personal perspectives, galvanized many of the events/dedications that were to follow his articles in 2008 after Mike was moved to his final resting place in Arlington. According to U.S. Army combat medic Bill Stafford, Bob Moran deserves a tremendous amount of credit for pushing the Cardinal Dougherty graduate and his actions of November 20, 1968, on a mountain in South Vietnam, into the limelight.

This story would not have been possible without the unwavering support of Joe Crescenz, the entire Crescenz family and a host of veterans, many who served in Vietnam: Joe Griffies, Frank Tacey, Jim Willard, Tom Gosse, Ron Burke, Jimmy Kirlin, Terry Williamson, Ken Briggs, Jim Engler, Jeff Jacobs, Bill "Doc" Stafford, Father James Breen (deceased), Bob Gleason, and Ray Miller.

I also want to thank the Michael J. Crescenz Medal of Honor Foundation, which was founded in 2008 by the aforementioned Tom Roberts, in conjunction with members of VFW Post 2819 in Philadelphia. (Post was renamed for Mike in 2014.) The Board also includes Ed Blanchard, Tom Christy, Bill Crean, Jack Crussard, Frank DeFranco, Len Francis, Dan Hazely, John Kosin, Jack McLaughlin, and Joe O'Rourke. And deep appreciation to all members of the post, as well as Philadelphia's Vietnam Veterans Memorial Society, and sculptor Chad Fisher.

John A. Siegfried

My thanks first to John A. Siegfried and Joseph and Valerie Crescenz for inviting me to join the team. The three of them did an incredible job of finding all these strands of Michael Crescenz's much-too-short life so they could be woven together to bring his inspiring story to a larger audience. Their patience and professionalism throughout the process has been a blessing.

There are so many great writers and journalists who, over the years, have set a high bar when it came to telling different parts of Michael's story. From Sgt. George Hawkins, who first wrote about the battle of Nui Chom Mountain six months after it happened in November 1968, to Chuck Williams, with his seven-part series on the 50th anniversary of that battle for the Columbus, Georgia, *Ledger-Enquirer*. Closer to Michael's Philadelphia home, Robert Moran not only did a masterful job of telling Michael's story for *Philadelphia Inquirer* readers, but he spent hours and hours interviewing Michael's friends, fellow soldiers and family members—and then generously shared those video interviews with the Crescenz family. Robert's *Inquirer* colleague Ed Colimore and the *Philadelphia Daily News*' Tom Schmidt have also had the pleasure of getting to know the Crescenz family and writing about Michael over the years. Two incredibly talented videographers also deserve thanks for capturing parts of Michael's story: television anchor and reporter Samantha Crawford and Tom Johnson. Michael Miller and Steve Cronin of the *Press of Atlantic City* and Beau Weisman of the *CMC Digest* in Cape May County, New Jersey, had the story covered from the Shore, the other part of the world where Michael grew up.

Then there are all the amazing people who enthusiastically shared their memories about Michael for this project: Joseph and Valerie Crescenz, Charlie Crescenz, Mary Lou Allen, Jack Bisbee, Timothy Brooks, Ron Burke, Tom Corcoran, William Dishon, John Dolan, James Engler, Rick Gallagher, Bob Gleason, Tom Gosse, Jeff Jacobs, Joseph Lynch, Denise McLaughlin, Ray Miller, John Norton, William Peglow, Tom Robinson, Benjamin Silver, Emanuel Silver, William "Doc" Stafford, Tom Stanton, Lieutenant General Sam Wetzel, Jim Willard, and Kathleen Zippilli.

I hope we've done a good job of sharing their stories, and we take full responsibility for any inaccuracies or misinterpretations.

Special shoutout to these veterans and many others who not only helped make this book happen but also work tirelessly to ensure that Michael and his fellow Vietnam veterans are honored and never forgotten: Frank DeFranco, Joe Griffies, Ray Miller, Tom Roberts, and Frank Tacey.

Thanks also to two veterans who generously offered their time and talent to ensure we were able to tell Michael's story in pictures: Patrick Hughes and Larry Kesterson. Forever grateful.

Appreciation to the Richard Nixon Library and Museum for the audio of the Medal of Honor ceremony that posthumously honored Michael and 20 other heroic soldiers. Any opportunity to learn more about Medal of Honor recipients is to be cherished.

There wouldn't be a book without Joseph Craig, director of the Book Program at the Association of the United States Army, who provided support, numerous helpful editing suggestions, and an introduction to Casemate Publishers. Ruth Sheppard and the Casemate team, Jackie Wilson Asheeke, Carl Zebrowski, and Chris McNab, have been gracious and patient and we are so grateful for their belief in the power of Michael's story.

Two other gentlemen deserve a thank-you because of their inspiring work with veterans, particularly Medal of Honor recipients. One is Peter Collier, the late best-selling author whom I never met in person but who was always available by phone or email to offer encouragement, direction, or good advice to a fellow writer. He is missed and I highly recommend to all his book *Medal of Honor: Portraits of Valor Beyond the Call of Duty*. The other is my friend Wallace Nunn, a Vietnam veteran, chairman emeritus of the Congressional Medal of Honor Foundation, and founder and first chairman of the Friends of the Medal of Honor Grove in Valley Forge, Pennsylvania. It was during a dedication ceremony in the grove that I first heard him mention how love is behind each act of valor that results in a Medal of Honor—as well as the countless actions performed in service to our country that go unrecognized. That stayed with me.

Thanks, of course, to Donna, for believing in me and the work I do and for making all things possible. You're amazing. And to Emily and Kieran, who make me proud every single day.

Finally, I have to thank Michael. Working on this project during the lockdown was not only inspirational, but also a much-needed reminder to count one's blessings and be grateful for it all. God bless him—and you for taking the time to read his story.

Kevin Ferris

Index